Boil, Bubble, Toil And Trouble

An Analytical Exploration Of Bubbles

Edited

William Rapp

H. J Leir Professor International Business

Director Leir Center For Financial Bubble Research

School of Management

New Jersey Institute of Technology

Newark, N.J. 07102

E-mail: rappw@njit.edu

Website: www.leirbubblecenter.org

Please address all correspondence to:

William Rapp

H J Leir Professor International Business,

New Jersey Institute of Technology

Newark, N.J. 07102

ISBN-13: 978-1489565365

ISBN-10: 1489565361

DEDICATION

This book is dedicated to the Memory of Henry J. Leir without whose. financial vision it would never have been written

CONTENTS

ACKNOWLEGEMENTS

Many people have contributed to producing this volume, which is intended to be the first in a series of books examining aspects of financial bubbles based on fundamental research and annual conferences supported by the Ridgefield Foundation and the Leir Retreat Center. Most notable are Mr. Arthur Hoffman, Esq., President of the Ridgefield and Leir Foundations and Ms. Margot Gibis, the Director of the Leir Retreat Center. It was Mr. Hoffman's interest in Bubbles that led to NJIT's School of Management's first bubble research papers and it was Ms. Gibis that suggested we present these at a series of conferences at the Leir Retreat, Mr. Leir's beautiful former estate in Ridgefield, CT.

The first conference was held in September 2011. This volume is one outcome of that meeting and its lively discussion about Bubbles. The conference Notes are available from the Leir Bubble Center's website: www.leirbubblecenter.org, critically maintained by its webmeister, Jordan Rapp. Thus there were important contributions not only by the NJIT School Of Management Professors who have actively participated in the initiation and development of the project and the Chapters in this book but also by the other participants from finance and academia who through their insights, experience and comments enriched the discussion and the final outcome. These contributions are seen in the Conference Notes and in the Introduction to this volume.

Also I wish to thank Dean Pius Egbelu of NJIT's School of

Management for suggesting the establishment of the Leir Center for Financial Bubble Research, NJIT's Administration for its institutional support, and Professor Robert Aliber for sharing his incites on Bubbles. Finally it is clear this editorial effort gained immeasurably from the love, support, and common sense insights of my wife Diane.

TABLES

FIGURES & EXHIBITS

PREFACE

Boil, Bubble, Toil And Trouble

The Leir Center For Financial Bubble Research and Leir Bubble Research Project at the New Jersey Institute Of Technology's School Of Management began with a student assignment in my global macroeconomics class in the summer of 2007. The topic was examining the US housing and mortgage market as a possible bubble using the Kindleberger-Aliber-Minsky paradigm as an analytical lens. The results were so compelling in the fall of 2007 I decided to also write a paper that was ultimately presented at a July 2008 Conference sponsored by the Indian Ministry of Finance and then published after the Subprime Mortgage Collapse and related stock market crash as "The Kindleberger-Aliber-Minsky Paradigm And The Global Subprime Mortgage Meltdown," in *Critical Perspectives on International Business,* Volume 5 Issue 1/2 [2009].[1]

However, I had distributed the paper prior to the Conference presentation to the Leir and Ridgefield Foundations that had established my chair at NJIT. The President, Arthur Hoffman, thus felt this type of predictive practical research should be given more scope and the Foundation provided funds to begin a research project at NJIT on financial bubbles that would be oriented towards operational concepts with a rigorous analytical base.

---

[1] This paper is available for download along with other working papers on financial bubbles from the Leir Center website: www.leirbubblecenter.org.

As the Project evolved and the first results were presented, it became apparent there was considerable scope to expand the understanding of financial bubbles, their consequences and related policies that combined both qualitative and quantitative methods. Therefore with more support from the Foundation the Leir Center For Financial Bubble Research was established at NJIT in its School of Management to do financial bubble related research and hold an annual Conference that would bring together academics, financial industry participants, and government officials with an interest in financial bubbles. The objective of both Center activities would be to produce solid academic research that would have practical value to industry participants and government policymakers.

Research working papers and Notes from the first two conferences can be accessed on Center's website: www.leirbubblecenter.org. This volume is a more detailed outcome of the presentations and discussion from the first Conference and examines financial bubbles generally. The second Conference in 2012 focused on government's various roles in bubbles acting at different times as contributor, regulator, last resort lender, aftermath manager, and writer of legislation against possible large future bubbles.

This Conference will be the source of material for the Center's next book on Bubbles and Government Policy. Some of the critical questions and issues regarding financial bubbles the Center is trying to address through this process of research and discussion include the fact that bubbles are economically and financially important globally and are becoming more frequent.[2] Thus it is important to study and better understand them.

Indeed because of these facts it is no longer sufficient to just look at financial bubbles retrospectively and state "Oh that was a Bubble" and to then see a flurry of books and articles on the subject with some policymakers saying the bubble's development, evolution and results could not be foreseen [mea culpa] after which the analysts and policymakers move on to a different topic.

So it is very appropriate that NJIT with support from the Ridgefield and Leir Foundations has undertaken to form a Center dedicated to exploring financial bubbles in depth over a period of time in order to produce research and related publications such as this volume that address the issue of knowing when one is involved in a Bubble, the type of Bubble it is, and what kinds of macro or micro policies might be appropriate either to manage it or perhaps even to just ignore it.

The current book begins to address some of these issues and questions in that it presents quantitative, qualitative and theoretical approaches to identifying and assessing a bubble and its stages of development. This multi-faceted approach should prove useful to practitioners, policymakers and academics because the concepts and data presented emerge from active discussions by participants from all these groups. Nevertheless

---

[2] Professor Aliber noted this at both the first and second conferences and has analyzed this situation in the 6th Edition of *Manias, Panics and Crashes* [2011].

the policy measures and the involvement of government addressed to some degree in the Chapter "Bubbles in Law" will require another book based on the 2012 Bubble Conference that was specifically on that topic and expanded the knowledge and perspective of government's various roles in financial bubbles.

The third conference to be held in September 2013 will apply the methodologies and insights developed in this book and subsequent research and discussion to three great Bubbles that have altered major economies, changed laws and created new institutions: 1929, Japan 1980s, and the dot.com boom and bust. Hopefully this volume has begun this journey towards a greater understanding of such financial bubbles. Please feel free to send your questions or comments to the editor, William Rapp, at rappw@njit.edu.

INTRODUCTION

When Shall We Three Meet Again?

This book is the outgrowth of a project at the New Jersey Institute Of Technology's School of Management funded by the Leir and Ridgefield Foundations that has evolved into the Leir Center For Financial Bubble Research dedicated to the study and understanding of Financial Bubbles. The Center's website is www.leirbubblecenter.org where working papers and other materials can be freely downloaded. The material and ideas for the chapters in this book were first presented at a Conference organized by the Leir Center at NJIT and supported by the Leir Retreat Center. However the ideas and concepts they contain have benefitted greatly from the comments and questions of the conference participants and their subsequent inputs and revisions.

The first question posed was whether the participants could agree on a definition of a financial Bubble or how it might be modified for different types of Bubbles. From this evolved the question how one would know when one was in a bubble as opposed to looking back after a bubble had burst and stating "Oh yes! That was definitely a bubble." Robert Aliber who attended the Conference has defined a bubble as "a non-sustainable increase in the prices of certain currencies and classes of assets."

However, others have defined it as a rapid rise in prices above an asset's basic economic value such as comparing the discounted rental value of a property to its selling price during a real estate boom. In both cases however a bubble refers to a rapid rise in asset prices that captures the attention of the bubble participants. These definitions appear related because rapid asset price increases are not sustainable when there is a large and increasing difference between an asset's price and its basic economic value.

While there appears to be general agreement that a rapid increase in real asset prices relative to other prices is a requirement for a bubble there is less agreement in how rapid that relative price increase has to be. Reinhart and Rogoff[3] for example state it should be 15% or more but this seems to too arbitrary. Rather the conference participants felt that other factors would signal whether it was a bubble such as the relative price increase being sufficient to attract speculators and to divert assets and capital from other uses. The chapters by A. Yan and B. Chou highlight the concept of herding that is needed in the later stages of the asset bubble to sustain its expansion.

There was agreement that one should use real prices since if asset prices are rising 15% a year but the CPI is rising 10% a year people feel less rich and the asset price increase is more sustainable than if the CPI is rising 1-2% per year. This was true in the recent US and Japan situations when real estate and housing prices were booming but the core CPI was relatively low. This situation will make people feel richer without forcing

---

[3] Reinhart, C. & Rogoff, K. 2009. *This Time Is Different*, Princeton University Press, Princeton, NJ.

analysts to rely on money illusion. In turn if they really feel richer then they will be more optimistic and euphoric fueling the mania and the development of the bubble. Core price stability may also keep central banks from intervening and restricting credit. This will support further expansion of the bubble.

There was little agreement over what period of time sustainability should measured and this is still an open research question as is the general time horizon for Bubbles in terms of their evolution and collapse. Yet research indicates there are more precise metrics that allow one to track a bubble's evolution and to understand when price increases are no longer sustainable and the collapse is coming. Indeed several participants felt it was not difficult to know if you were in a bubble but it was difficult knowing how close you were to the collapse or what one should do after recognizing it. The threshold rate appears to be the level that attracts the speculators that truly initiate the bubble and differentiates it from reasonable investments.

This entry of speculators is what leads to price acceleration, the entry of more speculators and the exit of investors. In turn price deceleration that causes some speculators to leave marks a maturing stage in a bubble's evolution and signals that the end is nearer. There do seem to be methods for identifying and measuring the entry of speculators or momentum investors compared to investors using more traditional valuation methods such as discounted cash flow. From this perspective movements above equilibrium and movements back [cobwebs] are not bubbles.

Bubbles are thus all about price action and investors and speculators reactions to changes in prices. Yet while there are commonalties to bubbles the participants agreed that there are important differences between bubbles such as asset, credit and technology related bubbles. However the participants disagreed on whether any bubbles were good even if due to over-investment with positive externalities such as canals, railroads and the Internet. At the same time it was agreed that exponential growth or price acceleration is not a bubble in and of itself if the associated price increases are justified by increased earnings [Google and Apple stock prices]. Rather there must be exponential increases in real prices not economically supported and this is what makes assessing when something is a bubble tricky and frequently more intuitive than analytic.

It was clear to the participants too that there are important differences between financial bubbles and economic instability or crises. Some crises such as a traditional bank run [Crash of 1907 or current Euro crisis] occur without the presence of any financial bubble. There may also be bubbles without an accompanying financial crisis such as the dot.com boom and bust or the collapse in social media stocks. This seems clear when there are investment overshoots that even after the collapse leave the economy better off due to beneficial improvements in infrastructure and capital capacity such as the railroad and mining booms of the 19th Century, the auto, appliance and oil booms of the 20th Century and the Internet boom of the 21st Century. The Conference called these Schumpeterian or industry bubbles.

Other bubbles include commodity bubbles but within this category some participants questioned whether gold was different because some people view it as an alternative currency. There may also be bubbles in biology when there are no natural predators or one outruns a host. In these cases the system changes due to the excess population and there is a crash. Chain reactions until there is an explosion may be similar. This also appears to be true for new types of leverage or resources that feed a system until that source is used up as illustrated by the Japanese boom discussed in Chapter One. Then there is a crash due to no further support. The boom in Japanese movie financing or defeased leases during the 1980s appear to have been such phenomena in that as the MOF saw revenues fall they closed what had been an attractive financing vehicle based on exploiting the Japanese tax Code.

In this way government incentives can create a bubble as in the housing mortgage guarantees or triple AAA ratings behind the recent Great Recession. Government regulations can also affect social attitudes towards risk taking as when the SEC changed capital requirements for investment banks in 2004. In general though as the Conference progressed the participants agreed that bubbles could be analyzed in more detail and thus rejected Garber's idea that bubbles are too fuzzy and vague to be analytically assessed and regulated. Research could move our understanding of bubbles beyond the intuitive.

One criterion for a bubble is that there does seem to be a need for an open system. Neither Communist Russia or China had any bubbles but the phenomena emerged quickly once their systems became more open and market driven with the possibility of asset ownership. Further the policy concern for bubbles is really due to their potential to disrupt a financial system. This is something that did not occur under command economies. Size and effect are also relevant considerations when assessing a bubble and what to do about it. Ones that affect access to credit are the most dangerous.

Economic growth and risk taking are part of the market and capitalistic system. Entrepreneurs and the creation of new companies or old companies entering new businesses or markets are all important aspects of economic growth. Indeed current macro-economic theory argues only technological progress can lead to increases in real per capita income. Yet decisions to develop a new technology, product or service entail risk since they may not succeed or progress may be erratic. On the other hand if they succeed very well they will draw in competitors and there may be overshoot in terms of the investment in that and related sectors. Therefore risk to the financial system in providing capital support to the new ventures is the aspect that needs to be carefully considered from a policy viewpoint.

That is changes in financial institutional arrangements can

contribute to a bubble's development. Perceptions and historical experience are relevant in this regard since they affect decision-making and the legal regime too. One signal in this regard is that as speculators enter the market it becomes more volatile even though the market may appear more liquid with more participants. Furthermore, these new participants can and do exit more quickly causing the bubble's collapse. This is covered in Ben Chou's chapter on using a Cobweb model to understand Housing Bubbles.

Still the question of whether some bubbles are good or beneficial to economic growth under some circumstances remains an open research question. This is because while it may be true that in the short-term all bubbles are bad and the larger they become the more this is likely to be true because they can be economically disruptive, in the longer term some may create economic benefits that more than pay for the adverse impact of the disruption and thus the actual cost of the bubble should be seen as a social investment.

Still this only seems to apply to the Schumpeterian bubbles that are part of the risk taking function in the economy, and thus these must be differentiated from financial bubbles that are always bad and that are frequently a function of bad government policy. Further because these are always bad it argues for regulatory policies such as margin requirements that restrict the banks' ability to lend into such situations and thus avoid the financial system being severely impacted by the spillovers from potentially good investment bubbles when they finally crash. Because banks are highly leveraged losses on such loans can wipe out their capital exposing them to runs and failure.

Bubbles do seem to require excessive optimism at least with respect to the particular asset acquisition opportunity and this can be tracked in terms of media statements, consumer confidence, and contracting. This is because there was general agreement that bubbles are psychological and social phenomena as well as economic phenomena. Thus perception is a key aspect of bubbles and the more obvious the opportunity to make money or that the asset is over-priced becomes, the more the bubble expands or becomes likely to collapse. In this respect mania is crucial to a bubble's development but it then becomes important to identify when the mania begins and how it evolves. The chapters on herding, speculative housing and institutional behavior address and analyze this.

Since Bubbles are based on over optimistic expectations, pressures to buy in order not to miss out on a sure thing are one potential bubble signal whereas anxieties about selling so as not to lose one's profit can be the signal of a top. However because it is very difficult to time them, asset bubbles may in fact be a bad investment from the beginning. Further going short a bubble early can be very painful. There are situations too as per the Kindleberger-Aliber-Minsky[4] paradigm where the bubble begins

---

[4] Kindleberger, C. & Aliber, R. 2011. *Manias, Panics And Crashes*, Palgrave Macmillan, NY.

for logical economic reasons but then at some point switches to mania and the bubble starts to evolve. This is why Garber called them vague, but is also the reason this book is initiating a research agenda to develop more concrete signals and measures to understand a bubble's type and where it is in its development.

In the case of bubbles that also result in financial crises as noted above leverage is usually involved. This leverage can take many forms and need not involve banks, though if it does the financial fallout is more severe. Subscription agreements are one of the most common forms. However systemic risk seems to require the involvement of banks. As noted above this is due to their high leverage and their close integration into financial systems. Even small changes in the value of collateral or other bank balance sheet items can severely and quickly impact a financial system.

Therefore from a policy standpoint policymakers should distinguish between global, national or large regional bubbles impacting bank assets and those affecting a limited group of assets such as nanotechnology or rare earths. The economic size of the bubble is relevant too as is the involvement of large international banks as opposed to small local banks.

This is because international financial markets such as the foreign exchange and international bond markets can propagate and spread leveraged risk as seen in the Asian and Emerging market bubbles and crashes of the 1990s. The current Euro-zone travails seem to reflect this phenomenon as well. Further the

Yen's revaluation in 1985 and related losses triggered this kind of effect for Japan. The BOJ's low interest rates designed to offset the deflationary effect of an appreciated Yen fueled the subsequent boom and bust.

The chapters in this book, though, seek to go beyond these primarily descriptive approaches to evaluate and understand bubbles by identifying more precise metrics [quantitative or qualitative] that all bubbles share and how they vary with the type of bubble. For example, certain words or approaches to accounting are used to market securities and other types of assets. These signals appear to vary by the stage of the bubble. However it is less clear how these signals impact a particular group of asset buyers or sellers [institutional players versus individuals, speculators versus investors, lending banks, investment bank packagers or underwriters, insurance company investors or guarantors, pension funds, mutual funds, foundations, academic institutions, or financial advisors].

What is clear, though, is that changes in investment attitudes of major investor groups can materially affect a group of assets and create a bubble. Thus William Synnott explained how in the 1960s pension fund managers were persuaded that combining risk free assets such as Treasuries with growth securities such a Polaroid and Xerox could over time produce better portfolio returns with no real increase in risk. This switch in portfolio management in turn created the "nifty fifty" whose stock prices soared as more pension and mutual fund managers bought their stock. This then attracted the speculative momentum investors and a bubble was born. The bust came in the early 1970s.

Of course not all bubbles find their origins in the private sector. The granddaddy of all bubbles from which it takes the name is the Great South Sea Bubble where its origins are found in the British Government's strong desire to refinance its War Debt and Parliament then passing the necessary laws to do this. Similarly as explained above aggressive Japanese monetary policy in the 1980s and by the Fed starting in 2001 initiated and fueled the Japanese and US real estate booms.

In addition no-action signals from regulators and central banks can keep the bubble expanding. For example during the recent financial bubble the Fed in its bank Supervisory Reports starting in 2003 and especially after 2005 was continuously and ever more explicitly highlighting deteriorating lending practices and increased loan risks related to real estate but they did nothing about it. Similarly the SEC in 2004 allowed investment banks to increase their leverage and count riskier assets as capital thereby setting Bear Stearns and Lehman on a dangerous and ultimately fatal path when the market value of those assets fell.

This raises the question whether adverse selection increases in the latter part of a bubble inviting riskier investments and lending. Certainly this was true for the bundling of subprime mortgages as prime mortgages became less available. B. Chou explains in his chapter that when speculators enter the market in large numbers and investors leave the market becomes more volatile and less stable but also prices rise. Here adverse selection can make speculators more optimistic and give them more persuasive arguments on why regulators should not take any action to counter the bubble. However this is deceptive and is actually a signal that regulators should become more proactive in administering existing regulations and in leaning against any liberalization of financial controls.

Indeed when "financial innovation" runs into legal or regulatory barriers put in place after past bubbles it can be a signal that this is not really an innovation but is an old problem masquerading as something new and which only seems new because it has not been tried recently due to the existing regulations. Thus some participants saw Structured Investment Vehicles or the SIVs described in the Chapter by M. Ehrlich as descendants of the 1920s leveraged trusts while the CDO squared and cubed securities seemed similar to the corporate pyramid schemes that emerged in the 1920s but collapsed in the 1930s when the production companies at the bottom of the pyramid were no longer able to provide the cash flow needed to support the securities of the shell companies at higher levels.

Further financial instruments can be disguised as something new when a new technology seems to facilitate an organizational change that helps initiate the bubble. For example large-scale computers and global telecommunications aided and expanded the size and globalization of the securitization process in the 2002-2010 real estate bubble and collapse just as the ticker tape and radio expanded and globalized the crash in 1929. In 1929 even bankers crossing the Atlantic could track the course of their investments or buy and sell. Now one can do this even more easily via a Blackberry or i-Phone from virtually anywhere.

Of course if prices could rise indefinitely we might not be concerned about bubbles and understanding them in more detail. But this is not the case and when the bubble pops that downward rush in prices is generally dramatic and many people feel the financial pain. Further if the Bubble is large and banks are involved the economic fallout and aftermath as explained above can be severe. This raises the question of when there might be a bottom and how one knows it. Are there similar signals as during the boom only reversed such as excessive pessimism or price reduction overshoot, or are bottoms a completely different phenomena since many investments cease to exist?

There was no consensus on this question though Bob Aliber did not think you should call them negative bubbles since each recovery is very different and do not show the same similar aspects as bubbles. A recent article by two British economists looking a news articles seems to support this view since it finds more uniformity in reporting on the upside of a bubble than on the downturn.

One participant noted that during the Nifty-fifty mania in the 1960s and early 70s investors only got a 6% return on growth stocks and questioned at the time whether that was enough and were told "If you buy the right stock it does not matter". He heard this same response again during the Internet boom and wondered if that standard answer is a signal of a bubble and coming crash since it shows investors are only looking at the upside.

It certainly appears to be the sign of a bubble when combined with herding and momentum since one sheep does not usually fall off a cliff but a herd can. Herding in asset prices such as stocks is when prices tend to move together in certain situations such as the one described above. Once this starts it can gain momentum on both the upside [greed] and downside [fear]. That is following the trend or imitating others can have power even if one does not believe the story. It is even more powerful if as in the case of the Railroads, the Nifty Fifty or the Internet one believes the story. This can then drive prices away from any fundamental value and the price action itself becomes the story.

This price action in particular can attract unsophisticated investors who will exit quickly on the downside since they are considered not to have "strong hands". Herding can be inefficient in this case but can be efficient when it is based on copying people that actually know the actual story. Thus high frequency trading increases a perceived but false liquidity by creating an artificial depth in the market that can quickly disappear, exacerbating any collapse. In this view one should look at momentum effects that lead to increased herding that then increases momentum as a signal that the mania phase has started. If the level of herding increases it shows the mania phase is developing further.

Though the chapter on herding views six months as the normal financial measure of momentum, herding seems to change and evolve with the bubble over a 3-5 year period. This is because the microstructure of financial markets and how traders are organized play a role in mania transmission and how the bubble develops. But the history of bubbles shows organizations may respond to bubbles too due to perceived profit opportunities and the two groups can interact to promote the bubble. Thus certain market phenomenon may disappear once the bubble finally bursts. This was true in the Japanese Bubble for example as stocks and real estate prices rose increasing bank capital that encouraged banks to make more real estate and stock loans. Once real estate prices began to decline so did bank capital and the ability to make the loans fueling the bubble leading to further real estate price declines, shrinking bank capital and their ability to lend.

The simple Cobweb model presented in Chapter 8 captures this herding effect and the different roles of speculators and investors. It is also possible to introduce government as a player and regulator. In this view bubbles are generally seen as demand side phenomena with supply responding to this demand from investors and speculators. If supply is limited, which is usually the case at least initially, prices will rise more quickly and the bubble will emerge faster.

When there is no more increased demand the panic and crash will come and new supply will disappear except for the existing but now expanded stock of assets. As already explained price increases affect both speculators and investors so as to make the market look more liquid despite increased price volatility. Thus positive price action for a time can be self-reinforcing. As prices reach the top, though, and the upward price action slows and this slowing causes some speculators to leave the market, this starts the price action moving in the other direction, ultimately leading to panic and crashes. This downward price action is exacerbated by the fact that by this time most investors, particularly value investors, have left the market leaving only speculators that are quick to sell since they were only in the market for the expected short term price increases.

Supporting and growing the bubble therefore requires growing aggregate demand that will always reach a limit based on the total value of the asset class and the resources investors and speculators have to buy at higher prices. Interestingly if there is too large an increase in supply, it will moderate the price action that led to herding and the start of the bubble. Thus a reduction in herding and a coincident reduction or leveling in upward price momentum created by more supply is a signal the bubble is close to the top and that a possible panic and crash is near.

In the final months of the Internet boom many new IPOs were not fully subscribed and underwriters even approached small net worth investors. In effect since the demand curve is composed of at least two basic groups of buyers, their different behavioral characteristics are key both to the development of the bubble and its crash. This model can accommodate more micro trading or buying groups as long as their reaction to the bubble's evolution is different. One important sub-grouping for example is that speculators themselves may be divided between rational and irrational speculators with the latter being more heavily influenced by price action and market peer pressure. Because some rational speculators will drop out of the market as the bubble evolves and prices rise this will eventually lead to a moderation of demand and a reduction in the upward price action that starts the downward price action process. This will happen more quickly if supply is growing as well such as more and more IPOs or CDOs.

The reaction of different buying groups is thus linked to herding in terms of price momentum. Therefore in understanding a bubble the reaction of these different groups to the price action is key. Investors that sell early may reenter the market later feeling they sold too soon, but there have to be enough speculators in the aggregate with access to resources that can push the price up from its current level even if all think prices are going up. If they do not have those resources they cannot translate their perceptions into reality and prices will not go up as expected. This will create a feedback mechanism that will force speculators to revise their price expectations or the perception that prices will continue to rise. Thus the bubble will not enter the mania stage or it will be short-lived. The same is true on the downside with respect to those that believe prices will fall indefinitely.

The Chapter on Institutional Behavior recognizes this psychological aspect of bubbles and tries to go behind the models and mathematics to examine why certain bubble promoting behavior occurs. That is it looks at relating the herding and momentum considerations to institutional considerations driven by human behavior that ultimately is exposed in the models and data that reflect or document that behavior.

It argues that the mix of financial and social incentives and pressures on the bubble participants represent a different type of social and economic phenomena. Some experts see bubbles as natural phenomena that emerge from capitalistic organizations. Thus their legitimacy evolves from perception they are related to innovation even if the participants do not really understand the innovation.

A successful situation is when the innovator understands the innovation and can legitimize and explain it to market participants. If the innovator or participants do not understand the innovation or change, then the innovation or change will legitimize itself especially if initially it seems profitable. This will lead to imitation and peer pressure where institutions will not question the results because everyone is doing it and making money. This seems to have been the case with bundled subprime mortgages rated triple A.

Signals this situation is occurring are when the innovation is extremely complex and cannot be easily explained to regulators or customers. So for example the Wall Street quants understood the models they were creating in terms of the mathematics but did not adequately understand the financial instruments and economic risks underlying their assumptions. Such a process becomes a Behavioral Commitment by organizations to a course of action that is then very difficult to stop without a complete crash.

Refusal or push back from providers of financial assets to regulators is part of this signal. Therefore when an institution keeps buying more of an asset, even when such action is being questioned by regulators, this is a bubble signal. Accompanying this signal are arguments that the firm is perfectly hedged and the risk is being managed. Yet the actual situation that evolves is a misperception of how much risk there actually is, a mispricing of this risk, and little understanding of how it is concentrated. In the recent crash the Government had to rescue AIG because it was the counterparty for billions of dollars in hedges by several major banks, a situation that had developed because AIG had underpriced the risks it had assumed.

There may also be a close relation between this type of organizational development and what is considered ethical. That is, if one really believes an investment is OK and low risk [sell self] then one can sell customers. But if one cannot really explain the investment and the risks in detail then maybe it is unethical or even illegal to sell the investment. Because the regulatory cycle tends to be pro-cyclical whereas it should be counter-cyclical this exacerbates the institutional biases and promotes the bubble when it should be countering it. This perception supports using a black line rule to control certain bubble promoting behavior as compared to trying to regulate a market or organizational actions.

In balancing the goals of an efficient market versus a resilient market, the policy response is therefore really important. However market-based rules seem subject to manipulation and appear too vague. If they are dependent on regulatory action there can also be co-opting of the regulators. Thus black line rules such as margin requirements appear to work best in countering a bubble's marketing hype.

This is because marketing is closely related to the misperception of risk and the commitment to a continued course of action prior to a crash. Once committed the organization will provide resources to selling this course of action to buyers, fully integrating sellers, organizers and buyers. So such marketing is a key aspect of what gets people optimistic, a critical element of the mania.

Using the recent real estate bubble as a proxy one can see lenders sought higher yields through lending to riskier buyers but believed the investment, securitization and payment risk was low due to bundling and pooling, though some questions remain whether they knew the risks but misrepresented them to buyers given that their jobs depended on selling these risky financial products. Marketing of course took place both by the mortgage providers and those selling the houses. Exploiting buyer's ignorance and optimism was a critical aspect of this marketing process. This point is highlighted in the Chapter Bubbles in Law that among other considerations discusses contracting and optimism as part of a bubble's historical development.

In marketing such products or innovations perception is everything. In order to access new homebuyers real estate mortgage lenders and packagers first went through the prime buyers and when they were exhausted started on the subprime borrowers. Lenders and developers needed ways to sell to these lower credit borrowers even though selling them a house they could not afford was clearly unethical since the lenders knew they were likely to default and this would stick the banks or more likely the investors that bought the securitized loan packages with the bill if servicers could not collect on loans and had to foreclose on behalf of the investors. This is an important example of the overly optimistic contracting created through financial marketing that the new Consumer Financial Protection Agency is meant to address.

This optimism was in turn supported by government behavior in both public statements and concrete actions through Fannie Mae and Freddie Mac for which the public ultimately paid a very high price via taxpayer guaranties and foreclosure prevention. These actions were supported by various statements: such as "everyone is doing it or I would not sell you something that was not value or home prices only go up". In this way one can relate the crisis to US individualism and the short-term performance pressures that created an environment for sales persons to deceive the buyer. But there were also incentives for the deceived to agree due to the promotion by the government and the press of the benefits of owning a home even if you cannot afford it. This generated a three-sided optimistic willingness to contract by the borrowers, the lenders [investors] and the government [guarantors and regulators]. Unfortunately for the homeowners as well as the ultimate investors the results were disastrous with huge negative externalities for the global economy.

Given evidence that regulators knew there was a potential problem within the housing boom as well as Alan Greenspan's famous remark about the dot.com bubble as "irrational exuberance" it has been suggested that recognizing bubbles is not that hard even when one is in it. Rather the issue is what to do about it as an investor or policy/regulator. This is especially difficult when the government as well as the general public seems to be benefitting. In addition regulators seem to frequently misperceive the eventual size and impact of the bubble on the economic and financial system when it pops.

Further because it is painful for an investor to be short if the bubble continues for a while [i.e. shorts too early], the best strategy may be for an investor to go into cash and wait for the bubble to burst and then buy back undervalued assets. However, exercising such patience can be difficult when others seem to be making money, especially for professional asset managers under pressure from their clients to invest their funds.

Yet the size of the bubble should be an important policy measure since very large bubbles can impact the financial system and the economy in its most critical aspects whereas a small tech bubble or a single commodity unless it is gold or oil seems much less critical to monitor and manage given the apparent patterns to investment by sophisticated investors that lead to a bubble's development as described above. Most bubbles rely on a good idea that can be promoted and where investors and speculators are willing to be promoted, such as with social media. This leads to optimism in contracting and herding.

Under these circumstances the available regulatory tools may be limited to the extent every bubble is new and different. The tools put in place to deal with the last bubble may not work for the next one. Still regulators must in any case actually want to act and thus cooption or pressure from bubble participants may be an issue particularly when there are both rational and non-rational players in the bubble and the rational players want to ride the bubble because they recognize the irrational players will drive up the asset prices and they can make money from this. Automatic circuit breakers such as a Tobin tax therefore may be an appropriate policy response in addition to increased margin and capital requirements.

Because contracting plays an important but generally underappreciated role in bubble development regulating such contracts is an important government function. This is especially true when the contracting parties misperceive and under price the actual risk. Sometimes this is by intent when one of the parties is more sophisticated and develops contracts that make the product look cheaper by putting costs towards the end and introducing complexity so that customer thinks it is cheaper. This process accentuates bubble optimism and will lead to taking on more credit and risk, promoting and expanding the bubble. For example generalizing beyond a mortgage to a situation where the probability of a $100 asset going to $150 is 50% and going to $40 is 50% but the investor only has $20 and needs to borrow $80.

The rational investor would not borrow but the optimistic investor might borrow and invest depending on the contract design, such as a back-end loaded cost. This then can exacerbate or fuel the demand for the asset by reducing its perceived cost. Securitization helped banks involved in the mortgage creation process to avoid some of the losses as compared to when banks held their own loans. This however has now become an agency issue for which the banks are paying a high price in terms of foreclosures, public perceptions, litigation headaches, administrative time and actual losses. Thus banks themselves were overly optimistic as to their ability to manage the actual risks given the large number of risky loans negotiated by all banks such that the global financial system and global economy were put at risk. Rating agencies mislabeling of this risk until well after the fact also played a role.

If the germ of an idea raises expectations, prices will rise.

Yet it should not rise too much. If it does, it will indicate a bubble. Looking at some industries one does not see this. But it did exist for the banks in the case of mortgage or other credit backed securities. Continued uncertainties about their exposure to real estate related loans and mortgage packaging suits reflect this and has an impact on their stock prices. The rapid demise of firms such as Countrywide shows how quickly prices can change as a factor in looking at the impact of a bubble. The size and rapidity of changing real prices is clearly a key to bubble topology.

In this respect while on a micro or individual institution level learning can create differences between players and customers in understanding complexity and being able to make rational as opposed to irrational decisions, at an aggregated or macro level the lenders in the recent lending boom were just as inexperienced as their customers. For example in the mortgage market customers had very limited experience and could be deceived by lenders or brokers with a lot of experience. This can also be seen in Credit Default Swaps, another financial contracting innovation contributing to the meltdown.

However when massive amounts of these risky innovations were contracted by multiple institutions globally, the lenders were also entering new unlearned and unchartered territory. In Credit Default Swaps as explained above an excessive amount of exposure became concentrated in one institution, AIG, such that the government had to save it in order for its counterparties to not also fail.

Professor Aliber put this view in context by noting that real estate bubbles in particular require credit and therefore their origins are usually found in the demand for securities denominated in specific currencies such as Euros or $. In a bubble the rate of growth in credit exceeds the interest rate by a substantial amount so that one is actually involved in Ponzi finance where the expansion of credit more than covers the interest the borrower must pay. This borrowing drives up real estate prices and as in Japan stocks in companies with large real estate holdings until the growth of credit slows.

When this happens the currency will weaken and prices will start to fall while repayment becomes a greater burden on leveraged borrowers. This was a key element in the Asian Financial Crisis of the 1990s. When increased borrowing can no longer cover interest the end is near and a crash will ensue. The Asian Financial Crisis for example was generated by an increasing demand for "Emerging Market" equities that was initiated by the rapid expansion of foreign direct investment [FDI] in these countries primarily from Japan and the US to develop a source of low-cost exports. These funds drove up stock and land prices. The trigger for decline came when inflation made these countries no longer low cost exporters and the balance of trade became adverse and was not covered by capital inflows. Increased imports and lower capital inflows put pressure on currency reserves and ultimately this was followed by devaluation. Borrowers in dollars saw their local currency obligations soar and they defaulted. A panic and crash followed as foreign investors and speculators exited these countries' markets.

The end of the recent US real estate bubble and bust came from the fact foreigners had enough US dollar assets. What happens when asset prices increase is that new wealth is generated that will then increase consumption. Thus a country whose assets are rapidly appreciating will have a larger increase in its current account deficit that will offset that increased demand for local assets. In effect the increased import consumption covers the increase in the export of securities to foreigners.

When the foreign demand for local assets such as US dollar assets in the form of securitized real estate loans collapses the real estate or other asset bubble will collapse too. Offsetting this effect will be a decline in the currency that will stimulate exports and reduce imports bringing the system back to a period of relative stability that existed before the bubble that resulted from the increase in the sale of dollar securities to foreigners.

Something similar happened after the Asian Financial Crisis and the collapse of those markets in 1990s when the decline in currencies led again to trade surpluses that had to be balanced by acquiring US dollar assets. These took the form of investment in Internet stocks and Treasury Securities. The latter even more so after the Internet bust, leading to a decline in US interest rates and an increase in home buying and mortgage refinancing. In this regard Real Estate is treated quite differently in terms of the way bankers around the world think.

Normally bankers lend against cash flow. But they perceive real estate as limited in supply and as always having value. Thus periodically they lend against real estate appraisals that become self-fulfilling prophecies when appraisers base their calculations on the selling prices for other comparable properties in an area. It is only after a bust that they return to cash flow calculations based a borrower's income.

This is why the world financial system is currently very unstable, compounded by the fact investors and bankers would like global prices to be less volatile. But floating exchange rates prevent this since real estate in particular cannot like goods be physically traded geographically by moving it from one place to another. Therefore floating exchange rates create more distortion than any trade barriers because owners of real estate in appreciating currencies can leverage this internationally as an appreciating asset to buy assets or goods in depreciating currency countries. This was the case in Japan in the 1980s, Iceland before 2008 and China more recently.

Such flows of capital can then lead to a spending boom in the country receiving the capital inflows that leads to a distortion in local prices such as happened in Hawaii in the 1980s due to large inflows from Japan. This increase in wealth then creates abnormal incentives that affect the allocation of local savings and consumption patterns. Such inward credit flows are not sustainable, though, and this means the prices that they are driving up are also not sustainable either. This is a classic bubble and bust scenario.

There is also the compounding effect of the mismatch of currency borrowings and earnings that has caused and continues to cause problems especially at the retail level where it looks cheap to borrow in a foreign currency supported by large capital inflows creating contracting optimism as in the Asian Financial Crisis but with a large foreign hidden exchange risk built into the loan the borrower ignores. Then when the inflows fall and the currency begins devaluing the borrower is unable to service the foreign currency loans through its local currency earnings. The result is defaults and panic.

The fact that this process seems to recur regularly in different economies and regions raises the issue of whether there is a global flow of capital or international money pool that sloshes around the world stimulating these developments.

From this perspective it is clear that such bubbles can impact managerial and financial behavior in various ways, most of which are not systemically benign. They have also impacted how managers are generally compensated for taking short-term risks, even though in retrospect they obviously did not understand the much greater but longer-term macro risks. The chapters on financial engineering and SIVs show how earnings and balance sheet manipulation can play a role in this process if banks take bad news on the downside while over emphasizing short-term earnings on the upside.

Looking at high tech firms' managers' behavior through the bubble, though, their behavior appears more cautious in their reporting because high growth and high P/E magnify reporting behavior related to earnings. Yet there does appear to be a pattern over the cycle from which one may be able to work backwards after observing certain types of behavior and thus identify where one is in a bubble.

This financial engineering chapter specifically looks at how management in their financial reporting treated volatility of earnings and discretionary items. Cash flow was examined to see if it affects reported earnings. Low volatility implies smoothing and earnings management. After the bubble period high tech firms appeared willing to report large losses given the crash. However, they wanted to see small earnings increases during the growth period. Therefore during the crash period there seems to be little earnings manipulation and they appear willing to report losses. Indeed they may use discretionary items to even push losses down more so that after crash they have more flexibility to manage the earnings back up and create a larger recovery in the stock price. Granting options after large drops in stock prices would of course incentivize such behavior.

There is, though, different behavior between low and high tech firms and some of this may be related to high tech's large R&D expenditures. Yet it is not entirely clear if the data shows one is in a bubble and if so at what stage. Nevertheless since bubbles are partly a behavioral phenomenon, one wants to know how managers are behaving during the bubble in terms of gaming the system. Further relative performance as a measure may be part of the story if all stocks of a certain type of high tech [innovative] firm rise together, such as in the case of social media. Nevertheless the outperformers do rise more among all semiconductor or all railroads, though in today's world for high tech firms the most important and relevant performance measure may be against its own stock price due to the importance of options to managers as noted above.

The ethics related to this behavior versus the difficulty of detecting it is apparent and is relevant to the chapters on herding and organizational commitment to a specific course of action. Restatement of earnings may be part of this process. Further earnings management is one way that Bubbles can spill over to hurt non-players. This is also true of Balance Sheet management as described in the Chapter on SIVs.

Structured investment vehicles or SIVs represented this type of bubble and developed from a financial innovation used to solve a specific business problem. They were designed by certain banks to get around Basle regulations by inflating bank capital.

Citibank particularly was hit by the higher Basle Tier 1 capital requirements compared to other US banks and the way they found around the rules were SIVs. Here they contributed asset backed loans to these vehicles and then negotiated with the rating agencies to get AAA ratings for SIV debt that was mostly in the form of 30-day Commercial Paper. Regulators were complicit in this accounting sleight of hand and other banks started copying Citi also issuing asset backed commercial paper. Using CP exploited a Basle loop-hole because asset backed paper with less than one year maturity required zero capital.

LTCM [Long-term Capital Management] changed the game however. This was because of a run on the fund that had also been issuing large amounts of asset backed CP as a funding source. After LTCM SIVs needed more capital, which they created using capital notes that would be rated BBB. However because this allowed SIV capital to be notes rather than equity held by the bank it shifted the skin in the game to the holders of the capital notes. The Banks and hedge funds made their money on managing the SIVs as in the case of Bear Stearns. Rating Agencies were complicit in this process since they wanted to keep the banks, funds and SIVs as customers. The scheme finally unraveled with Bear Stearns' two Cayman Island funds because their failure showed the assets in which they had invested the funds were not investment quality.

Critics argue given the new structures the SIV market would have collapsed regardless since SIV managers were buying the cheapest and lowest quality AAA assets they could find and ultimately the SIVs would have folded given the leverage used. However in folding given their leverage and connections to "too-big-to-fail" financial institutions they were putting the global financial system at risk.

The lesson is that when the doorkeepers under pressure

from the participants liberalize the rules whether Rating Agencies or Bank examiners they create a rush through the door that can create a bubble in those assets making innovation and government critical ingredients in the bubble mix along with complexity. Frequently asset transformation is part of this process. Thus when one sees this phenomenon happening it is another signal to be cautious and look for the coming crash.

While the SIV focus illustrates the interrelatedness of financial schemes and bubbles involving leverage there can also be micro or sublevel bubbles within a larger bubble. For example as a subcomponent of the real estate bubble there was a sub-bubble in golf retirement communities that hoped to benefit from and leverage the retirement of aging baby boomers and their accumulated wealth and income.

US residential construction is very large, about $500 billion a year with a critical element of this activity land acquisition that generally involves debt and thus leverage. Therefore over-optimism concerning retiring boomers and where they might settle could and did lead to excess land purchases in certain geographic areas and greatly expanded the related debt. The US real estate market including this subcomponent peaked in 2005 and the subsequent collapse was accelerated by the credit crisis and the use of Adjustable Rate Mortgages by retirees where lenders did not bear the risk due to securitization and bundling.

Many foreclosures were thus focused on new developments in the Sun Belt and retirement communities that included golf. Fort Meyers led the country in this regard. Further membership agreements in the form of optimistic contracts illustrated the intersection of law, leverage and economics explained above. Here though it was the developers more than the residential buyers that were overly optimistic, again showing that more experienced players at a micro level can be caught unawares by the creation of a macro bubble. They over promised buyers and over borrowed from banks to develop high-end properties.

One developer for example offered buyers money back guarantees on their deposits if they changed their minds because the developer was over-confident in thinking this would not happen or that there would only be a few buyers that could easily be replaced. That is over-optimism was reflected in a membership payback scheme where the developer never expected it to happen in volume, a kind of black swan event.

This and some other developers of high-end golf retirement communities continued expanding nationally even after it was clear the market had peaked. Several went bankrupt. Many were also affected by the housing crisis and stock market crash that forced many boomers to postpone retirement while in any case reducing the funds available to spend on a retirement home. One result is several golf and country club complexes have been sold to the members.

In addition it is not obvious the market will clear as the economy recovers. This is because second wave baby boomers may be different than first wave boomers because those that got jobs in the 1960s generally have defined benefit retirement plans whereas those that got jobs in the 1970s have 401(k) plans. This greatly affects how much they can risk and pay as does the effect of depressed stock markets and low interest rates on their retirement plans.

This tale reinforces several bubble signals. First real estate development is really leveraged land speculation and in some cases real land prices are negative. Thus real estate bubbles are almost always bad. Secondly one must always closely examine one's assumptions regarding why an asset should go up in price and then weigh the risk and consequences of being wrong or not hedging the related risk.

These truisms are especially valid when participating in a financial innovation, though real innovations are much rarer than Wall Street would have everyone believe. Yet one such financial innovation was the nifty-fifties and the Magic Five, where as discussed previously an asset manager created a financial innovation by persuading pension banks to invest half their managed assets in growth stocks and hold the rest in bonds.

However once again what was good idea at a micro level had adverse effects when aggregated. Here the innovative investment strategy created concentrated demand for those growth stocks and drove their prices to uneconomic levels that were unsustainable while keeping value stock prices relatively low. Then when high inflation came in 1970s value stocks that could raise prices became more attractive than the growth stocks and money moved out of the growth stocks. They thus dramatically lost value that took years to recover. Needless to say managers that had pursued the growth stock bond mix also took a big hit. Momentum and herding as expected played role in this nifty-fifty run-up and in the subsequent crash, another example of an innovation or idea that had logic at the time but then initiated a bubble. When the underlying assumptions changed the bubble collapsed.

While financial bubbles seem to always have bad outcomes, some micro technology bubbles can have profound economic consequences that in retrospect seem beneficial. For example comparing the Railroad booms of the 19th Century with the Internet boom as one presenter explained to the participants, one sees that both were technology innovations that reached a critical mass that affected the national economy and both were pushed by a government vision to tie the country together by creating network externalities. That meant the more people and towns that were connected the more valuable the network became. They also share the economics of high fixed and low marginal costs when adding someone to the existing network.

Due to this need for more and better interconnectedness, both these industries also had to develop complex organizational structures and information management systems involving matrix management that covered both geography and specific functions. Feeder railroads could become quite profitable because they could charge what the traffic would bear to get to trunk lines that might be subject to a greater degree of competition and marginal cost pricing. Something similar may have occurred for ISP providers and search engines that facilitated access and use of the Internet. Finally both industries provided opportunities for new firms and businesses to emerge using the network that could not have existed before the network was developed such as Sears catalogue sales through the RRs or Amazon and eBay using the Internet.

Financial innovations and raising capital thus were important aspects of the process as participants needed to raise large amounts of capital to build their networks. Morgan created the first mortgage railroad bond that reduced funding costs, an important idea given the large amounts of capital needed and the high fixed costs. However stocks in railroads and the Internet were both subject to bubbles because these were truly disruptive technologies that changed the world even after the investment bubble had passed. Even bankruptcies could be beneficial when they lowered the cost for the stronger competitors to acquire and operate network assets such as the telecom companies.

This makes it difficult in terms of bubble analysis to understand what were the indirect costs versus the long-term benefits. Morgan's mortgage bond idea solved the problem of reducing the risks associated with using stock or unsecured bonds to finance the railroad expansion by retaining access to foreign investors who had lost money on ordinary RR bonds or stock and were thus reluctant to finance additional expansions. This seems less of a problem today, though, since stock investors still appear ready to buy the next big Internet idea such as social media.

Finally commodity bubbles are frequently part of or closely related to other bubbles. Thus the recent boom in China for cars and housing have pushed copper prices and in turn the stocks of those producing copper or selling mining equipment to greater highs. One recent phenomenon in this vein has been the rapid price rise in Rare Earths and concern that this is a bubble directly related to the fastest growing parts of economy such as hybrid cars, cell phones and defense technologies.

It is estimated demand could double by 2020 due to their use in high tech magnets, batteries and glass. Recently after a gradual increase prices have risen dramatically, five to ten times in the year prior to September 2011. As explained above such price action is an important component of bubbles by drawing attention to an asset and initiating a bubble. However in evaluating whether it is a bubble one needs to understand the role of China and its export controls as well as its closing or restricting illegal mines and smuggling. Also for many years the Chinese underpriced the adverse environmental impacts.

In addition rare earth demand is very segmented by use and product. Thus there may be a bubble in certain rare earths but not in all. The ones in most demand for instance, heavy rare earths, involve very small quantities when they are used. So substitution effects can be important as well. Therefore despite the very rapid rise in prices it might not be a bubble because there is a constraint on supply and the price driver is not all on the demand side as new and existing production must price in the cost of environmental cleanup.

In addition there is the fact that rare earths are not actually that rare in terms or reserves and can be mined economically at these higher prices or from recycling. Rather rare comes from the problem of separating the rare earths from the ore. Here both Molycorp and some Australian mining companies have expertise. Actually short versus long-term supply issues are really related to price sustainability. That is, will the Chinese stop restraining supply or dump product to force other producers out of the market? Countering this possibility is the indication that governments such as the US and Japan seem prepared and able to subsidize output, and large users like Toyota appear willing to enter long-term contracts to break the Chinese monopoly.

This dynamic situation shows the role of expectations in whether a bubble will develop. In this case the price run up apparently can create supply that will eventually bring prices down to substantially lower prices. As long as investors perceive that this is the situation the mania required for a bubble will never develop. On the other hand in the short-term supply constraints could lead to hoarding that would have an upward impact on prices and could create a bubble. There will also be speculation in the stocks of firms that have particular rare earth resources or processing expertise.

This has happened to a degree in rare earths already though on balance it does not seem to be a bubble despite the price action. Yet this kind of phenomenon certainly was a factor in the run up of certain stocks during the Japanese real estate bubble of the 1980s. But the bubble will collapse or crash once investors and speculators believe that supply is no longer constrained. This is what happened in the Dutch tulip mania in the 1600s.

Nevertheless greed is always present and generally there always seem to be funds available to chase the next big thing. In the 1930s Colin Clark opined that based on his analysis of economic growth in different countries over several decades that capital grew much faster than other factors of production and that while growth in the capital stock was needed to support economic growth there were periods when it grew much faster than required to support such growth. Certainly bubble periods can do this as Robert Aliber has explained. Thus the cost of capital during such periods will decline driving down investor returns.

In response certain investors searching for higher returns will take on more risk and frequently will misperceive the actual degree of risk involved. This will lead to periodic booms where people move to purchase more risky assets but also to collapses as the true risks became apparent. This will reduce asset values and effectively burn up the excess capital while the re-pricing of risk will bring the system back into balance.

Something similar to this seems to have had happened in

the various crises examined in this book and again supports the idea bubbles may be a natural outcome of the capitalistic system and functioning financial markets. A policy question remains though on how to best moderate and balance their effects without frustrating investment in important disruptive technologies when bubbles can also adversely affect the global financial system.

W. Rapp, Editor

Henry J. Leir Professor International Business [rappw@njit.edu] and Director of the Leir Center for Financial Bubble Research at the New Jersey Institute Of Technology's School Of Management [www.leirbubblecenter.org]

CHAPTER ONE

EVERYTHING IS NOT A BUBBLE[5]

When The Hurley Burley's Done

W. Rapp

Introduction

Many books written after a financial or economic crisis including the collapse of a major bubble seem primarily designed to shock and scare the reader with respect to the just past economic catastrophe and the one looming just around the corner. Indeed after an economic crisis such as the recent Great Recession there seems to develop a bubble in books about bubbles as each author competes with other experts in explaining how it happened, how that particular author saw it coming and how the next one can be avoided.

In addition the popularity of the word "bubble" appears to result in every economic and financial problem becoming a bubble including the Euro Crisis centered in Greece but also involving Ireland, Portugal, Spain, Italy and even France. It is in this way that many financial gurus can identify several bubbles affecting the US or global economy that will come together to create a massive and coordinated bubble and crash that only they can help investors and policy makers avoid.

However, from the perspective of analyzing bubbles

---

[5] A preliminary draft of this chapter is posted as a Working Paper on the Leir Center For Financial Bubble Research website. A revision was presented at the IABPAD Conference in FL January 2013 and published in its *Proceedings*. This chapter is a further revision and has been related to other chapters.

generally or a specific bubble such as the one leading to the Great Recession, there are problems with this general labeling and analysis, especially if it is used as an investment or regulatory strategy.

Some authors justify this general "bubble" labeling by incorrectly stating there is no accepted definition for a bubble or that the definitions that do exist are so vague as to defy concrete analysis. Thus they feel free to use the word indiscriminately and can therefore define situations that are not bubbles as bubbles increasing the hype of their message while actually decreasing its analytical validity. The accepted definition of a bubble is when the real price of an asset rises rapidly to a significant level above it basic economic value such as the price of a house compared to its discounted rental value. At some point this differential becomes unsustainable and the bubble collapses. The authors in this volume use this definition in their analysis of bubbles and it is consistent with the one used by Professor Aliber in the current edition of the seminal work on bubbles, *Manias, Panics and Crashes* [Kindleberger & Aliber 2011].

There are three important components to this definition. First a bubble concerns assets that are unique in some respect and limited in supply such as real estate with a Hudson River View or great art such as a Matisse painting. Things that can be produced are rarely bubbles since the rapid rise in prices will bring increased production as noted in the Introduction with respect to Rare Earths. At the same time there must be enough of the asset or related assets available such that when prices begin declining it affects the entire class such as Japanese urban real estate or dot.com stocks or impressionist paintings.

Second the real price rise must be rapid, something that is captured in the analogized equation $E = MP^2$ where the explosive aspect of the bubble when it pops is equal to the money flowing into the market for the assets times the acceleration in real prices. If it takes 72 years for the real price of the asset to rise 100% above the asset's economic value, the price will only be rising above the asset's economic value at 1% per year and is unlikely to attract the speculators critical to forming an asset bubble. On the other hand if its real price [nominal price rise less the CPI] rises 15% or more per year it will double its real price in less than 5 years and will attract speculators who will accelerate the price rise and draw more money into the bubble increasing the negative impact on investor and speculator wealth when the crash finally occurs. Real prices are used because people need to feel they are getting wealthy as a result of the bubble. There is unlikely to be any money illusion if the CPI is also going up 15% a year or more.

Having the right statistics or price metrics is thus a key aspect in identifying a real bubble given that the cycle starts with an infusion of new cash into the market for the asset. So a bubble based investment strategy would be Cash to Investment back to Cash.

Examining some famous stock market bubbles, the top of

the US market bubble prior to the Great Depression was 1929 with the subsequent bottom in July 1932 but it did not regain that 1929 high until the peak of the defense related-conglomerate and nifty fifty boom of the 1960s and early 1970s. That bubble led to a new high in the Dow-Jones in January 1973 at 1022. It subsequently fell to a bottom in the subsequent crash at 570 in December 1974. It did not go over that 1973 high until 1983, reaching a new peak in January 2000 at 11,908 followed by another crash due to the dot.com bust.

We see in the first cycle that over a 41 year period the Dow went up by a factor of 26 times and in the second over a period of 26 years it went up twenty-one times. If we extend the analysis to the high of 14,280 in October 2007, it was 25 times over a 34-year period.

In any case financial bubbles involve asset prices. If there is no asset, then there is no bubble. Applying this criterion to bubbles that some authors associate with the US budget and trade deficits, there are in fact no bubbles. This does not mean ballooning trade and budget deficits are not worrisome trends. These expanding deficits have implications for investment strategies and helped facilitate the housing and subprime mortgage bubbles. Indeed as noted in the Introduction Professor Aliber has directly linked the financial flows associated with several different countries' trade and budget deficits to particular bubbles. Nevertheless they themselves are definitely not bubbles because there is no asset involved that is increasing rapidly in price.

If I build 50 houses during a five-year period at 10 houses a year and next year I build another 10 houses I have 60 houses and there is no bubble unless the prices for those houses rise dramatically creating an asset inflation. Similarly if I have a series of budget deficits or trade deficits I have just added to the national debt and the borrowing from foreigners. Since these obligations are all denominated in dollars and the price of one dollar does not change, there has been no change in price. Further from a US investor's point of view there is no asset involved since the trade deficit is not an asset nor is the US budget deficit. Therefore there is no change in any asset price.

For the same reason from a US investor's perspective there cannot be a dollar bubble because the price of a dollar is not rising or falling except compared to another currency or some benchmark commodity such as oil or gold.

This is not to say you cannot have a dollar bubble. You can. But you have to be a non-US investor and you have to be investing in US dollar assets such as US stocks or bonds. Indeed such a bubble occurred in Japan in the early 1980s after the US negotiated the Yen/Dollar Accord. US interest rates at that time were extremely high due to the Volker anti-inflation squeeze and this attracted investment by Japanese financial firms, especially big life insurance companies that due to the regulatory changes resulting from the Yen/dollar Accord were now permitted to invest in foreign currency assets. This dollar asset demand strengthened the dollar against the Yen creating foreign exchange gains for the insurers on top of the very high interest rates. Then in 1983 when US interest rates started falling there were capital gains on the bonds too. This combining of high interest rates, exchange gains and market appreciation attracted more Yen funds, further strengthening the dollar and lowering bond rates that created more capital gains.

However, the very strong dollar hit US exporters extremely hard, especially firms such as Caterpillar, Boeing and GM and strong political pressures developed to counter the appreciating dollar-weak yen environment leading to a collapse in the dollar bubble in 1985. Then as is not uncommon with a collapsing bubble the Japanese economic and policy reactions to the rapidly devalued dollar relative to the Yen established the preconditions needed for the Japanese real estate and stock market bubble that crashed in early 1990. This was because the investment funds that normally would have flowed from Japan now turned inward seeking local investment opportunities. This is described in a paper "Foreign Firms in Japan's Securities Industry in the 1980s and Post Bubble Economy,"[6]

> "Part of the bubble's origin is found in excess liquidity after 1985 due to a combination of the trade surplus and the sharp yen appreciation after the Plaza Accord. The

[6] See William V. Rapp, "Foreign Firms in Japan's Securities Industry in the 1980s and Post Bubble Economy," in *Post Bubble Japanese Business*, Raj Aggarwal, ed., Kluwer Academic Publishers, Chapter 7, 1999

balooning surplus greatly increased the money supply as companies converted dollars to yen and the Bank of Japan permitted the increase to counter the deflationary effects of a strengthening yen (Ito, 1992). Further, as already noted, portfolio investors had stormed into foreign assets in the early 1980s in response to higher rates, also keeping the yen weak (Shinkai, 1987). Now they took billions in portfolio losses, and sought the safety of yen assets and hedges for their dollar investments. This created additional upward yen pressure. So excess liquidity found outlets in government bonds, real estate and stocks with investors primarily large corporations, financial institutions, and wealthy individuals. No longer having attractive overseas investments, excess savings chased domestic assets, driving up prices (Ito, 1992). For instance government bond trading which had amounted to about to 200 to 500 trillion yen between 1980 and 1984 jumped to 2,200 trillion in 1985 and peaked at 5,800 trillion in 1987 (Japan Securities Research Institute, 1994).

However, the supply of Japanese bonds, real estate and stocks were restricted. Historically, financial institutions had bought government bonds by direct placement and held them to maturity (Shinkai, 1987) which was why trading activity was rather limited. Similarly, people and companies did not sell real estate because taxes were too high (Ito, 1992) and prices always went up (Frankel, 1991 and Yamamura and Hanley, 1992). Finally, firms did not sell stock because the market over time has trended up and because of stable shareholder relationships (Zielinsky and Holloway, 1991). Further, over time the proportion owned by institutions had risen since they were generally buyers, not sellers. Thus, by the late 1980s, unlike the U.S. 70% of stock was held by companies and individuals for business purposes (Zielinsky and Holloway, 1991). ...

This environment would have forced prices up more than normally in any case. But as stock and real estate prices rose, they created a compounding effect and the engine for the sharp upward price spiral and the bubble. The increase in bond, real estate and stock prices caused investors to value companies based on these hidden real estate and financial assets, bidding up their shares (Frankel, 1991 and Ito, 1992). They then used stock gains to buy real estate, either selling shares or borrowing against appreciation. Profits and loans on appreciated real estate were used to buy stocks and bonds, ratcheting up both on a continuous interactive basis as the bubble became full blown. Since rising rices for bonds, stock, or real estate affect all holders, this extended well beyond the immediate buyers and sellers to all owners, lifting the economy's borrowing capacity and paper wealth enormously. ...

The first indication of possible weakness in this boom scenario given a change in supply/demand dynamics came with the fall in the Government Bond Market in June 1987. Here, unique features of the market combined with the loose money policy to promote ramping by a syndicate of banks and securities houses. As money expanded and interest fell, money poured in during the first half of 1987, and the "benchmark's" price rose sharply. By June, the yield approached 2%. It was then rumored the reason for the rapid rise was a syndicate had cornered the limited supply of benchmark bonds. Other dealers caught short complained and the MOF moved quickly, unilaterally expanding the issue and eliminating the corner. The ensuing collapse, though, showed what could happen when the pressure of too much money chasing a restricted asset supply was eased. So while stocks recovered after the October 1987 crash, the bond market did not because the institutional dynamics restricting supply had been permanently altered. ...

Since bonds did not recover but stocks did with the Nikkei Index rising from about 18,000 in 1987 to 38,000 at the end of 1989 (Japan Securities Institute, 1994), the interactive upward price ratcheting in stock and real estate resumed with the speculative money in bonds adding to the pool."

Something similar, however, happened to stocks and real estate when the MOF in 1988 allowed the development of a futures market that could essentially create stock from thin air while at the same time restricting bank lending on real estate and revising the 1975 real estate pricing law (Rapp 1999). The decrease in available leverage for real estate combined with the de facto increased supply of stocks worked to dramatically reduce upward price pressures and then contributed to the downward acceleration. Many banks and insurance companies lost their hidden reserves plus there were losses on loans secured by real estate and stock. Over two trillion dollars in market value evaporated, completing a classic boom and bust bubble from which Japan has not yet fully recovered (Rapp 1999). The current Nikkei value is about one-third to one quarter of its all time high more than twenty years after the collapse.

At the same time it illustrates several important analytical benchmarks. A bubble occurs from the standpoint of some investor or speculator. Here the dollar asset bubble occurred from the standpoint of Japanese investors. When the dollar collapsed dollar investors did not lose but Japanese insurance companies did which is why in the subsequent boom they funneled money into Yen assets. However, in the Yen boom and bust both Japanese and foreign investors were active, though many of the latter made money betting against the bubble (Rapp 1999).

If one applies this type of analysis to a US based investor prior to and after the 2008 crash, one can examine whether there was a bubble in the dollar against some other currency's investor or against some other currency from a US perspective. Was there for example a bubble in the dollar from the perspective of the Chinese and Japanese governments even though those governments have historically purchased dollars to keep their currencies weak so their export industries will continue to generate employment.

Indeed many predict that the triggering event for a coming crisis will be when these governments get tired of buying US bonds because they predict this dollar accumulation cannot go on forever. Many well-known analysts argue this unwillingness to buy US bonds will trigger a very sharp rise in interest rates that the Fed will be unable to counter and this will bring about a bubble crisis as the dollar devalues.

However, there are many things wrong with this analytic scenario. In the case of Japan, for example, this accumulation has been occurring since the mid-1970s or more than 35 years. Therefore it is not clear why the Japanese MOF will suddenly change its mind. It is also true that in addition to the Japanese, the Chinese, the Koreans and the Taiwanese have been pursuing the same neo-Mercantilist export job creation strategy for several years. If they were to begin selling their dollar assets and exchanging them for another currency, though, such as the Euro or the Yen then those currencies would appreciate against the dollar and US exports would rise stimulating US employment and the US economy. Indeed the Japanese have accused the Chinese of buying Japanese bonds with the predatory purpose of weakening Japanese competitiveness in key industries such as automobiles and electronics.

Further as imports are only a small part of the US economy any inflationary impact would be modest. Finally any increase in bond market interest the Fed could easily counter through expanding its balance sheet, though this might not be necessary given the expansion in exports and reduction in imports, all of which would tend to stabilize the dollar at a new and more competitive level.

In retrospect of course we know the 2008-2009 crisis had nothing to do with the Japanese or Chinese refusing to accept dollars. Thus the Fed never had to raise interest rates to protect the dollar and it is not clear given the actions they did take that they would have. Rather this bubble and bust had everything to do with the subprime mortgage crisis where dollar trillions of over-priced securitized mortgage loans defaulted causing the bankruptcy of several major as well as minor financial institutions and a global financial meltdown with aftershocks continuing into 2012 and 2013.

The housing bubble developed because people's incomes were not rising in proportion to the rise in housing prices and when interest rates rose too they could not meet the rising monthly service costs. Therefore they borrowed to fill the gap. When this was no longer possible housing prices began to peak, defaults increased and the crash started and then expanded to the securitized mortgage backed securities market that was itself financed by a highly leveraged global financial system. Since some investment banks and hedge funds were leveraged over 30 to one (see Chapter 7 on Structured Investment Vehicles) even small changes in such asset values proved disastrous.

Predicting this crisis, as some did, thus required not a focus on what the Chinese and Japanese were doing but a focus on US housing, CDOs and the activities of US financial institutions. Under this scenario after US housing prices peeked in August 2005 and began declining people could no longer refinance their homes to payoff credit card bills, fund their monthly mortgage payments, or increase consumption spending. As Aliber has explained Ponzi finance where interest can be covered through refinancing ended for many US consumers [Kindleberger & Aliber 2011]. Morgan Stanley estimated this took a trillion dollars out of US consumption. This development then triggered mortgage defaults and decreased the value of trillions in US mortgage and credit card backed securities.

The collapse of the US housing market meant other economies built on similar economic structures such as Spain and Ireland would suffer similar fates. There would also be a dramatic fall in US consumption that had been financed by mortgages and credit cards. Yet the Bubble was not in consumer debt that had like the US government and trade deficits just grown. Rather it was in the securities or assets backed by mortgage and credit card debt and then packaged by investment banks and sold to investors worldwide. In fact as the Michael Lewis book the *Big Short* (Lewis 2011) informs us some of these securitized assets were "designed to fail". The issuance of these assets such as securitized subprime mortgages and CDOs grew rapidly but were over-priced relative to their true economic value and thus prices fell dramatically when the defaults began.

Under this scenario as financial institutions especially banks came under pressure they would do what they always do in these situations, they would become more conservative, providing less and less business and consumer credit. This would subsequently make the overall deflationary impact on the economy worse, leading to a collapse in stock prices for anything connected with homebuilding and the mortgage-backed securitization business including investment banks, commercial banks, specialized mortgage lenders, those providing credit default swaps [AIG], and mono bond insurers. Lewis (2011) does an excellent job of describing this development. These developments would of course make lenders even more conservative creating an adverse economic loop.

Given this set of facts a major recession was likely in response to which the Fed would lower interest rates dramatically and the Federal government along with other countries would begin aggressive fiscal stimulus. Under these conditions the Chinese and other neo-mercantilist countries would not stop buying US bonds because demand for their exports would drop significantly and they would want to maintain the export related employment. Again the bubble was thus not in the dollar but in housing and subprime mortgage backed securities. Everything related to these would collapse including bank stocks such as Countrywide or the mono-insurers of mortgage-backed debt or those writing Credit Default Swaps such as AIG.

Conversely due to a combination of low interest rates and fiscal stimulus, infrastructure would be expected to do well and did. An investment in a diversified portfolio of such stocks between the end of November 2008 and March 2009 would have yielded around 3 times one's investment. Similarly concern with financial safety saw a large move into Treasuries further lowering market interest rates. In the Spring of 2007 when the housing bubble collapse signals were fairly apparent 10 year Treasuries were paying 5% compared to a yield of 3.4% by 2009 and even lower in 2012. Thus investors moving into Treasuries in 2007 would not only have protected them from the crash it would have yielded a nice return plus a capital gain, until the collapse in stock prices was over. They could then invest in a potentially sharp and lucrative upside recovery.

This is not to say investment recommendations in gold or the Euro would not have yielded positive results. Gold almost doubled between 2005 and 2010 and the Euro has been selling at a premium to the dollar. However, investing is all about percentages and a doubling of the gold price between 2005 and 2010 is only a 15% rate of return, hardly comparable with the bounce in infrastructure stocks. The Euro in turn during this period only rose 25% or an average of 5% per year or comparable to Treasuries and clearly with more risk as seen by its fall relative to the dollar by the summer of 2012. In fact if one did not see Greece coming, US based investors might be slightly down on a 2005 Euro investment.

Actually in terms of a foreign exchange play given a prescient assessment of the coming 2008 collapse as being housing and financial credit focused, a Yen investment would have been a more logical choice. This is because the Japanese for the last several years have not been manipulating their currency as the Chinese have. Rather the continued deflation in Japan has led the central bank to keep borrowing rates close to zero. This has created something known as the "carry trade" where hedge fund managers would borrow Yen and then invest in securities in other currencies with higher yields including US dollar securities.

This use of borrowed Yen to buy dollar assets kept the Yen weak relative to the dollar and in some cases gave hedge fund managers a negative cost of funds.

Given the expected drop in US dollar rates resulting from the housing bubble collapse scenario, though, the reasons for the carry trade would disappear and the Yen should subsequently strengthen. In addition a global recession would lower oil prices and the Yen is an anti-petro currency. Therefore given a projected asset backed securities collapse scenario a Yen appreciation was likely and this turned out to be a correct call. On balance gold appears to have been among the better hedging options though it did not achieve the incredible multiples of those who shorted the subprime mortgage crisis [Big_Short, Lewis 2011]. Also gold prices as of July 2012 were down about 20% from their earlier peak.

It should also be recognized that gold's annual economic demand depends on use in industry and jewelry. If it rises in price in a downturn, industrial users will try to use less and jewelry demand will switch from demand to supply as the stock of gold jewelry is exchanged for cash. Thus, to know the top in the price of gold one needs to monitor whether there are long lines on 47th Street and its overseas equivalents to sell jewelry since the available gold stock accumulated since 5000BC will overwhelm demand. This is what happened to the gold price in 1980 when it collapsed.

Of course a bubble collapse of global consequences is not a

good thing even if one saw it coming and took the logical protective steps just outlined or just because some capital product industries have benefitted from infrastructure investments. Local and state governments not only in the US but also in other countries have been very badly hurt, especially in education and healthcare. This is because these governments are heavily dependent on property taxes, sales taxes and income tax revenues that all fell sharply at the same time that expenditures related to unemployment rose along with pension costs and unfunded benefits given layoffs and falling stock prices. This could be especially hard on communities that promised more than they could afford during the good times they thought would continue or that were sold toxic assets by investment bankers.

Therefore it is appropriate from a policy standpoint that governments understand and work to manage large financial bubbles. At the same time if one is going to manage bubbles it is critical that one understands them and is able to differentiate among the different types or when there is no bubble at all. This is not possible when one defines every dramatic rise in prices as a bubble along with every financial crisis. For example some commentators see the rise in CEO compensation relative to labor and middle management income as a bubble (Shiller 2012) or collage tuitions with both leading to financial as well as social crises.

Is There A Bubble In CEO Compensation Or College Tuition?

Robert Shiller in his latest book, *Finance and the Good*

Society (Shiller 2012), argues that there is a Bubble in CEO compensation. Others have argued that the increasing cost of higher education is now a bubble that has been exacerbated by the recent financial debacle because state and local governments have cut back on their support, forcing public colleges to raise tuitions and students to take on more debt.

Few deny these are large and serious financial problems in the aggregate for the United States with significant societal consequences. The income and wealth differentials between the top 10% and even more the top 1.0% and 0.1% are increasing and the Occupy Wall Street movement and political polarization over tax rates for the wealthy show these have clearly become important social and political issues (Ferguson, 2012). Similarly debt loads for many students are becoming overwhelming and the rates of default especially for those attending profit-making institutions are rising. Over a trillion dollars in student debt is a burden on family formation and has forced many new graduates to return home while trying to find employment in a difficult job market. Yet are these situations Bubbles? Applying the criteria used above the answer is no and they are examples of how the "bubble" word has been abused and can lead to a misleading impression of what is a bubble and the appropriate investment and/or policy response.

A bubble requires an asset that is tradable or at least interchangeable with similar assets in that class and where a rise in the price of related assets responds to increases in demand such as when all dotcom stocks went up together but where they will all also trend down together when the bubble bursts. Of course under the 13th Amendment to the US Constitution one cannot buy and sell human beings in the US as an asset. Yet one could argue that because CEO pay has steadily outpaced the CPI on the upside while workers and middle management income in real terms has remained relatively steady there is a CEO compensation bubble.[7] Indeed some CEO pay packages have been really outsized. However, though a CEO can leave to go to another firm for more money this can take weeks to accomplish not seconds as when selling a security. Further terminations do not seem to cause buyer's distress.

Further the number of CEOs seems not only limited but also highly segmented especially for large public companies where the issue seems to be most visible and political. Among the international Fortune 1000 there are only 1000 CEOs and the pay for some such as in large Japanese firms appears to be totally unrelated to American CEOs' compensation. Further when the CEO Merrill Lynch Stan O'Neal was fired his replacement John Thain's package seemed equally as rich. In addition the compensation in an industry such as steel appears unrelated to the compensation for CEOs in finance or autos.

This is not to say there cannot be bubbles in compensation

---

[7] In his book *Finance and the Good Society*, Shiller notes the Congressional Budget Office calculated that the real after tax income for the top 1% of US income earners grew 275% between 1979 and 2007 while for the bottom 20% of the population it only increased 18%.

but it appears to take place at lower levels such as freshly minted lawyers, MBAs and programmers who are hired at will or based on a standard employment contract rather than via the elaborately negotiated contracts for high paid CEOs. Since the recent financial collapse there have been numerous articles on how freshly minted lawyers even from top law schools are no longer guaranteed a spot at a big law firm with lucrative compensation packages to help meet their massive amounts of student loan debt.

At the same time the ABA has reported that for those lucky enough to be hired by a top tier firm, pay packages have remained relatively constant but have not yet collapsed. Thus the market seems to be working as supply exceeds demand, but with no bursting of a law compensation bubble. Similarly after Dewey & LeBoeuf went bankrupt the productive partners quickly found other rewarding slots.

On the other hand during the Asian Boom of the 1990s salaries for entry-level Thai programmers approached those that Microsoft was paying in the US for those with 10 years of experience. This was a good bubble indicator since the Asian boom began with a surge in FDI seeking educated workers at lower wages. Once this excess labor pool evaporated and wages rose FDI fell and imports rose, triggering the bust and a collapse in foreign exchange rates that returned market wages to a sustainable global level. Indeed after the baht collapsed in value, Toyota began exporting cars to Japan from their plant in Thailand.

This change in exchange values along with the dramatic drop in real estate prices helped set the conditions for an economic recovery without the prior mania.

Something similar seems to be happening in higher education with respect to tuition and students' willingness to take on debt. That is states and students are responding to economic realities but the very top colleges have no shortage of applicants just as the very top law firms continue to hire the very top law students. Further those students continue to sometimes pay higher and higher tuitions to those institutions.

I note "sometimes" because almost every college and university is involved in price discrimination and the elite ones even more so. Thus while the sticker price at an Ivy League School is currently around $50,000 a year many students pay substantially less than that based on need. Other private and state universities offer scholarships based on merit or athletic ability as well. In essence these schools are taxing those who can afford to pay in order to subsidize those that are less affluent. Under these circumstances it is not clear from what level a price collapse would come and whether even at these price levels applications to elite schools are not actually rising rather than falling.

In addition just as with the CEOs where is the tradable asset? As yet we have not entered the realm of science fiction where one can download one's educational experience and learning directly from one brain to another. Whatever education is acquired belongs uniquely to that individual and in turn by entering the job market that individual can rent that package of talent, experience and education to an employer making an economic and social contribution while gaining employment experience.

Of course due to the Great Recession many graduates are having difficulty finding jobs. Further given high unemployment and declining property values state and local governments are cutting back on support to public higher education shifting the cost of higher education from the general public to the actual consumers. At the same time many families feel financially stretched and thus they and their children will look for lower cost options putting pressure on financially weaker colleges and universities. These economic and fiscal forces are obvious and are creating big headaches for administrations.

Longer term this could also lead to a less well educated less productive population and to increased defaults on student loans. Therefore there is no denying that a crisis may be developing where public colleges and universities along with less well-endowed private institutions may have to make painful choices with respect to degree requirements, teaching loads and their current emphasis on research. Yet this crisis is not a bubble since there is neither an obvious tradable asset nor a clear market price for that asset which has risen relative to the CPI and is poised for collapse.

Rather if there is a bubble in higher education it only seems to be possible in the stock price of "for-profit institutions" such as the University of Phoenix (Apollo Group: APOL) or National American University (National American University Holdings Inc.: NAUH). But this bubble and bust may have already occurred since APOL as of August 2012 was selling around $28 a share down from a high of $90 in September 2009 and NAUH was around $4.25 down from $12.50. Thus both firms have seen their share price collapse between sixty and seventy percent from their highs.

Not All Financial Crises Are Bubbles –
Panic 1907 and Euro Crisis 2012

While many financial crises such as the Great Depression and the recent Great Recession involve financial bubbles not all bubbles result in a financial crisis. The dotcom bubble only hurt investors in those high tech stocks since margin requirements limited lender involvement. No "too-big-to-fail" bailouts were needed. A black letter rule put in place in response to the 1929 crash did its job. The Summer of 2012 drop in the share prices of social media companies has caused little or no economic fallout other than for those that invested or are working for them. Similarly not all financial crises involve bubbles.

Historically one of the most famous and important of US financial crises is the 1907 Panic where J. P. Morgan is credited with saving the US financial system and where Congressional hearings ultimately led to the formation of the Federal Reserve System. In their book *The Panic Of 1907* (Bruner and Carr 2007) Robert Bruner and Sean Carr describe how the 1906 San

Francisco earthquake led to very large nationwide capital demands and a national liquidity squeeze that there was no central bank to offset. This situation slowly depressed equity prices particularly mining shares, leading to financial problems for several related banks that then set off a series of bank runs.

What occurred was that a group of Wall Street manipulators used a pyramiding scheme to acquire several banks, trust companies and insurance firms. Having acquired a controlling interest in one financial institution the "pool" would then use that control to borrow money to buy a controlling interest in other financial institutions, securing loans with shares of the company being acquired. The investor pool's initial capital though came from success in mining and it used its shares in United Copper to secure the loans to start acquiring financial firms. Then

> "as equity prices fell broadly, the brothers became concerned about their holdings in United Copper, whose stock had been used to secure their positions in numerous banking concerns. In an attempt to support the price of their United Copper Company shares, the Heinzes began purchasing large quantities of the company's stock and placing them on margin with as many as 20 brokerage houses on Wall Street. A dangerous game was afoot."

After an attempted corner in United Copper stock failed the whole pyramid began unraveling with brokerage houses and in turn the banks from which they had received margin loans affected. It began with the Mercantile National Bank of which

Augustus Heinze was president but spread to several related banks and brokerages, the most important being the Knickerbocker Trust Company.

> "Should the Knickerbocker fall, its failure would signal to the public that something more endemic was threatening the financial system. By day's end, widespread fear and uncertainty would spread like brush fire."

Indeed what followed was a series of bank runs as rumors and reality merged since there was no deposit insurance, an idea that only emerged later during the Great Depression. Depositors thus rushed to withdraw money from any bank or trust company that seemed weak. This of course only made the situation worse. Further as New York was the country's financial capital whatever affected New York impacted the country and London too.

> "The crash and panic of 1907 reverberated in markets, governments, and the lives of individuals throughout the United States and around the world. Commodity prices fell 21 percent, eliminating virtually the entire increase from 1904 to 1907. Industrial production dropped more than in any other U.S. panic up to 1907. The dollar volume of bankruptcies declared in November spiked up by 47 percent over a year earlier ... Gross earnings of railroads fell by 6 percent in December, production fell 11 percent from May 1907 to June 1908, wholesale prices fell 5 percent and imports shrank 26 percent. Unemployment rose from 2.8 percent to 8 percent."

The situation was only stabilized due to the efforts of J. P. Morgan who used his personal power and influence to get the stronger banks to work together to become in effect lenders of last resort, a function now done by central banks. Nevertheless the establishment of a central bank while addressing the liquidity deficiencies of the US financial system clearly did not eliminate the possibility of financial crises, including those unrelated to a bubble but rather to natural catastrophes or fiscal mismanagement.

The Latin American debt crisis of the 1980s is an example of the latter as is the current Euro crisis. It is true that both Ireland and Spain had housing and construction bubbles similar to the U.S. that are exacerbating the crisis but its origins and underlying problems lie in Greece and the Eurozone's economic and political system not those particular housing and construction bubbles.

The Euro is from an historical perspective a unique modern currency experiment in that it is a currency not tied to a single country such as the dollar, yen or pound. Thus its exchange rate is not subject to any single country's monetary and fiscal policy. Yet exchange rates determine the international price of a country's goods, services and assets, so any currency regime will have winners and losers based on productivity.

If a particular country within a currency zone or region within a country with its own currency has a high level of productivity, the exchange rate from its perspective will look undervalued compared to countries or sectors with lower productivity. However, all sectors within the common population are importing goods and services based on the common exchange rate. The less productive sectors will therefore buy from the more productive sectors and from abroad. Given scale, scope and experience effects this will benefit the more productive sectors making them even more competitive while keeping the currency weaker than if the less productive sectors did not exist. Therefore over time more and more resources will flow to the more productive sectors, which benefits a country's economy if it is a single country but may not be so clearly beneficial if it is a currency zone composed of several countries.

In effect there is a symbiotic relationship between the less productive and more productive sectors or regions that would end if the former disappeared since then the less productive regions would no longer be importing and the exchange rate would appreciate reducing the more productive sectors' competitive edge. Political disagreements between the sectors would increase too.

This is why the UK Prime Minister David Cameron was correct when he stated that a successful currency regime required the winners to compensate the losers from some of their benefits through fiscal policy or other types of transfer payments such as pensions, national healthcare or social security. New York for example complains it contributes more to the Federal Budget than it gets back. However this view fails to account for the fact Wall Street and thus New York benefits from the less productive states or regions being able to keep consuming due to those transfer payments, thus weakening the dollar relative to other currencies and making Wall Street more competitive.

A similar economic dynamic has been unfolding with respect to the Euro but without the political and fiscal offset. Within the Eurozone there are high productivity countries such as Germany, Netherlands and Finland. There are also lower productivity countries such as Greece, Spain and Portugal. For several years the lower productivity countries consumed more than they sold but not out of transfer payments. Rather they borrowed. Indeed it seems in the case of Greece the government borrowed more than they were supposed to under Eurozone guidelines but disguised this fact through a series of derivative transactions arranged by Goldman Sachs. When this became known in 2010 it triggered the Euro crisis and a weakening of the Euro because investors fled the weaker countries' bonds. The main beneficiaries of this development were the stronger countries, especially Germany, which saw its exports soar and its unemployment drop even as unemployment in Spain jumped above 20 percent.

Given the free movement of labor within the Eurozone the logical result is for younger educated workers from countries such as Spain or Greece, especially those with engineering or technical skills, to migrate. Indeed demand for German language training is apparently soaring. Yet how long will those countries be willing to see their economic and intellectual futures leave and their economies negatively impacted while another country seems to be prospering at their expense. It is also short-sighted on the part of Germany and Finland to resist negotiating some fiscal compensation arrangement to keep these countries from leaving the Euro since that event would lead to the Euro's immediate appreciation and a reduction in their competitiveness and economic growth.

The idea the European Central Bank will buy the weaker countries' government bonds while helpful in the short-run is not a long term fix since it does not improve these countries economic situation in terms of productivity and employment. This requires FDI, job training and infrastructure investment. Providing capital from the European Fund directly to these countries' banking sectors is a move in this direction since it reduces the growth in their government debt and enables their banking sectors to provide loans to business.

However more is needed if those businesses are going to compete effectively under a strong Euro currency regime. Further by pulling up the bottom of the European economy the strong countries will be increasing the markets for their products. Henry Ford figured out this positive economic synergy 100 years ago. When he raised wages to $5 a day his competitors asserted he would immediately go bankrupt. Instead he prospered and it was his competitors he drove out of business with increased productivity and market share. The most productive and skilled workers flocked to his factories while also becoming some of his best customers.[8]

Conclusion – Bubbles

Are A Distinct Market Phenomena Of Misperceived Risk

If everything is a bubble then neither bubbles nor other financial problems will be properly identified, regulated or managed. As explained above bubbles involve the rapid rise in the real price of a tradable asset. If there is no tradable asset there is no bubble and the crisis or problem is due to something other than a bubble such as in the case of the Euro where large government deficits for certain countries combined with large differentials in productivity within a single currency zone have created the crisis.

While having a lender of last resort can effectively counter the aftermath of a collapsed bubble it will not address a financial crisis requiring the fiscal transfer of resources from a currency zone's winners to its losers. Also fiscal or monetary restraint or stimulus may not be the best way to manage a bubble. Apparently one reason the US has margin requirements is during the stock market boom of 1920s the Fed raised interest rates to try and control the boom. But due to perceived high returns in stocks relative to other investments this policy actually increased funds flowing into speculation and hurt the underlying economy by

---

[8] Some articles related to the these points about the Euro crisis are: N. Kulish and P. Geitner, "Euro Zone Crisis Boils as Leaders Fail to Signal New Steps, " *NY Times*, May 23, 2012; R. Atkins, "Migrants learn language of German boom," *Financial Times*, January 11, 2012; B. Marsh, "Its All Connected: An Overview of the Euro Crisis," *NY Times*, October 22, 2011; P. Krugman, "European Crisis Realities," *NY Times*, February 5, 2012; J. Ewing, "Euro Zone Crisis: A Primer," *NY Times*, May 22, 2012.

strangling normal business investment. This shortage of productive investment made the collapse's economic consequences vastly worse.

In sum having a proper understanding of what is and is not a bubble as well as the particular type of bubble is critical to developing appropriate investment and government policies. Therefore proper labeling as with food is critical to an economy's health.

References

Aliber, R. & Kindleberger, C. 2011. *Manias, Panics and Crashes*, 6th Ed. Palgrave Macmillan, NY.

Atkins, R. 2012. "Migrants learn language of German boom", *Financial Times.*

Bruner, R. & Carr, S. 2007. *The Panic Of 1907*, John Wiley, Hoboken, NJ.

Ehrlich, M. 2011. "Innovation, Regulation and Financial Bubbles: The Evolution of Structured Investment Vehicles", Leir Center For Financial Bubble Research, Working Paper #8, www.leirbubblecenter.org.

Ewing, J. 2012. "Euro Zone Crisis: A Primer", *NY Times*, NY.

Ferguson, C. 2012. *Predator Nation: Corporate Criminals, Political Corruption, and the Hijacking Of America*, Crown Business, NY.

Frankel, T. 1991. *Securitization: structured financing, financial assets pools, and asset-backed securities*, Volume 1, Little Brown, Aspen Institute, Aspen, CO.

Ito, T. 1992. *The Japanese Economy*, MIT Press, Cambridge, MA.

Kulish, N. & Geitner, P. 2012. "Euro Zone Crisis Boils as Leaders Fail to Signal New Steps", *NY Times*, NY.

Krugman, P. 2012. "European Crisis Realities", *NY Times*, NY.

Lewis, M. 2011. *The Big Short*, W. W. Norton, NY.

Marsh, B. 2011. "Its All Connected: An Overview of the Euro Crisis", *NY Times*, NY.

Rapp, W. 1999. "Foreign Firms in Japan's Securities Industry in the 1980s and Post Bubble Economy", in *Post Bubble Japanese Business*, Raj Aggarwal, ed., Kluwer Academic Publishers, Chapter 7.

Shiller, R. 2012. *Finance and the Good Society*, Princeton University Press, Princeton, NJ.

Shinkai, Y. 1987. "The Internationalization of Finance in Japan", *The Political Economy Of Japan*, Vol. 2, *The Changing International Context*, T. Inoguchi and D. Okimoto, Stanford University Press, Palo Alto, CA.

Yamamura, K. & Hanley, S. 1992. *Land Issues In Japan: A Policy Failure?*, Society for Japanese Studies, Seattle, WA.

Zielinsky, R. & Holloway, N. 1991. *Unequal Equities*, Kodansha International, NY.

CHAPTER TWO

BUBBLES IN LAW

When Birnam Wood Comes To Dunsinane

W. Rapp

An important and fascinating aspect of bubbles is the optimism of the participants that allows their greed and positive expectations to get ahead of basic economic sense. The overconfidence that prices can only rise for awhile becomes a self-fulfilling prophecy, when speculators seek to benefit from a sure thing. Thus like Macbeth who believed that Birnam Wood could never come to Dunsinane the bubble participants do not believe prices can fall or that black swans can exist because it has never happened or been seen before which of course is different than it cannot happen or exist [Taleb 2008].

This overconfidence is frequently expressed in a bubble's legal dimensions and especially with respect to government regulations and authorizations and to contracts entered into within that framework.[9] The very first great bubbles in Western financial history, the Tulip Mania of 1636, the Great South Sea Bubble of 1720 from which the term Bubble is taken, and the Mississippi Bubble of 1720 all involved contracting, while the latter two involved legislation that authorized the formation of stock companies that sold stock through subscription contracts.

---

[9] Contractual risk is another dimension of bubbles and is examined specifically in a forthcoming paper "Risk Management and Contractual Obligations" that will be available as a Working Paper on the Leir Bubble Center website: www.leirbubblecenter.org.

This chapter will examine and analyze how this interaction between the legal system and contracting has played a role in bubble formation and expansion and how more sophisticated participants in seeking to exploit the ignorance of less experienced participants have themselves been trapped by over-optimism in devising and entering contracts that appear to be beneficial and sure winners but in fact in the ensuing bubble collapses become losing propositions.

The latter effect comes about because the more successful the issuers of a security or asset are the more they issue. Then when the bubble bursts they are often caught with substantial amounts of the asset and must bear the costs of the aftermath.[10]

Optimism in Contracting

Professor Bar-Gill in an excellent paper [Bar-Gill 2009], "The Law, Economics and Psychology of Subprime Mortgage Contracts," has explained how during the 2002-2008 real estate boom ending with the Subprime Mortgage Crisis, sophisticated lenders exploited less experienced borrowers. He "argues that the contractual design features can be explained as a rational market response to the imperfect rationality of borrowers." Borrowers were overly optimistic in terms of their expectations that housing

---

[10] Investment banks such as Lehman and Bear Stearns that were huge underwriters of subprime mortgages during the US housing boom through their mortgage banking subsidiaries were apparent victims of this phenomena when their pipeline of subprime mortgages financed by short-term paper that were to be pooled and then sold to investors froze up and could not be liquidated or financed by rolling over the short-term paper. Ultimately Lehman filed for bankruptcy, while Bear Stearns was acquired by J. P. Morgan through a Fed arranged rescue.

prices would rise and that they would be able to refinance for more money at a later date.

Therefore their expectations incorporated the kind of Ponzi finance scheme identified by Professor Aliber [Kindleberger and Aliber 2011] where the banks would constantly be covering interest payments through lending higher and higher principal amounts. Furthermore the banks promoted this idea in their marketing and advertising programs as explained by D. Viola, W. Rapp and R. Mehta in Chapter 5 of this book.

Subprime mortgage lenders in turn front-end loaded fees and interest to increase current earnings while postponing principle repayments to the end of the loan period by which time borrowers were encouraged to believe they could refinance due to housing price appreciation [Chapter 5]. These loans were also unusually complex and included an ARM [Adjustable Rate Mortgage] feature where the rate would be reset, generally after two years according to a formula. Again borrowers usually believed they would be able to refinance before the rate was reset, which turned out not to be true. In addition some loans included early termination fees that raised a borrower's refinancing costs while again increasing a lender's near-term earnings on which their executives' bonuses and options were generally based.

Therefore borrowers frequently did not fully understand how much the monthly payment rates could rise once the introductory teaser period had expired or what the eventual cost of the loan would be. The idea from the lender's standpoint was to make the loan look affordable and to generate substantial upfront earnings through large and multiple fees on each loan or refinancing. Lenders and mortgage servicers were not worried about default because they also believed housing prices were going to rise and if a subprime borrower defaulted they could quickly foreclose and recover whatever was still owed on the mortgage loan.

In this respect, however, they were mistaken because when done in volume the underlying assumptions shifted. A large number of defaults particularly if concentrated in certain high growth real estate markets such as the golf course retirement communities discussed in the Introduction could saturate a market with supply forcing prices down. This phenomenon illustrates a bubble pattern that goes beyond the individual contracting that is the focus of Professor Bar-Gill's paper and that can be seen in other bubbles.

In this case the sophisticated lenders exploited the subprime borrower's lack of sophistication which given their assumptions about those borrowers and the housing market made sense even if results were not optimum for borrowers.[11] However, in the subprime mortgage case the banks along with the regulators did not think through the implications of macro aggregation and large numbers. Rather they were overly focused

---

[11] Professor Bar-Gill has analyzed how similar exploitation of consumer psychology is at work by banks in credit cards and by telecommunications firms' in wireless phone plans.

on the individual transactions and their ability to bundle and sell them as securitized mortgage-backed bonds to investors while retaining the lucrative service contracts.[12]

When a financial product is so lucrative it will naturally attract many participants and the product's supply will expand rapidly. In this case trillions of dollars in subprime mortgages were lent, bundled and securitized. This of course drove up housing prices making the whole scheme look more stable than it really was. This is similar to the role speculators play in making a market look larger and more liquid as they enter the market [see Dr. Chou's analysis in Chapter 8].

Yet as with the speculators this perceived increased liquidity and expansion of market participants was highly deceptive. Once defaults began investors were no longer willing to accept the securitized subprime mortgage pools and the support for rising housing prices not only collapsed but the increased supply of foreclosed properties further depressed

---

[12] Asset Managers can be involved in a similar type of Ponzi finance that can feed a bubble and increase contractual risk. Most investors enter a contract with their broker, mutual fund manager, and/or financial advisor that delegates them a certain amount of independence and authority in managing the investor's assets. History indicates in contracts incentives matter and a contract risk related to asset managers is making sure the investor's asset management goals and those of the asset manager are aligned even though the manager has a legal fiduciary duty in this regard. In reality some asset managers like the banks have been involved in Ponzi finance creating fictional earnings through taking unwarranted short-term risks to boost current earnings by optimistically acquiring bubble related assets. Much litigation has involved determining whether such investments were authorized or appropriate [Rapp 2010]. Still it is clear the collapse of the Bear Stearns hedge funds in June 2007 were due to such actions by the asset managers [Rapp 2009].

prices undermining the exit strategy the banks had assumed. In addition defaults increased as borrowers who had optimistically assumed they could refinance could not. So the Ponzi finance scheme came to an abrupt halt. This compounded the problems facing the subprime mortgage lenders. Several such as Countrywide, New Century, Washington Mutual, Bear Stearns and Lehman disappeared. It also trapped several asset managers as described in footnote 12 above such as those running the Structured Investment Vehicles [SIVs] analyzed by Professor Ehrlich in Chapter 7.

In effect the subprime mortgage lenders who were exploiting their "greater sophistication" to make money off unsophisticated borrowers were themselves overly optimistic in their assumptions concerning the rise in housing prices and their exit strategies. Such a pattern of over optimism by the originator of the bubble as well as the participants seems to be an important aspect of bubbles that is expressed in individual contracting which due to aggregation effects brings about both the bubble's expansion and its collapse as the expansion changes the underlying assumptions that supported the origination and evolution of the bubble.

Early Bubbles[13]

Tulipmania arose in the Netherlands in "the 1630s the first

---

[13] The material for this section comes from Galbraith, J. 1994. *A Short History of Financial Euphoria*, Penguin Books, NY; Balen, M. 2003. *The King, the Crook and the Gambler*, Harper Collins, NY; Kindleberger, C. & Aliber, R. 2011. *Manias, Panics and Crashes*, op. cit.

of the great speculative explosions known to history," (Galbraith 1994). While it was clearly a mania in that people sold or mortgaged their houses to procure a rare bulb from a more current perspective there were three important elements. The concept of a leveraged installment sale was introduced as a financial innovation. It was a contractual arrangement. The mania appears to have had Schumpeterian characteristics.

As described by Galbraith tulips grew wild in the Eastern Mediterranean and arrived in Europe in the 16th century. As appreciation of their beauty rose so did prices of bulbs of the rarer blooms. "The speculation became more and more intense. A bulb might now change hands several times at steadily increasing and wonderfully rewarding prices while still unseen in the ground. ... The demand for tulips of rare species increased so much in the year 1636, that regular marts for their sale were established on the stock exchange of Amsterdam, in Rotterdam, Harlaem, Leyden, Alkmar, Hoorn, and other towns. ... The tulip-jobbers speculated in the rise and fall of tulip stocks, ... Many individuals grew suddenly rich. A golden bait hung temptingly out before the people, and one after the other, they rushed to the tulip marts, ... The operations of the trade became so extensive and intricate that it was found necessary to draw up a code of laws for the guidance of dealers.

In keeping with the immutable rules governing such episodes, each upsurge in prices persuaded more speculators to participate. This justified the hopes of those already participating, paving the way for yet further action and increase, and so assuring yet more and ever-continued enrichment. Money was borrowed for purchase; the small bulbs leveraged large loans.[14]

In 1637 came the end. The wise and the nervous began to detach, ... others saw them go; the rush to sell became a panic; the prices dropped as if over a precipice. Those who had purchased by pledging property for credit ... were suddenly bereft or bankrupt. ... Those who had contracted to buy at the enormously inflated prices defaulted en masse. Angry sellers sought enforcement of their contracts of sale; the courts, identifying it as a gambling operation, were unhelpful." From this brief description one can see all the elements of a bubble.

It began for a logical reason, the appeal of beautiful flowers that in turn because of that appeal developed a commercial value that continues to this day. However once prices began to rise speculators entered the market driving out normal merchants [investors] dealing in tulip bulbs. As prices rose, sellers had to enter into installment sales contracts to attract buyers, the initial use of leverage. Say the price was 900 florins and one agreed to pay 150 down and 150 a month over the next five months. If the price went up to 1200, one could sell the contract for 450 florins recouping one's investment with a 200% return. More importantly one could use the 450 florins to enter into three new

---

[14] Something similar occurred respecting golf memberships in Japan trading at higher and higher prices on informal exchanges during its real estate mania of the 1980s. Even memberships in courses not yet built rose dramatically until the general real estate and stock market collapse in early 1990.

contracts of 1200 each with 150 down but with payments to be made over 7 months.

In this way time could leverage both the initial payment and demand, thus driving up prices and continuing the mania and the bubble. Ultimately, though, the longer and longer extended repayment period and the initial payment became contractual and financial constraints and speculators began borrowing against both the bulbs and other property to make the first payment. Therefore when the crash came, perhaps because some realized with time a bulb could reproduce itself, the financial system and the real economy were drawn into a downward spiral that slowed Holland's economic growth well into the 1640s.

However, a Galbraith [1994] notes "[t]here was one mitigating result: the cultivation of the tulip continued in Holland, and wide markets eventually developed for flowers and bulbs." Indeed today tulips in Holland alone are a $9 billion dollar a year business (Hill 2010) and the Dutch control the multi-billion dollar global cut flower business. Thus this bubble and bust appears to have had Schumpeterian aspects.

No such case can be made for the two great bubbles appearing in England and France roughly a century later. The Great South Sea Bubble and The Mississippi Bubble were contemporaries. Both occurred around 1719-1721 and there was interaction by some investors and speculators in both bubbles. According to Kindleberger and Aliber (2011) "Amsterdam profited from its position between Paris and London." Perhaps because they had had their own bubble they recognized the signs. In any case they sold their Mississippi stock at the right time and liquidated their South Sea stock as well buying Bank of England and East India Company shares instead.

As with Tulipmania we again see the leveraged installment sale contract playing a role in higher prices and high profits. People also mortgaged their properties in order to get shares and there was the organization of markets where the shares or contracts were exchanged. The two stock companies involved, the South Sea Company and the Mississippi Company, were both promoted based on the known success of the Dutch East India Company and the great wealth Spain was reaping from their colonies in South America.

The South Sea Company was given a charter by the English Crown to trade with the latter while the Mississippi was given a charter by the French to develop lands in the French controlled regions of North America. Neither had any real economic substance but access to riches was heavily promoted using arguments similar to those highlighted by D. Viola, W. Rapp and R. Mehta in Chapter 5. In both cases the two governments granted the charters as a way to reduce war debts.[15]

In the case of the Mississippi Bubble a man named John Law was given the right to establish a Banque Royale with the "authorization to issue notes, which were then used by the bank

---

[15] Governments similarly promoted, helped finance and loosely regulated the expansion of homeownership and real estate development in the recent housing booms and busts in the US, Ireland and Spain.

to pay current government expenses and to takeover past government debts. The notes, in principle exchangeable into hard coin if one wished[16], were well received. Some being well received more were issued.

What was needed, obviously, was a source of earnings in hard cash that would bring in revenues to support the note issue. This was provided in theory by the organization of the Mississippi Company ... to pursue the gold deposits that were presumed to exist in the great North American territory of Louisiana. ...

The proceeds of the sale of stock in the Mississippi Company went not to search for the as yet undiscovered gold, but to the government for its debts. The notes that went out to pay the debt came back to buy more stock. More stock was then issued to satisfy more of the intense demand, the latter having the effect of lifting both the old and new issues to ever more extravagant heights. ... In 1720, the end came. The leverage went sharply into reverse, ... there was a run on the bank – people seeking to convert their notes not into stock of the Mississippi Company but into gold. The notes were declared no longer convertible. Values ... collapsed. Citizens who a week before had been millionaires ... were now impoverished." (Galbraith 1994)

In the case of the South Sea Company established in 1711, it had origins similar to those of the Mississippi Company. "In return for its charter, the South Sea Company took over and

---

[16] Paper is much easier to carry than gold specie and can be written for any amount. Thus if really backed by gold in a safe place bank notes are more attractive than coin.

consolidated this diverse government debt." (Galbraith 1994) It was to receive 6% interest plus a monopoly on trade with the Spanish colonies in South America. As more government debt was issued more stock was issued to pay for it and "early in 1720, the whole public debt was assumed." This was considered a great benefit to the company and the stock that sold for 128 pounds in 1720 rose to 890 by May and to around 1000 in the summer. "As ever, the sight of some becoming so effortlessly affluent brought the rush to participate that further powered the upward thrust."

However after Parliament passed the Bubble Act in July 1720 and perhaps influenced by the Mississippi Company collapse things started to unravel and prices dropped to 175 pounds in September and 124 by December, ruining those who still owed money on their installment contracts since the British courts unlike their Dutch counterparts ruled they were valid (Balen 2003). The Sword Blade Bank that was intimately connected with the South Sea Company in the same way that the Banque Royale was intertwined with the Mississippi Company went down as well. Further there was a direct relationship between land prices and the South Sea and Mississippi share prices since speculators had taken their profits in shares and used them to buy landed estates. To the extent they had borrowed they lost these properties when the share prices collapsed.

Yet because of their severe economic consequences these bubbles became the subject of much observation and analysis and thus expanded the general understanding of these phenomena.

Further while sharing some common characteristics with Tulipmania in the excessive use of leverage, the installment sale contract and the rapid run-up in prices drawing in speculators and creating an established market, the South Sea and Mississippi Company bubbles introduced the joint stock company as well, a legal entity that was to play a major role in many subsequent booms and crashes.

They also illustrated a less recognized aspect of bubbles in terms of asymmetric contracting. Here the issuers of the stock knew there was little substance to the companies and their shares but were able to persuade investors to buy under the contractual subscription agreements. The very success of this arrangement and the entry of speculators then created further increases in prices and the development of the bubbles. When the collapse came the issuers themselves were caught in the aftermath. John Law for example died in poverty and several of the chief organizers of the South Sea Bubble either ended in jail or fled England. Similar outcomes met many involved in the events surrounding the 1929 Crash or the dot.com boom and bust of the 1990s.

Thus what exploiters of contractual and knowledge asymmetry fail to recognize is the risk their success puts the entities doing the exploiting and thus themselves. This misperception of concentrated macro risk emerging from micro contractual exploitation due to aggregation effects is a bubble theme seen frequently but not fully understood.

1929 Crash

For Americans the 1920s stock market boom, the 1929 crash and the Great Depression that followed are perhaps the defining economic events of the 20th Century that like the Civil War in 19th Century are seared into the National Consciousness. Further many institutions and regulations meant to protect investors and the public from financial machinations by lenders and companies emerged as the government worked to manage the aftermath of the great and economic financial collapse. The SEC, deposit insurance, and margin requirements are particularly notable in terms of addressing the issues of disclosure, bank runs and bank leverage that contributed to making earlier booms and busts more severe.

Investment banks, commercial banks and insurance companies were also separated from each other since it was determined that when these were combined in a single entity there were abuses with commercial banks using depositors' money to fund stock issues by the investment banking subsidiaries along the lines of the Mississippi Company and Bank Royale or the South Sea Company and the Sword Blade Bank.

Also Corporate Pyramiding schemes were no longer legal where a series of operating companies were combined into a series of holding companies that in turn were owned by a series of second tier holding companies with 49% of the stock at each level being sold off to the public. Of course while this is still illegal for stock ownership, as the Introduction notes there are strong similarities with the CDO squared and cubed pooling arrangements involving mortgage-backed securities up until the 2008 market collapse.

Conglomerates and the Nifty Fifty 1960s

Interestingly, perhaps due to individual and government financial caution born of the Great Depression followed by two intervening Wars [WW II and the Korean Conflict] there was no major bubble and related financial crisis between 1929 and 1959. Then because of Sputnik and the financial innovation of the conglomerate there was a boom in defense related stocks such as Morton-Thiokol in rockets and conglomerates such as ITT where the whole was seen as more than the sum of its parts. It was also a period of significant technological innovation such as semi-conductors [Fairchild, Intel and Texas Instruments], self-developing film [Polaroid], copying [Xerox], commercial jetliners [Boeing and McDonald-Douglas], and containers [Sea Land].

The latter were known as growth stocks and many became part of the "nifty fifty". As explained by Tom Synnott during the Conference these were the center of an important financial innovation in asset management that then became a bubble. Some investment banks and brokers were able to show pension managers that by combining a mixed portfolio of bonds and growth stocks they could achieve better returns with less price volatility. As more pension and other asset managers adopted the idea the price of the growth stocks as compared to value stocks rose and this in turn attracted speculators, further driving up prices in a classic bubble until it unraveled due the shocks of the first oil crisis and the abandonment of the Gold Exchange Standard by President Nixon.

In addition this period introduced another important bubble phenomena "Super Money" where firms with high stock prices such as ITT could use their stock to acquire firms with much lower Price/Earnings ratios. The market then for some reason felt that the acquiring firm would be able to transfer its management magic to the acquired firm and so the acquired firm's earnings were given the same P/E as the acquirer. This M&A mania and boom continued until it became clear that in many cases dogs continued to be dogs [Smith 1972]. Something similar would occur in the M&A boom of the 1980s only with high-yield ["junk"] bonds taking the place of stock as Super Money to fuel the stock market boom in "takeover" stocks [Smith 1990].

While there were many significant economic developments after the stock market collapse in the early 1970s that were related to soaring energy prices [another bubble], the important legal developments affecting financial markets and the likelihood of future bubbles during the period from 1959 through 1983 were the creation of the one-bank holding company, the abandonment of the gold exchange standard, the introduction of floating exchange rates, the development of syndicated asset backed loans, and M&A's emergence as an important management tool involving sophisticated legal support.

These developments show once again that changes in

legislation allow for the development of financial products that require legal support to put in place or that a business opportunity can result in legislative and regulatory changes that lead to bubbles.

Leverage Buyouts and Junk Bonds 1980s[17]

The origins and development of the leveraged buyout boom of the 1980s is an excellent illustration of this point. A regulatory legacy from the 1930s and the Great Depression was Regulation Q that allowed the Fed to restrict and set interest rates for both banks and thrift institutions. This was to prevent them from competing for funds and taking on undue risks to cover the higher rates. In addition thrifts were able to offer a slightly higher rate than commercial banks and this was considered helpful to the housing market since thrifts were generally restricted to financing long-term fixed rate mortgages.

However the two oil crises of the 1970s while creating a bubble in energy stocks and related assets as well as for companies involved in Mideast construction also caused this interest rate regime to unravel with unexpected consequences. Higher energy prices caused US inflation to soar. In 1979 and 1980 the CPI was 13.3% and 12.5% respectively [Blanchard 2009]. In 1979 the newly appointed Fed Chairman, Paul Volker, felt something had to be done and drove the Fed funds to almost 18% by April 1980 [Blanchard 2009].

---

[17] There are many excellent books on this period such as *Barbarians at the Gate* or *The Predators' Ball.*

These rates dramatically slowed growth, engineered the 1980 recession and collapsed the oil price bubble. Funds also flew from savings deposits into the Money Market Funds introduced in the 1970s [Geist 1997]. The result was thrifts holding mostly long-term mortgages were caught in a negative funding squeeze paying more for deposits but still limited by Reg Q relative to market rates. They were effective lobbyists, though, and in 1980 Congress passed the Deregulation and Monetary Control Act [DIDMCA].

This Act phased out Reg Q by 1986 but more importantly allowed S&Ls and savings banks to extend loans to businesses and to offer Federally Insured NOW accounts that bore a market rate of interest [Ciment 2010]. These changes were to have unexpected economic and financial consequences due to the introduction of the junk or high yield bond in combination with the hostile takeover via a leveraged buyout.

Michael Milken had done research on the risk versus return history of high yield bonds as a student at Wharton and having arrived at Drexel Burnham was able to persuade customers that a diversified portfolio of such bonds actually performed better than one composed of investment grade securities. However, having succeeded in this the available product was used up or rose in price eliminating the perceived advantage.

Thus he decided to create his own product in a move similar to what would happen two decades later when in response to the Fed lowering interest to historically low levels many prime mortgage borrowers refinanced. But having refinanced they were no longer interested when the Fed started raising rates. Yet having established a very profitable mortgage backed investment securitization business, the banks and investment banks switched to making and bundling subprime mortgages to keep the earnings flowing.

Milken found a ready issuers' market for his high yield securities in the form of corporate raiders that initially targeted cash rich firms in slow growth businesses. However again as those targets were acquired or broken up and the stock market boomed, the low hanging fruit disappeared and the green mailers and arbitragers switched to better-run companies such as Hertz and Disney [Smith 1990]. The frenzy was such that a firm's stock price would jump dramatically due to a takeover rumor.

Drexel was at the center of this bubble issuing letters to would-be acquirers that stated it was "highly confident" it could place billions in high yield bonds to finance a takeover.[18] The market for these bonds were in turn often S&Ls and savings banks such as Columbia Savings in Beverly Hills that now could raise funds by paying a market rate on Federally Insured deposits and had the investment flexibility to purchase such corporate

---

[18] Some bonds did not pay a real rate of interest. That is if after the LBO a borrower did not have the cash to pay interest, it would pay in kind [a PIK security]. This meant it would pay in more bonds, true Ponzi finance.

securities.[19] Other high flying financial institutions such as the insurance company, Equity Funding, were also buyers of these high-yield securities. Still what started out as a sound diversified bond portfolio strategy became warped into an invention of financial destruction as in the Nifty Fifty examined above or SIVs in 2008 [Chapter 7] when many highly leveraged takeovers failed or could not service the securities.

Yet while the eventual debacle was inevitable this was a period of great financial and legal innovation. Indeed without the legal innovation there might have been no boom and bubble. Hostile takeovers required teams of lawyers and two firms Wachtel Lipton and Skadden Arps emerged as kings of the hill more than willing to successfully engage more established white shoe firms such as Davis Polk, Sherman & Sterling or White and Case in providing the legal advice and engineering behind a hostile takeover of one of the latters' clients. Poison pills involving the issuance of massive amounts of stock given an unsolicited tender offer, golden parachutes for top managers, and greenmail

---

[19] "The Columbia Savings and Loan Association, which bought more "junk bonds" than any other savings institution, was taken over by the Government, paying the final price for its risky investment strategy. Columbia, based in Beverly Hills, Calif., had been suffering huge losses as the value of its portfolio plummeted along with that of the entire $200 billion junk bond market. Its takeover by Federal regulators was seen as inevitable. ... The seizure, ... , surprised no one. The Beverly Hills-based thrift faced massive losses in 1989 and 1990 as it was forced to write down its junk bond investments to market and announced in November that it would likely be seized by regulators. As of Sept. 30, 1990, Columbia had assets of $6.6 billion, making it the sixth largest S&L in Los Angeles County. Analysts already estimate the loss to taxpayers of bailing out depositors at $1 billion to $1.5 billion." Available at: http://scripophily.net/cosaandloasn.html

buying out a specific group of shareholders were all legal developments during this period. The issuance of junk bonds also required considerable legal support. In this way legislation, lawyers and finance merged to advance the M&A junk bond bubble.

Then when the collapse finally arrived in 1989 it not only took down Drexel Burnham and its investment bankers but precipitated the first major banking crisis and series of large financial scandals and related criminal prosecutions since the 1930s. This was largely because of the heavy investment of the S&Ls not only in junk bonds but also in other self-dealing transactions including significant insider trading of potential takeover stocks and questionable real estate development projects.

To manage the aftermath the US government did what governments seem to do in these situations, it passed legislation to deal with the collapse's economic effects and to try and prevent or moderate a future crisis. The former was the creation of the Resolution Trust Corporation that would buy troubled assets from the S&Ls while the FDIC closed and otherwise handled failed S&Ls. The latter legislation was FIRREA - *Financial Institutions Reform, Recovery, and Enforcement Act of 1989* – that increased the financial penalties and prison sentences associated with bank, mail and wire fraud and substantially tightened the controls over real estate lending where the S&Ls and affiliated developers had been particularly self-dealing [Rapp 2010]. However it is not clear given the recent crisis how effective FIRREA was in preventing or moderating the subsequent real estate bubble and its effect on the financial system.

Dot.com Bubble

During the 1990s the global financial sector had bubbles but mostly in Emerging Markets such as the Tequila Boom and Bust in Mexico due to the euphoria after it joined NAFTA, the Asian Financial Crisis following the boom in Asian FDI as the new global export platform and then the Rubble Crisis and collapse of LTCM [Long-term Capital Management] that followed the fall of the Soviet Union and its massive privatization boom.

The euphoric US bubble in the 1990s however focused on the Internet as a new disruptive technology with Schumpeterian echoes such as surrounded the Railroads in the 19th Century and then Electricity, Telecommunications, Radio, Automobiles, and TV in the 20th Century. This became a classic technology bubble and like its predecessors it displayed great and to a large degree initially justifiable though eventually "irrational" exuberance. At the same time due to safe guards put in place after the 1929 crash its collapse in 2000 did not have the same consequences as its counterparts in the 19th and 20th Centuries since given margin requirements it was investors rather than banks or financial institutions that lost money.

Yet the law did play a significant role both in the development of the bubble and in managing the aftermath of its collapse in 2000. Like many financial innovations just because the period when it was developed had passed, did not mean it had disappeared. Thus SuperMoney in terms of overvalued stock reappeared as the acquisition currency of choice such as in AOL's takeover of TimeWarner. Microsoft and Cisco also used stock to acquire start-ups with promising technologies. Further law firms were doing a booming business in IPOs [Initial Public Offerings] and Silicon Valley firms were able to compete with top Wall Street firms for the best legal talent especially in situations where lawyers could take part of their fees in stock.

However when the inevitable collapse occurred at the beginning of 2000, it was not the Federal government that took the lead in pursuing the usual bubble related malfeasance. Rather Eliot Spitzer the NY Attorney General took the lead as the "Sherriff of Wall Street" in exposing the cozy relationship between Wall Street Analysts and IPO investment bankers.[20] In turn some analysts such as Jack Grubman[21] became symbols of Wall Street deceptions that created public and legal pressure on financial institutions to enter a binding agreement with Spitzer to change their practices if not their culture.

However the Federal Government was not idle in this regard. It successfully prosecuted senior executives at WorldCom

---

[20] See *Time* magazine at http://www.time.com/time/magazine/article /0,9171,1003960,00.html

[21] Morrissey, B. 2002. "Salomon Telecom Analyst Jack Grubman Resigns," *Internet News.Com.*

such as Bernie Ebbers after it filed for bankruptcy in July 2002[22] and Enron's Jeffrey Skilling after its filing in 2001.[23] These and other Scandals then led to the passage of the 2002 Sarbanes-Oxley Act. As reported in Wikipedia [2013] it addresses policy concerns mostly related to corporate governance and financial reporting.[24] Thus unlike FIRREA or the legislation following the Great Depression there is little dealing with preventing bubbles per se but only the scams and scandals that inevitably seem to follow bubbles. This is perhaps why it did little with respect to preventing or moderating the US housing boom and bust that followed. In summary:

"The Sarbanes–Oxley Act of 2002 ... set new or enhanced standards for all U.S. public company boards, management and public accounting firms. ... As a result of SOX, top management

---

[22] As reported on Yahoo at www.google.com/url?sa=t&rct=j&q=&esrc=s&source=web&cd=4&ved=0CEkQFjAD&url=http%3A%2F%2Fvoices.yahoo.com%2Fworldcom-scandal-look-back-one-biggest-225686.html&ei=rGozUfHsKqiy0AGW-IHgCw&usg=AFQjCNHnGQ8NZhns9tzxCg8QjicvfqtbPQ&bvm=bv.43148975,d.dmQ, "On March 15, 2005 Bernard Ebbers was found guilty of all charges and convicted on fraud, conspiracy and filing false documents with regulators. He was sentenced to 25 years in prison. Other former WorldCom officials charged with criminal penalties in relation to the company's financial misstatements include former CFO Scott Sullivan (entered a guilty plea on March 2, 2004 to one count each of securities fraud, conspiracy to commit securities fraud, and filing false statements), former controller David Myers (pleaded guilty to securities fraud, conspiracy to commit securities fraud, and filing false statements on September 27, 2002), former accounting director Buford Yates (pleaded guilty to conspiracy and fraud charges on October 7, 2002), and former accounting managers Betty Vinson and Troy Normand (both pleading guilty to conspiracy and securities fraud on October 10, 2002) (MCI, 2006). Ebbers reported to prison on September 26, 2006 to begin serving his sentence."

[23] See *Wikipedia* at http://en.wikipedia.org/wiki/Enron.

[24] Available at: http://en.wikipedia.org/wiki/Sarbanes%E2%80%93Oxley_Act.

must now individually certify the accuracy of financial information. In addition, penalties for fraudulent financial activity are much more severe. Also, SOX increased the independence of the outside auditors who review the accuracy of corporate financial statements, and increased the oversight role of boards of directors.

The bill was enacted as a reaction to a number of major corporate and accounting scandals including those affecting Enron, Tyco International, Adelphia, Peregrine Systems and WorldCom. These scandals, which cost investors billions of dollars when the share prices of affected companies collapsed, shook public confidence in the nation's securities markets.

The act contains 11 titles, or sections, ranging from additional corporate board responsibilities to criminal penalties, and requires the Securities and Exchange Commission (SEC) to implement rulings on requirements to comply with the law. Harvey Pitt, ... , led the SEC in the adoption of dozens of rules to implement the Sarbanes–Oxley Act. It created a new, quasi-public agency, the Public Company Accounting Oversight Board, or PCAOB, charged with overseeing, regulating, inspecting and disciplining accounting firms in their roles as auditors of public companies. The act also covers issues such as auditor independence, corporate governance, internal control assessment, and enhanced financial disclosure. The nonprofit arm of Financial Executives International (FEI), Financial Executives

Research Foundation (FERF), completed extensive research studies to help support the foundations of the act.

1. **Public Company Accounting Oversight Board (PCAOB)**

   Title I consists of nine sections and establishes the Public Company Accounting Oversight Board, to provide independent oversight of public accounting firms providing audit services ("auditors"). It also creates a central oversight board tasked with registering auditors, defining the specific processes and procedures for compliance audits, inspecting and policing conduct and quality control, and enforcing compliance with the specific mandates of SOX.

2. **Auditor Independence**

   Title II consists of nine sections and establishes standards for external auditor independence, to limit conflicts of interest. It also addresses new auditor approval requirements, audit partner rotation, and auditor reporting requirements. It restricts auditing companies from providing non-audit services (e.g., consulting) for the same clients.

3. **Corporate Responsibility**

   Title III consists of eight sections and mandates that senior executives take individual responsibility for the accuracy and completeness of corporate financial reports. It defines the interaction of external auditors and corporate audit committees, and specifies the responsibility of corporate officers for the accuracy and validity of corporate financial reports. It enumerates specific limits on the behaviors of corporate officers and describes specific forfeitures of benefits and civil penalties for non-compliance. For example, Section 302 requires that the company's "principal officers" (typically the Chief Executive Officer and Chief Financial Officer) certify and approve the integrity of their company financial reports quarterly.http://en.wikipedia.org/wiki/Sarbanes%E2%80%93Oxley_Act - cite_note-5

4. **Enhanced Financial Disclosures**

Title IV consists of nine sections. It describes enhanced reporting requirements for financial transactions, including off-balance-sheet transactions, pro-forma figures and stock transactions of corporate officers. It requires internal controls for assuring the accuracy of financial reports and disclosures, and mandates both audits and reports on those controls. It also requires timely reporting of material changes in financial condition and specific enhanced reviews by the SEC or its agents of corporate reports.

5. **Analyst Conflicts of Interest**

Title V consists of only one section, which includes measures designed to help restore investor confidence in the reporting of securities analysts. It defines the codes of conduct for securities analysts and requires disclosure of knowable conflicts of interest.

6. **Commission Resources and Authority**

   Title VI consists of four sections and defines practices to restore investor confidence in securities analysts. It also defines the SEC's authority to censure or bar securities professionals from practice and defines conditions under which a person can be barred from practicing as a broker, advisor, or dealer.

7. **Studies and Reports**

   Title VII consists of five sections and requires the Comptroller General and the SEC to perform various studies and report their findings. Studies and reports include the effects of consolidation of public accounting firms, the role of credit rating agencies in the operation of securities markets, securities violations and enforcement actions, and whether investment banks assisted Enron, Global Crossing and others to manipulate earnings and obfuscate true financial conditions.

8. **Corporate and Criminal Fraud Accountability**

   Title VIII consists of seven sections and is also referred to as the *"Corporate and Criminal Fraud Accountability Act of 2002"*. It describes specific criminal penalties for manipulation, destruction or alteration of financial records or other interference with investigations, while providing certain protections for whistle-blowers.

9. **White Collar Crime Penalty Enhancement**

Title IX consists of six sections. This section is also called the *"White Collar Crime Penalty Enhancement Act of 2002."* This section increases the criminal penalties associated with white-collar crimes and conspiracies. It recommends stronger sentencing guidelines and specifically adds failure to certify corporate financial reports as a criminal offense.

10. **Corporate Tax Returns**

Title X consists of one section. Section 1001 states that the Chief Executive Officer should sign the company tax return.

11. **Corporate Fraud Accountability**

Title XI consists of seven sections. Section 1101 recommends a name for this title as *"Corporate Fraud Accountability Act of 2002"*. It identifies corporate fraud and records tampering as criminal offenses and joins those offenses to specific penalties. It also revises sentencing guidelines and strengthens their penalties. This enables the SEC to resort to temporarily freezing transactions or payments that have been deemed "large" or "unusual"." [Wikipedia 2013]

The Great Recession

As just explained above and as details concerning the Act reveal, Sarbanes-Oxley was not an attempt to control Schumpeterian bubbles but rather the greed and earnings manipulation [Chapter 6] often associated with such bubbles. Further because such bubbles often represent an overshoot of investment and risk taking in disruptive technologies from which the economy eventually benefits, this approach is probably a good thing as long as the financial system is not at risk. In this regard the margin requirements put in place after the 1929 crash seem to have worked in moderating such a development. In addition the new or revitalized multibillion-dollar companies that emerged after the dot.com crash and leveraged the heavy investment in the Internet and telecommunications during the boom such as Google, Apple, and Facebook seem to support this view. But from a legal or legislative standpoint this hands-off bubble philosophy was not so good since it saw financial markets as basically efficient and bubbles as posing little systemic risk to the global financial system. This view then led to the repeal of earlier legislation meant to constrain such developments.

Two events stand out in this respect. The first and most important was the effective repeal of Glass-Steagall's restraint on merging investment banking, commercial banking and insurance with the passage in November 1999 of Gramm-Leach-Bliley.[25] The second and less well-known but still significant law was Congressional passage in 2000 of a "law barring states from regulating credit default swaps under their gambling and 'bucket shop' laws". [26] New York State for example had passed a Bucket Shop law in reaction to the Panic of 1907 [Chapter 1] that made betting on a changed direction in a security's price illegal. These two changes in existing legislation passed in reaction to prior

---

[25] See n.wikipedia.org/wiki/Gramm–Leach–Bliley_Act.
[26] *WashingtonWatch.Com* available at http://www.washingtonwatch.com /blog/tag/bucket-shop-laws/

crises that had had significant impacts on the US financial system and the economy at the time were precursors of the events to come, especially as the worst, 1929, had been preceded by a great real estate and stock market bubble.

The economic part of the process was initiated by the Fed reaction to the dot.com bust and then the terrorist attacks of 9/11. It flooded the market with liquidity driving interest rates down to historically low rates, almost the exact opposite of what had happened under Chairman Volker roughly twenty years earlier as described above. This initiated a boom in mortgage refinancing and the packaging and placement of the related mortgage backed securities. As examined in Rapp (2010, 2009) the complex mortgage origination to investment chain that developed involved several integrated participants that included investment banks that had acquired mortgage banks to originate their mortgage backed securities product and commercial banks that had acquired investment banks to package and sell their mortgages to investors.

Neither of these options would have been possible under Glass-Steagall. However these institutions now expanded role over the mortgage chain meant that during the bubble period the potential profits relative to the size of the firm were greatly magnified, increasing the incentives to keep the "dance" going. But the converse was also true. When the collapse came the large integrated firms were stuck with a bigger piece of the lending chain funded by short-term debt. The consequences for Lehman and Bear Stearns in particular were evaporation.

Structure And Evolution Of US Mortgage Market[27]

Traditional Mortgage Between Lender And Borrower

The US residential mortgage market is a multi-trillion dollar market that dramatically increased from 2002 onwards. As of June 2007 residential and non-profit mortgages outstanding amounted to $10.143 trillion up from $5.833 trillion as of September 2002.[28] The number of firms and organizations participating in this huge market proliferated as well. Twenty-five years ago a local bank or local savings and loan [S&L] issued the typical home mortgage to a local borrower and the bank or S&L would hold that mortgage subject to local real estate laws and land registry regulations on its books to maturity or until the home was sold or the mortgage refinanced.

But starting in the 1980s and expanding into the 1990s and the first years of this century, that all changed. Banks and S&Ls discovered the benefits of securitization and balance sheet turnover. They realized mortgages and other regular payment credit instruments such as auto loans and credit cards had steady

---

[27] Residential mortgages are where the market, technical changes, and number of players is largest and the players are both sophisticated and unsophisticated ranging from large financial institutions to public entities to individual homeowners and investors.

[28] Source Federal Reserve Bank, *available at* https://www.f ederalreserve.gov/datadownload/Review.aspx?rel=Z1&series=dd6e0a 09170055cee26a1e11b50710fc&lastObs=10&from=&to=&filetype=csv&label= include&layout=seriesrow&type=package. This compares with $2.3 trillion in single-family mortgage debt in 1989 and $3.5 trillion in that year for all mortgage debt. *See* Korngold, G. and Goldstein, P. 2002. *Real Estate Transactions*, Foundation Press, NY.

cash flows that if bundled could provide investors with a large and seemingly steady income stream that could be capitalized and sold. They were securitized, generally through trusts constructed by lawyers. This meant banks and S&Ls rather than holding the loans in their investment portfolios[29] would bundle them and sell them to investors while retaining the servicing function for which they deducted fees.[30] These structures as well as the related contractual purchases and sales of mortgages and the securities they backed were very complex legal documents. Since the market collapse they have also been the source of much litigation.

This innovation meant the bank or S&L could now turn over their balance sheet on a rapid basis since they did not have to wait until a loan was repaid or their capital increased to make new loans and thus expand their revenues from the loan servicing and origination fees. This process increased their return on capital, earnings per share, and shareholder value,[31] benefiting shareholders and corporate officers with stock options.

---

[29] Any statistically steady stream of payments can be discounted to determine a present value that sets the price of an obligation that can be sold to investors who receive the future cash flows. This process is called asset securitization. Home mortgages are attractive to securitize due to the long payment periods and underlying assets.

[30] *See* for example the business model description of Countrywide Financial Corporation, *2006 10K*, pp 3-17 *available at* http://about.Countrywide .com/SECFilings/Form10K.aspx.

[31] In the 1980s under the Basle agreements and The Resolution Trust Corporation Act, banks and S&Ls became subject to more stringent capital requirements relative to the loans on their books. This gave them an incentive to no longer hold loans to maturity or payoff. Rather it made sense to package and sell these loans to long-term investors such as life insurance companies. *See* Chapter on Citibank in Rapp, W. 2004. *Information Technology Strategies*, Oxford University Press, NY.

As this new system evolved, however, and became national or even international rather than local[32], other financial intermediaries emerged that specialized in specific functions within the overall mortgage packaging and sale to investor business chain. For example, mortgage brokers realized they could sell a New York mortgage to a California or Washington S&L that might price it more aggressively on rate and term than a local New York bank. This situation could arise due to the other lender's lower funding costs, its desire to diversify lending risks across more markets, or an interest in expanding its servicing portfolio where it had economies of scale. Indeed the reasons could be a combination of all these factors. The broker could thus help a borrower find the best rate within an increasingly competitive and integrated national market for residential mortgages that ultimately squeezed out the small local bank or S&L.

Further as the market expanded, economies of scale in specialization at different points in the mortgage financing and investment chain emerged. The Internet and greater computer power only increased this benefit as technological progress created significant cost improvements in sourcing and processing mortgage applications and approvals on-line. In the same way a prospective home buyer could now virtually tour several houses in an afternoon without leaving home they could compare mortgage rates from several sources while the lenders could

---

[32] *See* Countrywide, *supra*, relative to their UK operations.

quickly scan a buyer's credit score and outstanding loans from many different sources. Similarly huge increases in computing power and telecommunications introduced economies of scale in servicing the mortgages and ultimate investors.

Under this new and evolving structure it was quite possible that no federally insured bank or S&L would ever be involved in the loan or that any one investor would even hold the mortgage as security. A mortgage broker could find a lender such as GMAC or GE Credit Services or Merrill Lynch rather than a traditional bank or S&L.[33] Such lenders would subsequently bundle the mortgages into pools of cash flows usually in the form of a trust and either themselves or via investment banks such as Lehman Brothers or Bear Stearns[34] place them with investors. But they did not sell these pools as a whole or percentages of the pool to an insurance company, hedge fund, or structured investment vehicle [SIV]. Rather they sold pieces of the mortgage pool's cash flow tailored according to the investor's requirements. Thus long-term investors might only want the final monthly payments of the pool while another, shorter-term investor, might desire only the first three years' interest payments.

---

[33] In 2005 GMAC Bank was the country's 6th largest prime mortgage lender with $314 billion outstanding while Lehman Brothers Bank was the 9th largest subprime lender with $142 billion outstanding. *See* Gramlich, E. 2007. *Subprime Mortgages*, Urban Institute Press, Washington, DC. Bear Stearns' bank was called EMC Mortgage.

[34] A client study by Yamada, Y. a bank analyst at Merrill Lynch, indicates Bear Stearns and Lehman were the number one and two underwriters respectively of sub-prime mortgage backed securities. *See* Yamada. Y. & Kubo, T. 2008. *Japanese Major Banks*, Merrill Lynch Japan Securities.

The longer dated monthly payments would then be sold to a different investor group. Thus in many cases no one investor owned an entire mortgage and none were involved in the loan administration or the handling of the security.[35] The power of large computer systems supported servicing these many different complex financial and legal structures that favored those firms that could source and service in volume and thus could spread the system and legal costs over a large number of mortgages, customers and structured investments. This resulted in a factory mentality in creating the pools including the supporting legal documentation, a practice that has carried over to foreclosure activity in the current economic downturn and housing crisis.[36]

Because the initial lenders only expected to hold the mortgages[37] for a short period they frequently funded the initial mortgage loan using commercial paper. This caught firms such as Lehman in a maturity mismatch between their funding and the inventory in their mortgage backed security pipeline when the crisis came in the summer of 2008 and short-term funding froze and could not be rolled over. Others such as GMAC, GE, and several specialized mortgage lenders also used this technique, including those focused heavily on the subprime mortgage market.[38] The Countrywide Financial Corporation perhaps the

---

[35] For a deal based view of this process *see* Sloan, A. 2007. "House of Junk", *Fortune,* NY.

[36] *See* Morgenson, G. & Glater, J. 2008. "The Foreclosure Machine," *NY Times,* NY.

[37] *See* Countrywide's 10K for description of their business model, *supra.*

[38] In their 2005 annual reports GM and GE indicate this kind of activity. Indeed

largest US mortgage lender at the time did this extensively with its commercial paper backed by its mortgage loans.[39] It did this even though a subsidiary was a federally insured S&L. It continued this funding practice until 2006, probably to avoid the more stringent capital requirements the government had imposed on S&Ls in 1989 as part of The Resolution Corporation Trust Act and FIRREA.[40]

The collapse of the subprime market, though, forced Countrywide to change its business model. In 2006 it applied for changed status to a Federally Regulated Savings and Loan Holding Company. Still even this move did not save it from being ultimately absorbed by Bank of America. Nevertheless, the size of the mortgage financing market, its rapid growth and its increasing complexity combined with the current meltdown and billions in losses by financial institutions and investors, did create many opportunities for legal actions including both criminal

---

GM indicated $4 billion in mortgage servicing rights on its balance sheet. Examples of GMAC's mortgage activities are *available at* http://www. gmacmortgage.com/index.html. The *ABA Journal* has published several articles on the subprime mortgage meltdown and the related collapse in the US housing market. These are *available at* http://www. abajournal.com/topics/real+estate+property+law. They include discussions of mortgage fraud, *see* Gibeaut, J. *supra*, or Neil, M. 2007. "N.Y. Lawyer Stole $24M, Gets 10 Years", *ABA Journal*, Washington, DC. However they also note the increase in related litigation and the fact some law firms are setting up special practices to sue banks or to pursue owner claims. *See* Weiss, D. 2007. "Judges Crack Down on Law Firm 'Foreclosure Mills'", *ABA Journal*, or Weiss, D. 2007. "Suits Follow Mortgage Meltdown", *ABA Journal*, or Neil, M. 2007. "More Law Firms Seek to Sue Banks", *ABA Journal*.

[39] *See* Countrywide's 10K, *supra*.

[40] Financial Institutions Reform, Recovery, And Enforcement Act Of 1989, P.L. 101-73 or FIRREA

prosecutions for mortgage fraud and numerous civil causes of action seeking a legal remedy and some restitution of the lost billions [Rapp 2010, 2009].

Not surprisingly these points of legal altercation are generally at the intersections that represent handoffs of the loans and mortgages in some form between institutions such as the mortgage broker to the lender or between the lender and the packager or the packager and an investor or GSE [Government Sponsored Entity such as Fannie Mae] because these points have usually been accompanied by contractual documentation representing the warranties and responsibilities of the party doing the handing off[41] or the offering to the one receiving or accepting the securities. These contractual obligations then become the basis for recovery.

However the cookie cutter approach used to produce these securities on a mass production basis is now creating some problems.[42] Therefore while litigation situations may exist at all points in the mortgage origination to investment chain, it is much easier for those that invested in mortgage related products to pinpoint possible knowledge of potential problems and risks when only one holding company is involved and when various actions are between related financial institutions acting as the

---

[41] Facilitating these handoffs and reducing the possible causes of action were changes in UCC Article 9 that legalized the automatic transfer of security interests in mortgage loans to subsequent investors while simultaneously eliminating or substantially reducing a borrower's defenses against the initial lender being extended to purchasers.

[42] *See* Morgenson, G. & Glater, J. *supra*, and also Bajaj, V. 2008. "If Everyone's Finger-Pointing, Who's to Blame?" *NY Times*, NY

originators, packagers, security purchasers and ultimate marketers to the investors or GSEs [Chapter 5].[43]

The market developments described above have combined with changes in the legal regime regulating financial institutions to significantly complicate what plaintiff lawyers must do to develop a complaint or pursue a specific course of action. This legal complexity is then amplified by the fact loan pools were sliced into tranches or pieces with varying rights to specific mortgage payments coupled with a multiplicity of documentation at each point in the mortgage to securitization investor chain. There is also the split between servicing and loan ownership that makes it unclear who controls the pool or underlying loans and mortgages and payment streams. In many cases the servicing agent holds the mortgage in trust for the pool, while the pool is controlled by the super senior tranche for a diverse group of investors with conflicting interests.[44] If the servicing agent has a second mortgage related to a HELOC conflicts of interest and

---

[43] "A wave of lawsuits is beginning to wash over the troubled mortgage market and the rest of the financial world. Homeowners are suing mortgage lenders. Mortgage lenders are suing Wall Street banks. Wall Street banks are suing loan specialists. And investors are suing everyone." Bajaj, V. op. cit. This article also notes two important legal issues underpinning these cases. Whether lenders and packagers alerted borrowers and investors to the risks involved and how much they were legally required to disclose.

[44] The mortgages are bundled into pools and then the cash flows from the pool are separated into tiered tranches each with its own documentation and rights to the cash flow including proceeds from the sale of the property after foreclosure. The super senior sits on top and as recently reported can force liquidation wiping out the more junior tranches. *See* van Duyn, A. & Mackenzie, M. 2008. "Tranche warfare breaks out over CDOs," *Financial Times* and Mackenzie, M. 2008. "Super-senior CDO investors begin to flex their muscles," *Financial Times*.

issues of fiduciary responsibility are raised another notch.

In sum the Fed's accommodative response to the economic downturn following the Internet related stock market collapse combined with its reaction to 9/11 led many prime mortgage borrowers to refinance at historically low rates creating a mortgage backed security and housing boom that was just too profitable. Thus when the Fed started to tighten and the number of prime mortgage borrowers fell, participants in the mortgage to investor chain, just like Milken for junk bonds in the 1980s, sought to maintain a supply of mortgage backed securities to put through their expanded and highly profitable organizational structures by creating an alternative mortgage supply, subprime mortgages. They also expanded products such as HELOCs [Home Equity Line Of Credit] so existing borrowers could tap the increasing equity in the homes as housing prices rose. But because the latter were subordinate to the primary mortgage they put lenders at greater risk in a downturn. Still since both subprime mortgages and HELOCs bore higher interest rates relative to funding costs, lenders pushed these products and investors found them attractive just as in the case of junk bonds in the 1980s or the unit trusts prior to 1929. Thus the money flowed in this direction with the percent of US subprime mortgages originated in 2006 roughly 20% compared to 8% in 2004.[45]

In effect as in earlier periods higher rates due to Fed tightening fueled the subprime bubble due to the higher

---

[45] http://en.wikipedia.org/wiki/Subprime_mortgage_crisis

"perceived" return by investors on those speculative assets relative to funding costs. When reality finally hit in the summer of 2008, the collapse in MBO security prices and the freezing of the short-term commercial paper market pushed these perceptions aside.

Meanwhile in an echo of what happened in Japan in the 1980s housing boom, the related stocks of lenders like Countrywide, GSEs [Government Sponsored Entities] like Fannie Mae, investment banks like Bear Stearns, home builders like Toll Brothers, and commercial banks like Citicorp that had soared during the boom collapsed along with the subprime backed CDOs [Collateralized Debt Obligations]. Some were rescued; others were not. Trillions of dollars in market values disappeared. This by itself probably would have been sufficient to put the country into the economic and financial crisis that led to the Great Recession. However, it was magnified by the existence of Credit Default Swaps.

Prior to their creation in the 1990s and full legitimization by the Congress in 2000, if a company such as GM went bankrupt and defaulted on any of its debt only those holding such debt would be directly affected. However as Michael Lewis [2010] lucidly explains in *The Big Short* a CDS enables non-holders of GM's debt to bet on its bankruptcy. Thus when GM did file for bankruptcy in 2009 those holding the related CDS expected to be paid by those that had written them, magnifying the risk to the financial system from this event if the issuers could not pay those holding the swaps.[46] As it turned out AIG had written several hundreds of billions in Credit Default Swaps on a range of securities that included subprime MBOs along with the debt of firms such as GM.[47]

In this way the world's largest and one of its most profitable insurance companies put itself into danger of failing and thus forced a very expensive government [taxpayer] rescue since it failure would have unraveled the series of credit default swaps that other large financial institutions such as Goldman Sachs or J. P. Morgan Chase had used to hedge their asset portfolios. This is why Mr. Geithner stated the government needed to honor AIG's "contractual" obligations. However the government could not be selective so using taxpayer money AIG also had to pay those that had merely speculated as describe by Lewis [2010]. After the fact it was clear that AIG's ability to write unlimited credit default swaps from London with no internal or required capital allocation had put the global financial system at risk and had greatly magnified the economic costs of the subprime mortgage market collapse. It also caught regulators and policymakers by surprise since in early 2008 the Fed Chairman and the Treasury Secretary were claiming the damage could be

---

[46] A forthcoming paper by the author "Risk Management and Contractual Obligations" examines this situation relative to current economic environment in more detail. It also argues there is a need for greater regulation and control over these instruments.

[47] GM was particularly vulnerable because the seemingly profitable mortgage business of GMAC noted above had been subsidizing a weak auto business. The Great Recession then hammered both together.

contained.[48] But in major financial crises the risks participants have assumed often turn out to have been much deeper and pervasive than is known to policymakers. Thus the fallout from the $1.2 trillion of outstanding subprime loans combined with the huge expansion in credit default swaps could not be contained [Cassidy 2008, Lewis 2010].

Similarly from an historical perspective [Kindleberger & Aliber 2011] observers should not have been surprised that after this major bubble there was a rash of litigation [Rapp 2010, 2009] and several scams and scandals were revealed including the largest Ponzi scheme in history and several high-profile insider trading cases[49]. In Bernie Madoff's case and other fund advisors and financial managers that had been running elaborate Ponzi schemes reporting stable earnings, the financial collapse following Lehman's bankruptcy meant many investors saw other investments sour. They thus decided to tap those "stable" investments. Madoff and others running such Ponzi schemes could not meet the payment requests triggering their collapse and exposure.

Greed and pressures to meet expectations as in the M&A boom of the 1980s also resulted in an explosion of insider trading cases the most prominent involving the Galleon Group and Rajat Gupta, a former head of McKinsey and a Goldman Sachs director.

---

[48] Cassidy, J. 2008. "Anatomy Of A Meltdown," *New Yorker*, NY.
[49] The Madoff Ponzi scheme and the insider trading cases were seen by some as regulatory failures especially the SEC. They also raised concerns about "revolving doors" and industry cooption.

"The Raj Rajaratnam/Galleon Group, Anil Kumar, and Rajat Gupta insider trading cases are parallel and related civil and criminal actions by the United States Securities and Exchange Commission and the United States Department of Justice against three friends and business partners: Galleon hedge fund founder-owner Raj Rajaratnam and former McKinsey & Company senior executives Anil Kumar and Rajat Gupta. In these proceedings, the men were confronted with insider trading charges: Rajaratnam was convicted, Kumar pleaded guilty and testified as key witness in the criminal trials of Rajaratnam and Gupta, and Gupta was convicted in Federal district court in Manhattan in June 2012." (Wikipedia 2013)

Dodd-Frank

The reaction to these developments and the crisis itself again conformed to historical precedent. The Congress held hearings and passed major legislation[50], Dodd-Frank, to try and fix what were the perceived weaknesses in the financial system that had led to and exacerbated the collapse and its aftermath. It is an extensive document that created new organizations such as a Financial Oversight Board and a Consumer Financial Protection Agency but also expanded the regulatory and rule making authority of existing organizations such as the Fed, the SEC and the Commodity Futures Trading Commission.

As noted elsewhere in this book the increased capital requirements for financial institutions including against derivative transactions and the use of exchanges seem

---

[50] Government's role relative to bubbles in their formation, evolution and aftermath was the subject of the second Leir Conference in September 2012 where Dodd-Frank among other topics was examined. The Notes from this Conference are posted on the Leir Center's website: www.leirbubblecenter.org.

appropriate especially in light of the consequences of the 2004

SEC decision to ease capital requirements for US investment

banks. Also efforts to control the optimism of market participants

through standardized and transparent loan documentation for

borrowers and living wills for very large financial organizations

also make sense.[51] However the intense lobbying by financial

institutions to blunt the rule making process shows the system

---

[51] A brief summary of the 2010 Dodd–Frank Wall Street Reform and Consumer Protection Act's main provisions is as follows [Wikipedia 2013] making "changes in the American financial regulatory environment that affect all federal financial regulatory agencies and almost every part of the nation's financial services industry. ... 4.1_Title I – Financial Stability; 4.2_Title II – Orderly Liquidation Authority; 4.3_Title III – Transfer of Powers to the Controller, the FDIC, and the Fed; 4.4_Title IV – Regulation of Advisers to Hedge Funds and Others; 4.5_Title V – Insurance; 4.6_Title VI – Improvements to Regulation; 4.7_Title VII – Wall Street Transparency and Accountability; 4.8 Title VIII – Payment, Clearing and Settlement Supervision; 4.9_Title IX – Investor Protections and Improvements to the Regulation of Securities; 4.10 Title X – Bureau of Consumer Financial Protection; 4.11_Title XI – Federal Reserve System Provisions; 4.12_Title XII – Improving Access to Mainstream Financial Institutions; 4.13_Title XIII – Pay It Back Act; 4.14_Title XIV – Mortgage Reform and Anti-Predatory Lending Act; 4.16_Title XVI – Section 1256 Contracts.

The main objectives of the Congress and the Obama Administration were: 1) The consolidation of regulatory agencies, elimination of the national thrift charter, and new oversight council to evaluate systemic risk; 2) Comprehensive regulation of financial markets, including increased transparency of derivatives (bringing them onto exchanges); 3) Consumer protection reforms including a new consumer protection agency and uniform standards for "plain vanilla" products as well as strengthened investor protection; 4) Tools for financial crises, including a "resolution regime" complementing the existing Federal Deposit Insurance Corporation (FDIC) authority to allow for orderly winding down of bankrupt firms, and including a proposal that the Federal Reserve (the "Fed") receive authorization from the Treasury for extensions of credit in "unusual or exigent circumstances"; 5) Various measures aimed at increasing international standards and cooperation including proposals related to improved accounting and tightened regulation of credit rating agencies. 6) At Obama's request, Congress later added the Volcker Rule separating the banks' proprietary trading by into separate subsidiaries.

remains at risk to potential cooption or regulatory lapses as indicated by the multi-billion dollar portfolio "hedging" losses at J. P. Morgan Chase.[52]

While Dodd-Frank[53] deals with the legislative and regulatory fix that typically follows a major financial crisis similar to Sarbanes-Oxley after the dot.com bust or FIRREA after the S&L crisis, the TARP [Troubled Asset Relief Program] was designed to deal with the economic fallout similar to the RTC after the S&L crisis or the WPA [Works Progress Administration] after 1929. Through the TARP the government lent funds or bought equity in major financial institutions such as AIG or GMAC as well as most major banks including Bank Of America, Citicorp and J. P Morgan Chase. It also rescued GM and Chrysler directly by providing loans in bankruptcy, and there were funds for handling the growing

---

[52]
http://topics.nytimes.com/top/news/business/companies/morgan_j_p_chase_and_company/ index.html

[53] Its enhanced prudential standards are meant to address aspects of the recent crisis identified in this chapter and elsewhere in this book as having magnified its adverse consequences on the financial system. These include single counterparty credit limits, greater public disclosure to support the evaluation of a financial firm's risk profile, limitations on funding with short-term debt, a requirement to establish risk committees, and capital plans to be reviewed by the Federal Reserve that demonstrate a financial firm has robust, forward-looking capital planning processes that account for its unique risks and leverage limits. Further systemically important bank holding companies and nonbanks will be subject to a resolution plan or "living will" requirement ("DFA Rule"). The plan must provide for the rapid and orderly liquidation or restructuring of a systemically important firm under the Bankruptcy Code or other resolution regime; must provide the Federal Reserve and the FDIC with information to understand a firm's structure, complexity and internal operations; and must propose a way to fund critical operations during a firm's resolution. Finally the plan must be evaluated under "baseline", "adverse" and "severely adverse" economic conditions.

problem of foreclosures that subsequently have gone through several iterations.

While the Federal government has developed a series of programs such as HAMP [Home Affordable Modification Program] to deal with foreclosures to eliminate the housing overhang and keep people in their homes the overwhelming amount of legal and legislative involvement has taken place at the state and local level. State Attorney Generals have been involved with the Federal government in negotiating settlements with banks involved in abusive foreclosure practices. NY State for example has passed laws requiring lenders go through a set of procedures overseen by the courts. Yet the process is time consuming due to the legal complexities surrounding real estate and only at the end of 2012 did the housing market begin to show signs of recovery.

Conclusions

Changes in laws and regulations have thus frequently led to bubbles fed by financial innovations with implicit leverage that have also required legal support. These developments have uniformly ended badly with a crash, resulting in large investor losses and the exposure of criminal activity such as insider trading and fraud. This series of events then leads to new legislation to both manage the aftermath and attempt to prevent similar future occurrences. Therefore in the beginning, evolution and aftermath of bubbles existing laws and rules matter; changes in legislation and regulations matter, and lawyers' activities matter.

References

Bajaj, V. 2008. "If Everyone's Finger-Pointing, Who's to Blame?" *NY TIMES*, NY

Balen, M. 2003. *The King, the Crook and the Gambler*, Harper Collins, NY

Bar-Gill, O. 2009. "Subprime Mortgage Contracts," *Cornell Law Review*, Vo. 94.

Blanchard, O. 2009. *Macroeconomics*, Pearson Education, Upper Saddle River, NJ.

Bruck, C. 1989. *The Predators' Ball*, Penguin Books, NY.

Burrough, B. & Helyar, J. 1990. *Barbarians At The Gate*, Harper & Row, NY.

Cassidy, J. 2008. "Anatomy Of A Meltdown," *New Yorker*, NY.

Ciment, J., Ed. 2010. *Booms and Busts*, Sharpe Reference, Armonk, NY.

Countrywide Financial Corporation, *2006 10K*, pp 3-17 *available at* http://about. countrywide.com/SECFilings/Form10K.aspx.

Geist, C. 1997. *Wall Street*, Oxford University Press, NY.

Gramlich, E. 2007. *Subprime Mortgages*, Urban Institute Press, Washington, DC.

Gibeaut, J. *supra*, or Neil, M. 2007. "N.Y. Lawyer Stole $24M, Gets 10 Years", *ABA Journal*, Washington, DC.

Korngold, G. and Goldstein, P. 2002. *Real Estate Transactions*, Foundation Press, NY.

Lewis, M. 2010. *The Big Short*, W. W. Norton, NY.

Morrissey, B. 2002. "Salomon Telecom Analyst Jack Grubman Resigns," *Internet News.com.*

Mackenzie, M. 2008. "Super-senior CDO investors begin to flex their muscles," *Financial Times*, London, UK.

Morgenson, G. & Glater, J. 2008. "The Foreclosure Machine," *NY Times*, NY.

Neil, M. 2007. "More Law Firms Seek to Sue Banks", *ABA Journal*, Washington, D.C.

Rapp, W. 2010."The Global Mortgage Crisis Litigation Fallout". *After the Crisis: Rethinking Finance*, Lagoarde-Segot, T., ed., Nova Science Publishers, Inc., Hauppauge NY.

Rapp, W. 2009. "Clash Of Titans - The Barclays v Bear Stearns Case and the Current Financial Crisis," *Proceedings Association For Global Business*, VA.

Rapp, W. 2004. *Information Technology Strategies*, Oxford University Press, NY.

Sloan, A. 2007. "House of Junk", *Fortune,* NY.

Smith, A. 1972. *SuperMoney*, Random House, NY.

Smith, A. 1990. *The Roaring 80s.* Penguin Books, NY.

Taleb, N. 2008. *Fooled By Randomness.* Random House, NY.

van Duyn, A. & Mackenzie, M. 2008. "Tranche warfare breaks out over CDOs," *Financial Times*, London, UK.

Weiss, D. 2007. "Judges Crack Down on Law Firm 'Foreclosure Mills'", *ABA Journal*, Washington, DC.

Weiss, D. 2007. "Suits Follow Mortgage Meltdown", *ABA Journal*, Washington, DC.

Yamada. Y. & Kubo, T. 2008. *Japanese Major Banks*, Merrill Lynch Japan Securities.

Wikipedia, 2013.

CHAPTER THREE

HERDING AND MOMENTUM AT THE INDUSTRY LEVEL[54]

When The Battle Is Lost And Won

Z. Yan   Y. Zhao L. Sun

Abstract

Theoretical models on herd behavior predict that under different assumptions, herding can bring prices away (or towards) fundamentals and reduce (or enhance) market efficiency. In this chapter, the joint effect of herding and momentum at the industry level often associated with stock price bubbles is examined. This examination indicates that the momentum effect is magnified when there is a *low* level of investor herding. Investor herd behavior thus helps move asset prices towards fundamentals and enhances market efficiency. A trading strategy taking a long position in winner industries and a short position in loser industries when the herding level is low can thus generate significant returns. However when the herding involves speculators the effect is to move away from the fundamentals and results in forming a financial bubble.

Introduction

---

[54] This chapter is based on material presented at the 1st Leir Conference on Bubbles September 2011. This material was subsequently published as an article in *The Journal of Investing*. See Yan, Z., Zhao, Y. & Sun, L. 2012. "Industry Herding and Momentum", *The Journal of Investing*, Vol. 21, No. 1. In this chapter the authors explain how the herding effects often associated with stock price bubbles can be identified and tracked on an industry basis and how using this information an investor might achieve superior portfolio returns.

Herd behavior, or the tendency of individuals in a group to "follow the trend," has frequently been observed in equity markets. Herd behavior in investors leads to a convergence of action (Hirshleifer & Teoh 2003).

There are at least two important strands of literature on herd behavior. The first is that mutual imitation among investors may temporarily drive asset prices away from fundamental values, and move the market towards inefficiency in an information cascade (Banerjee 1992; Bikhchandani et al. 1992; Bikhchandani & Sharma 2001). This is thus potentially a bubble formation signal. The second strand shows that uninformed traders can become informed by imitating the observed movement in the market. In that way, herd behavior in investors may help impound information about fundamentals into asset prices, and enhance market efficiency (Froot et al. 1992; Hirshleifer et al. 1994; Hey & Morone 2004).

There is a large body of empirical studies that has investigated herd behavior in equity markets. However, the empirical studies thus far do not focus on testing any particular herd model proposed in the theoretical literature. They either focus on the herd behavior of professional investors or on market-wide herding.

In the first case, professional investors such as institutional money managers and financial analysts are evaluated compared to the performance of their peers or to benchmark index returns. Thus they tend to buy or sell assets following each other. For instance, Grinblatt et al. (1995) provide evidence that mutual funds tend to buy and sell the same stocks at the same time (i.e., herd) in excess of what one would expect from pure chance. Voronkova and Bohl (2005) show that pension funds in the Polish stock market to a great extent exhibit herd behavior. Dass, Massa, and Patgiri (2008) find empirical evidence that mutual funds herded around the technology and Internet bubble.

In the second case, the empirical studies aim to establish the presence of herd behavior in the stock market. Chang, Cheng and Khorana (2000) show significant evidence of herding in South Korea and Taiwan. Hwang and Salmon (2004) use the cross-sectional (market-wide) standard deviation of individual security returns to measure herd behavior. They find that herd behavior in the market is significant and independent from market conditions in the US and South Korean stock markets. Caparelli et al. (2004) also find herd behavior in Italian stock markets. Caporale, Economou, and Philippas (2008) test and establish the presence of herding in extreme market conditions based on data from the Athens stock exchanges. Tan et al. (2008) examine herd behavior in Chinese stock markets, and provide evidence of herding within both the A-share and B-share markets.

Most of the existing empirical studies focus on the herding of individual stock or market index returns. Few study herd behavior at the industry level. Using Fama-French 49 industry classification, Choi and Sias (2008) find institutional investors follow each other into and out of the same industries. Jame and

Tong (2009) document that retail investors herd on the industry level on both weekly and monthly investment horizons. In this chapter, the focus is on the industry level. Using a different approach from Choi and Sias (2008) and Jame and Tong (2009), it does not utilize changes in investor holdings as a measure of herding. Instead, it uses stock return dispersions (cross-sectional standard deviation and absolute deviation) at the industry level to measure industry-level herding.

This chapter thus fills the gap of isolated theoretical and empirical studies to address the question of whether herd behavior creates price bubbles or enhances market efficiency at the industry level? In order to answer this key question it studies the joint effects of herd behavior and momentum. By linking herding and momentum at the industry level, it builds on the two strands of literature.

Stock market price momentum was first documented by Jagadeesh and Titman (1993, 2001). Stocks that have previously exhibited positive returns (winners) continue to outperform stocks that have previously exhibited negative returns (losers). Chan, Jegadeesh, and Lakonishok (1996) suggest this predictability of future returns is due to the market's under-reaction to information. They show that the stock market responds only gradually to new information.

If momentum is the result of a gradual movement of the stock market towards efficiency and if herd behavior temporarily drives asset prices away from fundamental values, then we can expect investor herd behavior to slow down the rate of movement towards efficiency. Stocks with a *high* level of herding will then exhibit a larger momentum effect than will stocks with a *low* level of herding. [See Introduction's discussion of how pension funds' herding with respect to the "nifty fifty" created the growth stock boom and bust of the late 1960s and early 1970s.] If, on the other hand, herding can help impound fundamental news into asset prices, and enhance market efficiency, investor herding will accelerate the rate of movement to efficiency so stocks with a *low* level of herding will exhibit the momentum effect more than stocks with a *high* level of herding.

The existing theories of herding make no definite *a priori* predictions about the impact of investor herding activity on the momentum effect at the industry level. Thus the approach used here is strictly empirical. The results indicate that stock price momentum is significantly enhanced given a *low* level of herding. Winner industries with a low level of herding generate higher subsequent returns than those with a high level of herding.

Loser industries with a low level of herding generate lower subsequent returns than those with a high level of herding. The conclusion is that herding effects play an important role in the momentum effect and have predictive power with respect to future price movements. These empirical findings are consistent with the second strand of the herd behavior literature. Acting in a herd, investors can help move asset prices towards fundamentals and enhance market efficiency.

This chapter thus extends the current literature by linking herd behavior and momentum at the industry level and by providing evidence that herd behavior can under certain conditions enhance market efficiency. Understanding these conditions can help investors and regulators to separate unstable herding by speculators the leads to bubbles [see Chapter 8] from those that improve market efficiency. The remainder of the chapter is organized as follows. Section 2 discusses the data and methodology. Section 3 presents the empirical evidence, while Section 4 presents checks for robustness and Section 5 the conclusions.

Data and Methodology

Data on individual stock returns, and industry classifications (SIC codes) comes from the Center for Research and Security Prices (CRSP). All ordinary shares (CRSP share code 10 or 11) from January 1980 to December 2008 are included. Each stock has been assigned to one of 49 or 30 Fama and French industries. The updated industry definitions are available on Ken French's website.

Following Christie and Huang (1995), the cross-sectional standard deviation of single stock returns with respect to industry mean returns was estimated and expressed as:

$$CSSD_t = \sqrt{\frac{\sum_{i=1}^{N}(R_{i,t} - R_{m,t})^2}{N-1}} \quad \dots\dots\dots\dots\dots\dots\dots\dots\dots\dots\dots$$

(1).

Here, $R_{i,t}$ is the observed stock return of firm *i* at time *t,* $R_{m,t}$ is the cross-sectional average return of N stocks in the industry at time *t,* and N is the number of stocks in the industry.

Although the cross-sectional standard deviation of returns is an intuitive measure used to capture herd behavior, it can be considerably affected by the existence of outliers. That is why Christie and Huang (1995) and Chang, Cheng and Khorana (2000) proposed the use of the cross-sectional absolute deviation (CSAD) as a better measure of dispersion:

$$CSAD_t = \frac{\sum_{i=1}^{N} \left| R_{i,t} - R_{m,t} \right|}{N}$$

As a dispersion measure, either CSSD or CSAD indicates a high level of herding when its value is low. In other words, when stocks in the same industry move in tandem, or herd, the dispersion is small.

Each stock is assigned to one of the 49 Fama and French industry portfolios according to their historical industry classification. The assignment of each stock to an industry portfolio is at the end of June of year t based on its four-digit SIC code at that time. Not only CRSP, but also Compustat is used as a source of SIC codes. The Compustat SIC codes (for the fiscal year ending in calendar year t-1) were used whenever available.

Otherwise, the CRSP SIC codes are used for June of year t. Each stock's return is equally weighted to generate industry returns. Results are very similar if the value of each stock's return is weighted. In each month, the past 6-month returns in each industry is calculated as a proxy for winners and losers. The past 6-month returns are the 7- to 1-month returns. The most recent one-month return are intentionally excluded to attenuate problems associated with microstructure issues such as the effect of the bid-ask bounce (see Asness, 1995). The herding level is calculated using the previous 1-month returns. Different window lengths of herding and momentum measures are also considered. To ensure the herding measure is not influenced by a few deviant observations, the approach requires that each industry have at least 10 stocks. Thus the tobacco industry is not included in our analysis as on average it has only 6 stocks.

Table 1 reports the summary statistics. On average, the largest industry in terms of market capitalization is the beer and liquor industry, which accounts for roughly 13% of the total stock market capitalization for the 49 industry classifications. The banking industry has the largest number of firms among all industries.

Monthly average returns range from a low of 0.11% for Coal to a high of 1.74% for Candy & Soda. The computer software industry is characterized by the highest volatility with a CSSD of 19.85% and CSAD of 13.60%; the utilities industry enjoys the lowest volatility with a CSSD of 6.47% and a CSAD of 4.32%. This is not very surprising due to the fact that the utilities industry is heavily regulated. For instance, many utility companies during our sample period confronted rate of return on capital or price cap regulation. With similar regulatory constraints, utilities firms should have relatively similar performance and therefore, have highly correlated stock returns.

Empirical Results

Table 2 reports the empirical results using monthly data. At the end of each month, there is a calculation of the previous 6-month (t-7 to t-1) returns for each industry where the top 50% group are winner industries and the lower 50% are loser industries.

Independently, we calculate the CSSD and CSAD for each industry using the previous 1-month returns. Based on CSSD or CSAD, the bottom 30% are labeled as having a high level of herding while the top 30% are designated as having a low level of herding; and the middle 40% are categorized as having a medium level of herding. In this way, all industries are organized into 6 portfolios.

Looking first at the loser industries, the subsequent 1-month, 2-month and 3-month cumulative returns of these industries with a *low* level of herding (CSSD) are 0.78%, 1.28% and 2.09%, respectively. These returns are significantly *smaller* than those loser industries with a high level of herding, whose returns are 0.86%, 1.63%, and 2.53%, respectively. This result demonstrates that a low level of herding enhances the momentum effect. That is loser industries with a low level of herding perform worse than loser industries with a high level of herding.

Examining winner industries the story is similar. Winner

industries with *low* herding (CSSD) levels have *higher* subsequent cumulative returns than winner industries with a *high* level of herding. The subsequent 1-month, 2-month and 3-month cumulative returns of winner industries with a *low* level of herding (CSSD) are 1.66%, 3.11% and 4.71%, respectively. These returns are significantly *higher* than those of winner industries with a high level of herding, whose returns are 1.21%, 2.43%, and 3.82%, respectively. The patterns are the same when we use CSAD as the measure of herding. In sum herding tends to moderate returns on both the downside and upside.

The empirical results thus show that winner industries with a low level of herding generate higher subsequent returns than those with a high level of herding. Loser industries with a low level of herding generate lower subsequent returns than those with a high level of herding. The fact that the momentum effect is more significant when the herding level is low is consistent with the notion that herd behavior helps incorporate news of fundamentals into asset prices. Thus the future returns of industries with a high level of herding are less extreme compared with those of industries with a low level of herding. This lends support to the second strand of herding theories - herding will accelerate the rate of movement to market efficiency.

Based on these findings, we can easily design a long-short portfolio. A trading strategy taking a long position in winner industries and a short position in loser industries when herding level is low can generate significant returns. Under the 49industry classification, the spread of 1-month, 2-month and 3-month cumulative returns are 0.88%, 1.85%, and 2.62% using CSSD as the proxy for herd behavior, and 1.19%, 2.18%, and 3.10% using CSAD as the proxy for herd behavior. All the spreads are statistically significant.

Figure 1 shows the annually cumulative long-short portfolio returns during the sample periods. The strategies incur losses in 3 out of 29 years. Maximum gain is in 1999, and maximum loss in 2002. Average Sharpe ratios are 1.15. This is not entirely surprising, considering the strategy is an enhanced momentum strategy. Most momentum strategies did quite well in the late 1990s when the Internet bubble was at its peak.

Since some industries, such as computer Software, have relatively low levels of herding, investors may consistently go long some industries and short other industries. Then this herding-momentum strategy is just an industry bet in disguise.

If by pure chance, the possibility of an industry being in either a long or short portfolio is 15 percent, which equals the product of 50 percent being either a loser or winner industry and 30 percent of being a low herding industry. Table 3 lists the occurrence percentage of an industry appearing in either long or short portfolio during the sample period. From this it seems that the portfolio choice is not random. The utilities industry, which consistently has a very high level of herding, is not selected even once during the sample period. Some industries, such as Computers, Pharmaceutical Products and Computer Software, are selected much more often than other industries, such as Defense, Candy & Soda, and Coal.

To reduce the selection bias towards industries with low levels of herding, the approach normalizes the herding measures for each industry.

$$z - CSSD_{j,t} = \frac{CSSD_{j,t} - \mu_{CSSD_j}}{\sigma_{CSSD_j}}$$

Here, $CSSD_{j,t}$ is the original CSSD for industry j in month t; μ_{CSSD_j} is the mean value of CSSDs of industry j over our sample period; σ_{CSSD_j} is the standard deviation of CSSDs of industry j; $z - CSSD_{j,t}$ is the normalized value or z-score of CSSD for industry j in month t. Similarly, $z - CSAD_{j,t}$ for each industry in each month is calculated.

In Panel A of Table 4, the occurrence percentages are provided for industries when z-scores of CSSD or CSAD are used in the portfolio construction. The industry selection bias is greatly reduced with normalization. Most occurrence percentages are around 15 percent and much more evenly distributed than those in Table 3. Panel B reports portfolio performance. The patterns are very similar to those in Table 3. Winner (loser) industries with a low level of herding generate higher (lower) subsequent returns than those with high herding levels. The long-short portfolios also generate positive and significant returns, but the degree of significance is slightly smaller than that in Table 3 when original CSSD and CSAD data are employed.

Being more conservative to alleviate industry selection bias using z-scores only in the empirical tests should suffice.

According to Christie and Huang (1995), herding is more likely during stress periods in the market when investors tend to suppress their own beliefs and follow the market consensus. Demirer and Kutan (2006) show that return dispersions during extreme downside movements of the market are much lower than those for upside movements. That is stock returns behave more similarly during down markets. Thus, it is important to investigate whether or not the above patterns hold during economic recession periods including panics and crashes.

Investigating the two most recent crisis periods of the dot com crisis aftermath from 2001-2002 and the financial collapse from 2007-2008, gives the results presented in Table 5. Although all the subsequent reported returns are negative, the previous findings still hold. For example, the 3-month cumulative returns of loser industries with *low* herding levels (CSSD) is -4.32%, which is *lower* than those loser industries with a *high* level of herding (-3.40%). The high-herding winner industries have a 3-month cumulative return of -2.62% that is *lower* than that of the winner industries with low-herding (-1.18%). The spread of the trading strategy taking a long position in low-herding winner industries and a short position in low-herding loser industries can generate 1.12%, 2.5%, and 3.15% spread over the following 1-month, 2-month and 3-month periods. All the spreads are statistically significant.

To summarize, sorting Fama-French 49 industries by the industry-level momentum and herding, demonstrates that high-level herding reduces the momentum effect whether original herding measures or normalized herding measures are used, and whether it is during a crisis period or not. These findings support the second strand of theories on herding (Froot et al. 1992; Hirshleifer et al. 1994; Hey & Morone 2004) that herding may enhance market efficiency, at least, at the industry level.

Robustness Checks

So far, only the Fama-French 49 industry classifications were used. The first robustness check is to employ different industry classifications. Table 6 reports on the results for the Fama-French 30 industry classification. The main results remain the same. For loser industries with a low level of herding (CSSD), the subsequent 1-month, 2-month and 3-month cumulative returns are 0.61%, 1.19% and 1.80%, respectively, *lower* than those of loser industries with a *high* level of herding (0.89%, 1.81% and 2.62%, respectively). For winner industries with a low level of herding, future 1-month, 2-months and 3-months cumulative returns (1.68%, 3.18% and 4.72%, respectively) are *higher* than those of winner industries with a high level of herding (1.10%, 2.27% and 3.65%). The long-short trading strategy conditional on a low-level of herding also generates significant returns. In an unreported table, defining industries according to the 3-digit SIC codes, the results will remain the same.

Previously the past 6-month returns in each industry were

calculated as a proxy for winners and losers, and the herding level was calculated using the previous 1-month returns. If different window lengths are used to measure herding and momentum, the results are presented in table 7. In Panel A, the past 12-month (t-13 to t-1) returns are used as the proxy for momentum. The patterns are similar. The trading strategy will generate spreads of 0.64%, 1.18%, and 1.86% over 1-month, 2-months and 3-months periods when CSSD is employed as the proxy for herding; and 0.69%, 1.16%, and 1.71% when CSAD is the proxy for herding. All spreads are statistically significant. Panel B reports results for herd behavior that is calculated using the previous 6-month returns, and momentum past 6-month returns. Again the patterns are similar; all trading strategies yield significant returns.

Finally, the above pattern is examined using weekly data, instead of monthly data. At the end of each week, the previous 6-week returns for each industry is calculated with the top 50% group as winners and the bottom 50% as losers. Independently, the CSSD and CSAD are calculated using the previous 1-week returns. The bottom 30% based on CSSD or CSAD are labeled as having a high level of herding, and the top 30% as having a low level of herding. Table 6 reports the empirical results using weekly data. All main results still hold at the weekly level.

Conclusions

The analysis presented in this chapter fills a gap in the theoretical and empirical studies of investor herding behavior, and examines if herd behavior creates price bubbles or enhances market efficiency at the industry level. It studies the joint effect of herd behavior and momentum. The empirical findings show strong evidence the momentum effect is magnified when there is a low level of investor herding. By acting as a herd, investors help move asset prices towards fundamentals and enhance market efficiency. Winner industries with low herding levels generate higher subsequent returns than winner industries with high herding levels. Loser industries with a low level of herding generate lower subsequent returns than loser industries with a high level of herding. A trading strategy taking a long position in winner industries and a short position in loser industries when herding level is low can generate significant returns.

TABLE 1. SUMMARY STATISTICS Each month January 1980 to December 2008, we classify stocks into one of Fama and French 49 industries. **# Firms** reports time series average number firms each industry. **ME** is time series average industry market equity value as % whole market. **Return** is mean monthly returns. **CSSD1** and **CSAD1** are cross-sectional standard deviation returns and cross-sectional absolute deviation returns using previous 1 month data.

49 Industries	# of Firms	ME	Return	CSSD1	CSAD1
Aircraft	23	5.67%	1.53%	12.62%	8.66%
Agriculture	14	0.72%	1.04%	16.04%	10.84%
Automobiles and Trucks	62	2.18%	0.83%	13.02%	9.01%
Banking	417	1.84%	1.35%	9.51%	6.25%
Beer & Liquor	14	12.89%	1.16%	10.96%	7.59%
Construction Materials	107	1.15%	1.10%	14.29%	9.33%
Printing and Publishing	43	2.29%	0.82%	12.30%	8.02%
Shipping Containers	18	1.39%	1.28%	12.78%	8.91%
Business Services	240	0.75%	1.31%	18.09%	11.68%
Chemicals	80	2.60%	1.04%	13.41%	8.69%
Electronic Equipment	259	1.67%	1.48%	18.44%	12.49%
Apparel	67	0.82%	1.01%	14.92%	10.02%
Coal	11	2.90%	0.11%	13.46%	9.42%
Construction	58	0.77%	0.90%	15.95%	10.75%
Pharmaceutical Products	200	3.38%	1.74%	18.99%	12.96%
Electrical Equipment	76	1.78%	1.08%	16.08%	10.83%
Fabricated Products	25	0.18%	0.88%	14.87%	10.23%
Trading	168	2.04%	1.57%	14.30%	9.01%
Food Products	77	3.06%	1.18%	12.97%	8.58%
Entertainment	69	1.70%	0.91%	18.69%	12.37%
Precious Metals	21	0.65%	0.75%	18.66%	12.73%
Defense	11	1.58%	1.54%	11.21%	8.07%
Computers	137	3.56%	1.15%	19.55%	13.44%
Healthcare	82	0.63%	1.46%	18.29%	12.48%
Consumer Goods	88	3.07%	0.96%	14.75%	9.85%
Insurance	141	3.56%	1.36%	11.29%	7.40%
Measuring and Control Equipment	111	0.71%	1.39%	16.49%	11.26%
Machinery	167	1.13%	1.16%	15.63%	10.37%
Restaurants, Hotels, Motels	90	1.07%	0.69%	14.89%	10.08%
Medical Equipment	142	0.99%	1.33%	18.36%	12.49%
Non-Metallic & Industrial Metal Mining	16	1.47%	0.73%	15.33%	10.73%
Petroleum and Natural Gas	192	3.79%	0.96%	16.95%	10.76%
Almost Nothing	36	1.53%	1.02%	17.07%	11.74%
Business Supplies	63	2.56%	0.88%	11.41%	7.79%

Personal Services		53	0.70%	1.01%	15.93%	10.78%	
Retail		233	2.57%	1.06%	15.70%	10.48%	
Real Estate		42	0.38%	0.77%	16.29%	10.48%	
Rubber and Plastic Products		48	0.50%	1.14%	15.24%	10.22%	
Shipbuilding, Railroad Equipment		12	2.60%	0.11%	11.45%	8.59%	
Candy & Soda		13	1.79%	1.74%	9.81%	6.98%	
Computer Software		267	1.65%	1.42%	19.85%	13.60%	
Steel Works Etc		65	1.32%	1.06%	12.99%	9.09%	
Communication		103	5.82%	1.32%	17.69%	11.29%	
Recreation		41	0.50%	0.65%	16.98%	11.69%	
Transportation		100	1.75%	1.13%	14.29%	9.61%	
Textiles		35	0.53%	1.13%	13.75%	9.61%	
Utilities		145	3.09%	1.19%	6.47%	4.32%	
Wholesale		187	0.73%	1.11%	16.70%	10.87%	

Table 2: Momentum and herding Two-way Sort, 49 industries

Each month, from January 1980 to December 2008, all stocks are assigned to one of Fama and French 49 industries. **M6** is the previous 6 month cumulative returns (from month t-7 to month t-1), which is used as a proxy for momentum. **CSSD1** and **CSAD1** are the cross-sectional standard deviation of returns and cross-sectional absolute deviation of returns using previous 1 month data. **1 month**, **2 month** and **3 month** are the cumulative subsequent returns.

Herd	Mom	Obs	CSSD1	M6	1 month	2 month	3 month
High	loser	2111	0.1	3.33%	0.86%	1.63%	2.53%
Low	loser	2221	0.21	-4.49%	0.78%	1.26%	2.09%
High	winner	2340	0.1	10.96%	1.21%	2.41%	3.82%
Low	winner	2228	0.22	20.13%	1.66%	3.11%	4.71%
Spread (low-herding winner – low-herding loser)					**0.88%****	**1.85%*****	**2.62%****
Herd	Mom	Obs	CSAD1	M6	1 month	2 month	3 month
High	loser	2087	0.07	4.03%	0.89%	1.77%	2.57%
Low	loser	2256	0.14	-5.29%	0.63%	1.19%	1.79%
High	winner	2366	0.07	10.42%	1.17%	2.30%	3.72%
Low	winner	2193	0.14	21.61%	1.82%	3.37%	4.89%
Spread (low-herding winner – low-herding loser)					**1.19%*****	**2.18%*****	**3.10%*****

Note: *, **, *** represents the difference between the two portfolios is significant at the 10%, 5% and 1% level respectively.

Table 3: **The Occurrence Percentage of each industry, using original CSSD and CSAD** There are 348 monthly portfolios during our sample periods. The occurrence percentage for any industries equals the number of appearances of the industry in one-side of the portfolios divided by 348.

49 Industries	Long		Short	
	CSSD	CSAD	CSSD	CSAD
Aircraft	7.47%	5.75%	4.02%	2.59%
Agriculture	7.18%	8.91%	20.69%	22.99%
Automobiles and Trucks	4.31%	2.87%	6.90%	6.32%
Banking	0.86%	0.00%	0.57%	0.86%
Beer & Liquor	4.89%	4.31%	6.32%	5.75%
Construction Materials	8.33%	4.31%	6.90%	2.59%
Printing and Publishing	2.59%	0.86%	5.46%	4.02%
Shipping Containers	6.32%	6.32%	4.89%	4.89%
Business Services	34.77%	31.90%	23.56%	21.26%
Chemicals	8.33%	3.74%	5.46%	2.59%
Electronic Equipment	29.60%	34.20%	36.21%	37.36%
Apparel	9.20%	8.62%	11.49%	8.33%
Coal	2.01%	2.01%	0.57%	0.86%
Construction	11.21%	10.92%	14.94%	17.24%
Pharmaceutical Products	33.91%	37.93%	31.03%	36.49%
Electrical Equipment	16.09%	14.08%	17.82%	18.68%
Fabricated Products	3.74%	3.45%	13.51%	13.79%
Trading	9.48%	4.60%	4.31%	0.57%
Food Products	6.61%	2.30%	3.45%	1.44%
Entertainment	24.71%	26.72%	33.05%	37.64%
Precious Metals	12.36%	13.79%	20.11%	22.13%
Defense	4.89%	5.75%	2.59%	3.16%
Computers	29.31%	34.20%	40.52%	49.43%
Healthcare	31.03%	37.64%	24.71%	29.02%
Consumer Goods	6.32%	6.32%	12.64%	6.90%
Insurance	1.72%	0.29%	2.30%	0.29%
Measuring and Control Equipment	22.41%	24.71%	14.08%	17.24%
Machinery	12.36%	9.48%	11.21%	7.47%
Restaurants, Hotels, Motels	7.18%	6.03%	14.08%	14.37%
Medical Equipment	32.18%	38.22%	29.31%	38.22%
Non-Metallic & Industrial Metal Mining	10.06%	12.64%	20.98%	21.55%
Petroleum and Natural Gas	18.10%	14.94%	25.57%	21.55%
Almost Nothing	16.09%	18.10%	18.97%	21.84%
Business Supplies	2.30%	0.86%	2.87%	1.15%
Personal Services	16.38%	15.80%	15.52%	15.52%
Retail	10.34%	7.76%	13.79%	11.78%
Real Estate	10.34%	9.48%	19.25%	18.68%
Rubber and Plastic Products	14.08%	13.51%	12.07%	8.91%

Shipbuilding, Railroad Equipment	0.00%	0.00%	1.15%	1.44%
Candy & Soda	0.86%	1.15%	1.15%	0.86%
Computer Software	38.22%	43.39%	37.64%	40.80%
Steel Works Etc	5.46%	5.46%	3.45%	2.59%
Communication	22.99%	18.68%	18.97%	18.10%
Recreation	14.66%	16.95%	26.72%	31.32%
Transportation	8.62%	5.75%	6.32%	4.89%
Textiles	5.17%	6.03%	10.06%	9.77%
Wholesale	20.11%	19.54%	16.95%	13.22%

Table 4: The Occurrence Percentages and Portfolio Performance, using Z-scores of CSSD and CSAD Each month, from January 1980 to December 2008, all stocks are assigned to one of Fama and French 49 industries. **M6** is the previous 6 month cumulative returns, which is used as a proxy for momentum. **z_CSSD1** and **z_CSAD1** are the z-scores of cross-sectional standard deviation of returns and cross-sectional absolute deviation of returns using previous 1 month data. **1 month**, **2 month** and **3 month** are the cumulative subsequent returns.

Panel A: The Occurrence Percentage of Each Industry, Using Z-scores of CSSD and CSAD

49	Long		Short	
Industries	z_CSSD	z_CSAD	z_CSSD	z_CSAD
Aircraft	15.23%	16.67%	12.07%	11.78%
Agriculture	11.21%	11.78%	13.51%	13.79%
Automobiles and Trucks	15.52%	14.66%	14.66%	15.23%
Banking	18.39%	17.53%	15.23%	14.94%
Beer & Liquor	18.39%	19.54%	11.78%	13.79%
Construction Materials	13.79%	15.23%	10.92%	12.64%
Printing and Publishing	17.82%	17.24%	9.77%	10.92%
Shipping Containers	14.37%	17.24%	15.23%	14.94%
Business Services	13.51%	14.37%	6.90%	6.32%
Chemicals	15.52%	19.25%	14.66%	13.79%
Electronic Equipment	11.78%	9.20%	12.93%	13.22%
Apparel	13.51%	16.38%	9.20%	9.77%
Coal	2.01%	2.30%	0.86%	0.86%
Construction	9.77%	10.63%	13.51%	17.82%
Pharmaceutical Products	17.24%	15.80%	14.08%	11.78%
Electrical Equipment	15.23%	14.37%	16.38%	16.09%
Fabricated Products	13.22%	15.23%	15.23%	15.52%
Trading	14.94%	16.95%	7.18%	7.76%
Food Products	19.54%	18.68%	14.08%	12.93%
Entertainment	10.92%	13.79%	13.51%	16.67%
Precious Metals	4.89%	5.17%	14.94%	16.09%

Defense	8.05%	8.91%	6.61%	7.47%
Computers	6.90%	8.05%	12.64%	14.94%
Healthcare	18.10%	17.82%	10.34%	10.34%
Consumer Goods	16.67%	16.38%	12.93%	12.93%
Insurance	18.97%	16.38%	12.64%	11.49%
Measuring and Control Equipment	15.80%	12.36%	15.23%	12.07%
Machinery	13.22%	10.06%	17.53%	15.23%
Restaurants, Hotels, Motels	15.23%	13.79%	15.23%	15.23%
Medical Equipment	13.51%	10.92%	15.80%	13.79%
Non-Metallic & Industrial Metal Mining	16.38%	16.67%	18.97%	19.83%
Petroleum and Natural Gas	17.82%	23.28%	12.93%	15.23%
Almost Nothing	14.66%	13.51%	16.38%	14.66%
Business Supplies	17.24%	16.38%	15.80%	12.93%
Personal Services	15.80%	16.67%	15.23%	14.66%
Retail	11.49%	12.93%	9.77%	9.48%
Real Estate	10.06%	12.07%	13.22%	15.23%
Rubber and Plastic Products	20.69%	19.25%	13.51%	13.22%
Shipbuilding, Railroad Equipment	4.31%	6.32%	3.74%	4.02%
Candy & Soda	4.31%	5.46%	4.02%	3.16%
Computer Software	11.21%	11.21%	9.20%	8.33%
Steel Works Etc	13.51%	11.78%	18.68%	16.09%
Communication	13.22%	13.51%	6.61%	7.18%
Recreation	15.80%	15.23%	16.67%	14.08%
Transportation	20.40%	18.68%	11.21%	10.34%
Textiles	12.64%	12.93%	15.52%	15.80%
Utilities	22.13%	23.28%	15.52%	14.08%
Wholesale	17.53%	14.08%	14.08%	11.21%

Panel B: Momentum & herding 2-way Sort, Using Z-scores CSSD and CSAD

Herd	Mom	Obs	CSSD1	M6	1 month	2 month	3 month
High	loser	2300	-0.65	0.43%	0.82%	1.67%	2.49%
Low	loser	1979	0.76	-2.04%	0.56%	1.49%	1.83%
High	winner	2169	-0.66	11.65%	1.17%	2.43%	3.92%
Low	winner	2490	0.94	17.88%	1.69%	3.17%	4.41%

Spread (low-herding winner – low-herding loser)					1.13%***	1.68%***	2.58%***

Herd	Mom	Obs	CSAD1	M6	1 month	2 month	3 month
High	loser	1946	-0.66	4.03%	0.89%	1.77%	2.57%
Low	loser	3147	0.72	-1.04%	0.88%	1.65%	2.55%
High	winner	2508	-0.69	10.42%	1.17%	2.30%	3.72%
Low	winner	2089	0.84	21.61%	1.82%	3.37%	4.89%

Spread (low-herding winner – low-herding loser)					0.94%**	1.72%***	2.33%***

Note: *, **, *** represents the difference between the two portfolios is significant at the 10%, 5% and 1% level respectively.

Table 5 – Crisis Periods, 2000-2001 and 2007-2008

Each month in the dot com crisis and recent financial crisis, all stocks are assigned to one of Fama and French 49 industries. **M6** is the previous 6 month cumulative returns, which is used as a proxy for momentum. **z_CSSD1** and **z_CSAD1** are the z-scores of cross-sectional standard deviation of returns and cross-sectional absolute deviation of returns using previous 1 month data. **1 month, 2 month** and **3 month** are the cumulative subsequent returns.

Herd	Mom	Obs	z_CSSD1	M6	1 month	2 month	3 month
High	loser	213	-0.57	-7.26%	-1.84%	-2.77%	-3.40%
Low	loser	367	1.13	-14.27%	-1.58%	-3.18%	-4.32%
High	winner	388	-0.49	3.99%	-0.81%	-2.04%	-2.62%
Low	winner	234	1.17	8.68%	-0.46%	-0.68%	-1.18%
Spread (low-herding winner – low-herding loser)					1.12%***	2.50%***	3.15%***
Herd	Mom	Obs	z_CSAD1	M6	1 month	2 month	3 month
High	loser	217	-0.54	-6.46%	-1.57%	-2.63%	-3.59%
Low	loser	381	1.26	-14.39%	-1.64%	-3.20%	-4.33%
High	winner	384	-0.44	3.88%	-0.95%	-2.18%	-2.72%
Low	winner	220	1.37	9.36%	-0.60%	-1.00%	-1.53%
Spread (low-herding winner – low-herding loser)					1.04%***	2.20%***	2.79%***

Note: *, **, *** represents the difference between the two portfolios is significant at the 10%, 5% and 1% level respectively.

Table 6 – **Fama-French 30 Industry Classification**

Each month, from January 1980 to December 2008, all stocks are assigned to one of Fama and French 30 industries. **M6** is the previous 6 month cumulative returns, which is used as a proxy for momentum. **z_CSSD1** and **z_CSAD1** are the z-scores of cross-sectional standard deviation of returns and cross-sectional absolute deviation of returns using previous 1 month data. **1 month**, **2 month** and **3 month** are the cumulative subsequent returns.

Herd	Mom	Obs	z_CSSD1	M6	1 month	2 month	3 month
High	loser	1317	-0.65	3.77%	0.89%	1.81%	2.62%
Low	loser	1402	0.76	-3.64%	0.61%	1.19%	1.80%
High	winner	1416	-0.65	10.24%	1.10%	2.27%	3.65%
Low	winner	1369	0.91	19.43%	1.68%	3.18%	4.72%
Spread (low-herding winner – low-herding loser)					**1.06%***	**1.99%***	**2.92%***
Herd	Mom	Obs	z_CSAD1	M6	1 month	2 month	3 month
High	loser	1264	-0.66	4.45%	0.89%	1.76%	2.65%
Low	loser	1417	0.74	-4.39%	0.63%	1.13%	1.74%
High	winner	1471	-0.67	9.58%	1.09%	2.16%	3.38%
Low	winner	1354	0.78	20.31%	1.54%	3.03%	4.59%
Spread (low-herding winner – low-herding loser)					**0.91%****	**1.89%***	**2.85%***

Note: *, **, *** represents the difference between the two portfolios is significant at the 10%, 5% and 1% level respectively.

Table 7: Robustness Checks: **Various combinations of momentum and herding definitions** Each month, from January 1980 to December 2008, all stocks are assigned to one of Fama and French 49 industries. **M6** and **M12** are the previous 6 and 12 month cumulative returns, respectively, which are used as proxies for momentum. **z_CSSD1**, **z_CSAD1**, **z_CSSD6**, and **z_CSAD6** are the cross-sectional standard deviation of returns and cross-sectional absolute deviation of returns using previous 1 and 6 month data. **1 month**, **2 month** and **3 month** are the cumulative subsequent returns.

Panel A: 12 month window used in computing momentum

Herd	Mom	Obs	z_CSSD1	M12	1 month	2 month	3 month
High	loser	2018	-0.64	8.25%	0.84%	1.78%	2.71%
Low	loser	2266	0.84	-2.45%	0.82%	1.61%	2.22%
High	winner	2351	-0.66	22.32%	1.00%	1.99%	3.28%
Low	winner	2094	0.88	36.46%	1.45%	2.79%	4.08%
Spread (low-herding winner – low-herding loser)					**0.64%***	**1.18%***	**1.86%***
Herd	Mom	Obs	z_CSAD1	M12	1 month	2 month	3 month
High	loser	2016	-0.66	9.03%	0.91%	1.81%	2.54%
Low	loser	2284	0.80	-3.52%	0.84%	1.73%	2.45%
High	winner	2354	-0.68	21.84%	1.10%	2.14%	3.44%
Low	winner	2077	0.78	38.68%	1.53%	2.89%	4.16%
Spread (low-herding winner – low-herding loser)					**0.69%***	**1.16%***	**1.71%***

Panel B: 6 month window used in computing herding measures

Herd	Mom	Obs	z_CSSD6	M6	1 month	2 month	3 month
High	loser	2996	-0.65	0.86%	0.73%	1.44%	2.23%
Low	loser	1275	0.85	-4.17%	0.55%	1.27%	2.05%
High	winner	1453	-0.66	8.49%	1.24%	2.45%	3.82%
Low	winner	3174	0.90	21.47%	1.56%	2.95%	4.31%
Spread (low-herding winner – low-herding loser)					**1.01%***	**1.67%****	**2.26%****
Herd	Mom	Obs	z_CSAD6	M6	1 month	2 month	3 month
High	loser	2957	-0.64	1.71%	0.65%	1.34%	2.12%
Low	loser	1224	0.86	-5.17%	0.53%	1.32%	2.06%
High	winner	1492	-0.65	8.14%	1.27%	2.51%	3.79%
Low	winner	3226	0.79	22.13%	1.67%	2.99%	4.44%
Spread (low-herding winner – low-herding loser)					**1.14%***	**1.67%****	**2.38%****

Note: *, **, *** represents the difference between the two portfolios is significant at the 10%, 5% and 1% level respectively.

Table 8: **Robustness Checks: Using weekly returns** Each week, from January 1980 to December 2008, all stocks are assigned to one of Fama and French 49 industries. **M6** is the previous 6 week cumulative returns, which is used as a proxy for momentum. **z_CSSD1** and **z_CSAD1** the cross-sectional standard deviation of returns and cross-sectional absolute deviation of returns using previous 1 week data. **1 week, 2 week** and **3 week** are the cumulative subsequent returns.

Herd	Mom	Obs	z_CSSD1	M6	1 week	2 week	3 week
High	loser	9442	-0.66	-0.02%	0.25%	0.50%	0.74%
Low	loser	8806	0.85	-3.55%	0.13%	0.30%	0.49%
High	winner	9506	-0.67	3.06%	0.26%	0.58%	0.91%
Low	winner	10142	0.77	7.41%	0.60%	1.05%	1.44%
Spread (low-herding winner – low-herding loser)					0.47%***	0.75%***	0.96%***
Herd	Mom	Obs	z_CSAD1	M6	1 week	2 week	3 week
High	loser	9340	-0.70	0.23%	0.28%	0.55%	0.82%
Low	loser	8916	0.93	-4.05%	0.08%	0.22%	0.39%
High	winner	9608	-0.67	2.83%	0.26%	0.57%	0.89%
Low	winner	10032	0.88	7.95%	0.66%	1.13%	1.55%
Spread (low-herding winner – low-herding loser)					0.58%***	0.92%***	1.16%***

Note: *, **, *** represents the difference between the two portfolios is significant at the 10%, 5% and 1% level respectively.

Figure 1

Each month, from January 1980 to December 2008, all stocks are assigned to one of Fama and French 49 industries. We use M6, the previous 6 month cumulative returns, as a proxy for momentum; CSSD1 and CSAD1, cross-sectional standard deviation of returns and cross-sectional absolute deviation of returns using previous 1 month data. 1 month, as a proxy for herd. Annual cumulative subsequent returns by taking a long position in winner industries with low herd level and a short position in loser industries with low herd level are presented in the following figure.

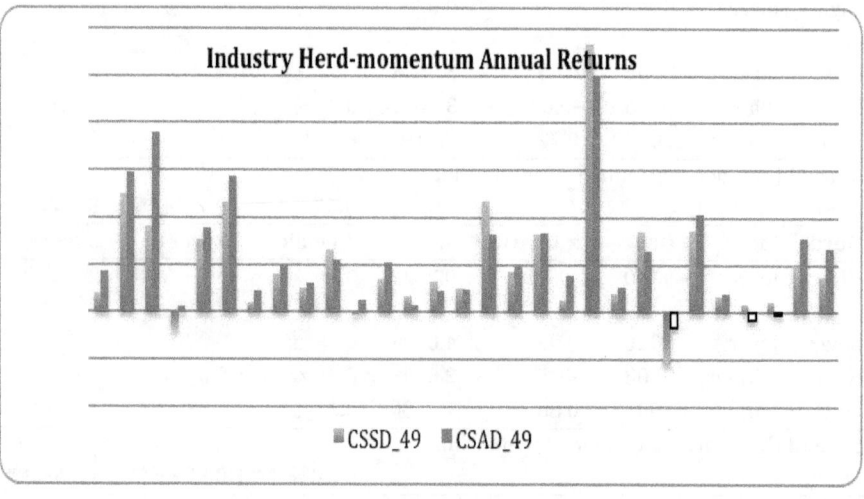

References:

Asness, C. 1995. "The power of past stock returns to explain future stock returns", Unpublished working paper, Goldman Sachs Asset management.

Banerjee, A. 1992. "A Simple Model of Herd Behavior", *The Quarterly Journal of Economics*, 107, 3.

Bikhchandani, S., Hirshleifer, D., & Welch, I. 1992. "A Theory of Fads, Fashion, Custom, and Cultural Change as Informational Cascades", *Journal of Political Economy*, 100, 5.

Caparrelli, F., Arcangelis, A., & Cassuto, A. 2004. "Herding in the Italian Stock Market: A Case of Behavioral Finance", *Journal of Behavioral Finance*, 5, 4.

Caporale, G., Economou, F., & Philippas, N. 2008. "Herding behavior in extreme market conditions: the case of the Athens stock exchange", *Economics Bulletin*, 7, 17.

Chan, L., Jegadeesh, N., & Lakonishok, J. 1996. "Momentum Strategies", *Journal of Finance*, 51.

Chang, E., Cheng, J., & Khorana, A. 2000. "An examination of herd behavior in equity markets: an international perspective", *Journal of Banking and Finance*, 24.

Christie, W., & Huang, R. 1995. "Following the pied piper: do individual returns herd around the market?", *Financial Analysts Journal*, 51, 4.

Choi, N., and Sias, R. 2008. "Institutional industry herding", *Journal of Financial Economics* (forthcoming).

Dass, N., Massa, M., & Patgiri, R. 2008. "Mutual funds and bubbles: the surprising role of contractual incentives", *Review of Financial Studies*, 21.

Demirer, R. & Kutan, A. 2006. "Does Herding Behavior Exist in Chinese Stock Markets?", *Journal of International Financial Markets, Institutions and Money*, 16, 2.

Froot, K., Scharfestein, D., & Stein, J. 1992. "Herd on the Street: Informational Inefficiencies in a Market with Short-Term Speculation," *Journal of Finance*, 47.

Grinblatt, M., Titman, S., & Wermers, R. 1995. "Momentum Investment Strategies, Portfolio Performance, and Herding: A Study of Mutual Fund Behaviour", *The American Economic Review*, 85, 5.

Hey, J., & Morone, A. 2004. "Do Markets Drive out Lemmings - or vice versa?", *Economica*, 71.

Hirshleifer, D. 2001. "Investor Psychology and Asset Pricing", *Journal of Finance*, 56, 4.

Hirshleifer, D., Subrahmanyam, A., & Titman, S. 1994. "Security Analysis and Trading Patterns When Some Investors Receive Information Before Others", *Journal of Finance*, 49.

Hirshleifer, D., & Teoh, S. 2003. "Herd behavior and cascading in capital markets: a review and synthesis", *European Financial Management*, 9.

Hwang, S., & Salmon, M. 2004. "Market stress and herding", *Journal of Empirical Finance*, 11.

Jame, R., & Tong, Q. 2009. "Retail investor industry herding, working paper", Emory University.

Jegadeesh, N., & Titman, S. 1993. "Returns to buying winners and selling losers: Implications for stock market efficiency", *Journal of Finance*, 48.

Jegadeesh, N., & Titman, S. 2001. "Profitability of momentum strategies: An evaluation of alternative explanations", *Journal of Finance,* 56.

Tan, L., Chiang, T., Mason, J., and Nelling, E. 2008. "Herding behavior in Chinese stock markets: An examination of A and B shares", *Pacific-Basin Finance Journal*, 16.

Voronkova, S., & Bohl, M. 2005. "Institutional Traders' Behavior in an Emerging Stock Market: Empirical Evidence on Polish Pension Fund Investors", *Journal of Business, Finance and Accounting*, 32.

CHAPTER FOUR

INSTITUTIONAL BEHAVIOR, ETHICS AND ASSET MARKETING

What, will these hands ne'er be clean?

M. J. Somers

Introduction

Bubbles occur when market factors distort the value of a financial asset such that it greatly exceeds its intrinsic value. At least some of the theory and research in this area has operated from the perspective that asset bubbles are inevitable; that is, bubbles are a characteristic of markets, and under the right conditions, will develop, grow and ultimately burst (Kindleberger & Aliber 2011). Not surprisingly, a great deal of interest has been expressed in identifying the stages (life cycles) of asset bubbles not to prevent them, but rather to avoid or mitigate the consequences of crisis and collapse when bubbles deflate.

Information from financial markets generated *in vivo* as a natural consequence of the formation, growth and unraveling of asset bubbles has provided a rich source of data to model the stages of asset bubbles. Scholars working in the areas of finance and financial economics have built complex quantitative models designed to assess market risk and the degree to which any given asset might be dangerously overvalued (West 2002). These models are typically built retroactively after the fact and then used predictively to identify potential and emerging asset bubbles.

This objective is accomplished by identifying extreme levels of market indicators that have been predictive of future steep declines in asset values. As these models are based on underlying financial theory, it is a mistake to consider them "black box" or a-theoretical because hypotheses (either implicit or explicit) about the nature of markets are being tested empirically. Further, as data are collected and predictive models are refined, the underlying financial theory is modified accordingly. [See Chapter 9 for a Survey of some of these econometric models and their application to past Bubbles.]

Perhaps because, in recent years, asset bubbles are perceived to be both more common and/or more severe (Krugman 2009; Posner 2009), this phenomenon has attracted interest from disciplines outside of economics and finance (Davis 2010; Palmer & Maher 2010). In contrast to the quantitative models typical of research in finance, scholars in the areas of management, psychology and organizational theory have offered a different perspective on asset bubbles. This research is best understood as focused on the factors underlying aggregate behavior that research in finance captures with quantitative models. That is, while financial research addresses the level at which any given asset diverges from its intrinsic value, the behavioral perspective attempts to understand why these "nosebleed" levels are seen as attractive and why rational assessment of risk is suspended.

This chapter takes a behavioral perspective to asset bubbles by integrating research from management theory and psychology to gain a different perspective on how bubbles form and why they persist. It differs from financial and economic research in two significant ways. First, the theory and concepts employed are more abstract reflecting differences between management and financial theories. Second, it is based on qualitative data and, as such, comes with the advantages and disadvantages of this type of research.

It begins with a discussion of the stages of asset bubbles. It is important to understand this process because doing so is central to finding clues indicative of possible asset bubbles. It then turns to a brief discussion of how asset bubbles have been studied. Next comes the development of a conceptual framework that is based on concepts from institutional theory and behavioral research. To some extent, this is a cross level approach since institutional theory is concerned with the influence of systems on individuals and the commitment to a course of action focused on the persistence of irrational economic behavior. Once this framework is established, its application to asset bubbles is examined empirically using archival data drawn from public sources. The chapter concludes by presenting some behavioral indicators of potential asset bubbles and a brief discussion of the ethical issues involved in their formation and development.

The Life Cycle of Asset Bubbles

The process by which asset bubbles are formed is well understand and well established (Kindleberger & Aliber 2011). Although the duration and staging of each bubble varies, the sequence through which bubbles form and burst appears consistent:

- Displacement: The basis for an asset bubble begins with a discernable displacement in markets and/or industries. The displacement changes opportunities for profit based on new ways of doing business. The displacement can be large and pervasive (such as the development of the Internet or Railroads as described in the Introduction to this book) or more circumscribed (such as the financial innovations that triggered the financial collapse in 2008).

  It is important to note that the displacement that triggers a bubble frequently represents a legitimate innovation; that is, the changes that are taking place in industries and markets that are not trivial and that are not necessarily bad for society or a country as a whole. For example, the Internet bubble was based on an array of radically new technologies that continues to transform businesses and societies. This transformative change has clearly been beneficial and continues to be so today. The "bubble" problem was not with the Internet technologies per se. Rather it was with how these assets were valued as investments or businesses in a "new" economy.

• Boom Period: Once the displacement takes hold, there is a period of rapid expansion. It is often associated with the expansion of bank credit as firms and individuals rush to take advantage of the innovation and the high perceived returns on the related investments. Increased investment and loose credit leads to growth in the money supply, and increased demand generates more firms, investors and the entry of speculators. The result is steep increases in asset prices as demand outpaces supply.

In the early stages of the asset boom, investment can be viewed as rational. [See Chapter 8.] Most displacements create opportunity and, up to a point, it is economically rational to invest in those opportunities. At some point, however, asset valuation begins to exceed the intrinsic and future value of the asset leading to the beginning of a bubble. However, and importantly, those that have invested in these assets and those seeking to do so do not perceive the asset valuations as becoming risky or developing as a bubble. Rather there is a sense due to over optimism that it is riskier not to be invested because of a lost money making opportunity.

• Euphoria: Speculation then leads to overestimation of potential profits and the minimization of the actual risk. Speculation also leads to greater investment and greater increases in prices. [See Introduction and Chapter 8.] In the later speculation stage, money is transferred from valuable to less valuable assets and the market approaches a mania or sickness as Dickens wrote in *Little Dorrit* during the 1850s. Indeed some participants must have the desired asset at almost any price. In this late stage speculation, money flows into the asset on higher and pyramids of credit so that leverage is leveraged. At this point, the mania may cross national borders and become pervasive internationally.

Euphoria is associated with suspension of rational judgment and the ability to objectively assess risk. As assets become increasingly overvalued, rationalizations are necessary to justify increased investment and increased leverage. The most common rationalization "this time is different" demonstrates that lack of rationality in markets and the lack of concern with downside risk.

• Crisis: During the crisis phase, the bubble bursts. It comes clear that all of the explanations for the high asset prices are not credible and that anticipated profits based on even higher prices will not materialize.

The crisis is precipitated by an event that changes perceptions and bursts the bubble. In some cases, it is a bank failure. In others, it is a bankruptcy or a credit default. Often, a precipitating event is related to a change in the perception of a continuingly rising asset price relative to the general consumer inflation rate. This in turn can be due to deceleration in the money flow needed to expand the bubble further, which can then trigger or be reflective of the credit event.

In this sense, crises are triggered by objective reality intruding on the rationalizations that were used to justify asset price speculation. For example, in the case of the Internet bubble, bankruptcies of dot.com companies made it clear that many Internet companies had unrealistic business models with little or no real profit potential. When viewed in terms of their lofty stock prices, it became apparent to many investors that the Internet did not suspend or change fundamental business principles and that these assets were greatly overvalued. Thus stock prices of Internet companies began to lose momentum and eventually fell as new money did not flow into the bubble and existing investors then tried to convert their Internet related assets into cash.

• Panic: Panic follows crisis in that the event, which actually bursts the bubble, triggers an extreme emotional reaction and money moves out of the objects of speculation at an increasingly rapid pace as bubble asset prices fall. The panic feeds on itself as the market implodes and money moves to perceived safe havens such as US Government securities. The phrase "this time it is different" is replaced with "cash is king" and prices of the inflated assets fall to very low levels or zero in the case of bankruptcies.

The panic phase of a bubble is the most traumatic and the most public as losses mount and the effect widens to impact the general public (including non-investors). Depending on the nature of the displacement and the assets involved, value can be found as assets fall below their intrinsic values.

• Stabilization: Markets stabilize when prices fall so low that investors are enticed back into the market and further price declines are limited. In a severe bubble, a lender of last resort is identified to stabilize markets and new regulations are usually proposed to limit the possibility of future bubbles of that particular type.

This process of stabilization was evident in the financial crises of 2008. The Federal Reserve Bank became the lender of last resort in the United States and eventually stocks of money center banks were perceived as greatly undervalued leading to price stabilization and then strong appreciation. As the financial stocks rebounded, confidence in the economy and the financial system returned slowly and the overall stock market rebounded strongly. Changes in financial regulation were also proposed and reforms were enacted.

Theories of Asset Bubbles

The most interesting aspect of asset bubbles from the point of view of behavioral theory is their recurrence. It would be one thing if the process and cycle of bubble formation was not well understood thereby leaving practitioners and scholars with limited or few insights (or clues) about how bubbles form and evolve. This, however, is clearly not the actual situation. Yet bubbles persist to the point where some researchers have suggested that they are a natural consequence of markets and capitalistic risk taking and thus should be seen as such (Abolafia 2005; 2006; 2010).

In order to get a better sense of the degree to which bubbles can be identified and to consider the possibility that they might be managed, it is useful to briefly review theory and research on asset bubbles. This literature complements studies of the formation and destruction of bubbles and also serves to frame this chapter. With regard to the latter, a central objective of this chapter is to explain how to use management and behavioral theory to augment research on asset bubbles. Understanding how scholars have conceptualized them is therefore critical to this goal.

Abolafia (2010) presents an excellent review of modern theories of bubbles on which the chapter will heavily rely as a framework to classify and discuss theories of asset bubbles. Abolafia (2010) suggests that there are three modern bubble theories: market fundamentalism, financial instability hypothesis, and the social construction perspective. For purposes of this chapter, the social construction perspective seems the most relevant, but for completeness each theory will be discussed.

Market fundamentalism is based on the assumption that markets are efficient in pricing assets and that regulation should be kept to a minimum so as not to interfere with the market's natural tendency to ensure assets are properly priced (Flood & Garber 1980: Flood & Hodrick 1990; Garber 1990). The strongest derivative of market fundamentalism (which is best viewed as a set of interrelated concepts) is the widely known efficient market hypothesis that is based on the proposition that asset prices always reflect their true values (Stiglitz 2002).

Market fundamentalism is, thus, grounded in the core assumptions of rationality and determinism. That is, there is a critical and pervasive assumption that markets are rational (although individual behavior might not always be so) and that collective behavior exhibits a deterministic effect on asset prices that greatly inhibits or precludes substantial and sustained mispricing of an asset class.

It its strongest form, market fundamentalism leads to the inexorable conclusion that asset bubbles are not possible. This view, of course, runs contrary to fact and observed market behavior. Bubbles do indeed occur and there is strong evidence that they are not uncommon when the proper conditions are present. Indeed they can persist for a relatively long_time. Thus there are "softer" versions of the theory to account for the clear presence and occurrence of asset bubbles. Specifically, market bubbles are seen as rare events that occur when there are external shocks to the market so that it is not possible to determine that a bubble is developing until after it bursts (Abolafia 2010). For example, Kindleberger & Aliber (2011) argue that bubbles are a consequence of destabilized credit markets (an exogenous event) leading to mania and herding from an oversupply of money.

In contrast, the financial instability hypothesis is based on the assumption that bubbles are a property of markets in capitalist economies, which are inherently unstable during certain periods. As such, bubbles are seen as endogenous to financial systems and happen as normal if periodic economic events. This model was put forth by Minsky (1986; 1993) who reasoned that long periods of prosperity can lead to instability in financial markets as financing mechanisms evolve and financial capital grows. Therefore stability leads to instability as risk-taking and innovation increase (Papadimitrou & Wray 2008).

We have seen this behavior in the Internet bubble as innovation led to large increases in investments in Internet related firms, first from venture capitalists and then from more traditional sources as investors sought increased opportunities for profit. Similarly, the 2008 financial meltdown was fueled by financial innovations, which were then expanded by newer innovations and the increased use of leverage to pursue profit opportunities.

Unlike market fundamentalism, which is grounded in rational processes, the financial instability hypothesis relies heavily on emotion to explain asset bubbles. Thus, the greed/fear balance is seen as increasing, tipping toward the former in the mania phase, leading to herding and euphoria as the bubble forms, and to distress or fear as it bursts. In this respect, it is compatible with views on the life cycle of asset bubbles where suspension of reason is a key force fueling expansion of credit and misperception of risk.

Finally, the social construction perspective is based on the notion that individual activities such as investment or speculation occur within a broader social context that includes political and economic institutions, social relationships, and cultural values (Abolafia & Kilduff 1988). As such, bubbles are seen as endogenous to financial systems, but are created by insiders and not by the herding of investors or manias (Akerlof & Romer 1993; Ferguson 2008). Specifically, insiders using complex innovations and asymmetrical information to their advantage use market mechanisms to create bubbles. This is accomplished by political influence to create favorable rules and conditions and by marketing tactics (sales) to entice investors. [See Chapter 5 on the Marketing Bubbles.]

The market collapse of 2008, thus, would be interpreted by these analysts as caused by financial institutions using political influence to relax government regulation of their activities to permit entry into new, lucrative markets. Once these barriers fell, these institutions developed and aggressively marketed complex financial instruments that were not well understood by customers (and often not by those selling them) and that were then "certified" as appropriate or attractive investment by other financial institutions (rating agencies) using questionable methods.

Conceptual Framework

The social construction perspective is most suited to a behavioral analysis of asset bubbles because it is grounded in the social context of financial activity. This model of asset bubbles is also helpful because it highlights those elements of management theory that apply directly to the issues related to the social construction of markets and actors. Further and importantly, Abolafia's (2010) view that these social relationships determine markets and not *vice versa* raises the possibility that asset bubbles can be managed. Although this might well be the case (at least in theory), our goal, in this chapter, is to use the social construction perspective to identify relevant concepts from management and behavioral theory that allow asset bubbles and their stages to be identified rather than controlled.

To that end, a conceptual framework to meet this objective is presented in Exhibit A. It is intended to be integrative by linking the social construction perspective with institutional theory to understand the "sell" side of bubbles and the institutional factors and behavioral theory to better understand the "buy" side. In this regard, while the social construction perspective diminishes the role of herding and manias in the formation and destruction of bubbles as set forth in Chapters 3 and 8, this latter view cannot and does not fully address the emotions and decision-making of investors.

Although established social relationships and peer influence are factors in enticing investors to commit funds to new assets, the psychological factors involved in the assessment of risk and the willingness to continue to invest in assets as their prices become increasingly unrealistic cannot be ignored. For this reason, the social construction perspective is augmented with theory and research on how commitments to a course of action are made and maintained. An outline of this conceptual framework is presented below in Exhibit A.

As indicated in the Exhibit, institutions start the process of creating a bubble by developing the displacement that disrupts the current social order of markets and the social and political networks associated with them. This process begins with the innovation itself, which is introduced into the market. It is accompanied by an influence process designed to entice investors (customers) to first see the innovation in a favorable light and then to participate in its expected gains. As noted by Abolafia (2010), these innovations are heavily marketed as firms seek to use their reputations, existing social networks and other advantages to meet *their* goals. [See Chapter 5.]

Exhibit A

Conceptual Framework

Institutions (sellers)

Institutional Influence-------> Marketing Political Influence

Participation

Innovation-------> Widespread Adoption

Institutional

Legitimacy ------> Inverted Legitimacy------------

>Contextual Justification

Investors (buyers)

Distortion of Risk

Contextual Factors: Asymmetric Information, Trust,

Established Social Relationships

Behavioral Factors: Commitment to a Course of Action

Political influence comes into play if there are regulatory or legal barriers to the innovations being proposed as explained in Chapter 2. In this case, both individually and collectively, firms seeking to introduce the innovation will use their influence and related social or political capital to have these barriers relaxed or removed. The argument almost always takes the form of an appeal to the greater good as seen in the successful effort to have the Glass-Steagall Act repealed by using the argument American banks would be at competitive disadvantage internationally if these restrictions were retained.

Institutional theory is also relevant to understanding the process by which innovation is introduced into the market. As indicated by its nomenclature, institutional theory is concerned with the influence of networks or organizations on their behavior and the behavior of the individuals within them (Powell & DiMaggio 1991; Scott 1987). Further, from the perspective of institutional theory, maintaining legitimacy is a key objective for individual firms since they must demonstrate their value to society and to a network of partners, customers, regulatory agencies and counterparties.

Developing new and valuable innovations that have benefits that go beyond a particular firm or industry is one path to gaining legitimacy. Indeed, it is very much in the interest of a specific firm to do so. Problems, occur, however when the innovation that serves as the basis for the displacement that drives an asset bubble is not well understood. Based on the social construction perspective and on institutional theory, the firm or industry is expected to give legitimacy to the innovation based on its reputation, expertise, integrity, and on the expectations of society. That is, there is the expectation that the innovation is legitimate and that it gains legitimacy on the basis of the expertise and integrity of the firms that developed it.

As was evident in the financial crisis of 2008 and in the Internet bubble, the innovations on which the displacement was based were not well understood. Yet, there was widespread marketing of both innovations within an institutional context to the point where it was necessary for many firms to be associated with the innovation to retain their legitimacy. I refer to this situation as inverted legitimacy since it is the innovation that is legitimizing the firm and not vice versa. That is, in this situation, the institutional context places enormous pressure on even the most conservative managements to become involved with the displacement because they must achieve the same status within the institutional and market context as their competitors. Further the higher stock valuations associated with the innovation may expose traditional firms to takeover threats as in the case of the merger of Time Warner and AOL.

This notion of inverted legitimacy places a different perspective on the rapid proliferation of the displacements that lead to bubbles. Viewing this widespread adoption strictly from a herding perspective leads to the view that there is mindless adoption and marketing of a new product or service simply because competitors are doing so. Inverted legitimacy suggests that the firm's reputation and efficacy come into play so that the decision is carefully considered in that it has strategic import.

While this might seem like a relatively minor distinction, it is critical because a firm's reputation and its perceived management expertise come into play making the decision very difficult to reverse once it is finalized. Of course, it is naïve to suggest that the stream of early profits typical of a successful displacement and the promise of even greater future profits are not important factors in a firm's commitment to an innovation, the issue of legitimacy pressured by the public's and the investment community's perception that the innovation has explosive profit potential also seems relevant to understanding why the commitment is so strong and why associated risks are minimized even by board of directors composed of experienced business executives. Not going along with the boom and the excessive asset valuations can label a director as a Neanderthal.

The institutional context also affects those who make investments in inflated assets as bubbles develop. Abolofila (2010) points to information asymmetry as a key component of the institutional context because those firms who develop and market the assets (and the innovation behind them) have a different information base than those who invest in them. This asymmetry can be exploited in the same way as the complexity in lending explained in Chapter 2, raising the same issues of ethics and integrity, and thereby straining the social capital that is inherent in financial transactions. As such, firms operating on the "sell" side of the transaction can exploit their advantage by not adopting the conventions and behaviors expected of them. This can then have a high social and economic cost when the bubble explodes.

It is important to note that these expectations are governed by the conventions and norms of the institutional system and not by legal and regulatory mandates. Further, it is important to note that there is an element of trust involved in these transactions that is embedded in the institutional networks in which they take place. Unfortunately in the recent economic collapse these norms of trust were misplaced and have as a result largely evaporated as indicated by the current low public regard for banks and other financial institutions.

The terms fads and manias conjure up images of an irrational craving for assets in which all elements of reason are suspended in pursuit of the coveted assets and expected high returns. Although these terms are very colorful and have some explanatory utility with respect to asset bubbles, it is unlikely that the distortion of risk that is necessary for bubbles to develop comes solely from emotional decisions and herding behavior.

To begin with, bubbles develop over a relatively extended period and result in repeated investment in an asset class. Emotions, in contrast, are fleeting and while they can drive fads in consumer markets, these fads are usually short-lived (Hirsch 1972; Kotler 2008). Second, from the point of view of institutional theory and the social construction perspective, many participants in bubbles are not naïve investors with unrealistic expectations. Rather, they are expected to make reasoned and careful decisions that demonstrate an acumen that justifies their positions such as the boards of directors noted above and illustrated by Time Warner's board decision to merge with AOL. Even the appearance of making large bets based on little more than emotion or following the herd is not acceptable in this cases.

Irrational exuberance, thus, cannot fully explain the sustained behavior that is necessary for asset bubbles to persist. Behavioral scientists have thus looked elsewhere to explain such persistent irrational behavior. Indeed, the tendency for both individuals and institutions to pursue a risky and ultimately losing course of action is one that has generated long-standing interest among behavioral scientists. One approach to gaining insight into this phenomenon has been an interest in behavioral commitment to a specific course of action. Behavioral commitment leads to persistence in the face of risk and loss based on prior actions. Specifically, actions that are volitional and important (affect significant resources) are seen as building a level of commitment that locks individuals and institutions into continuing in that course of action (Arkes & Blumer 1985; Brockner 1991; Staw 1976, 1981; Staw & Ross 1989).

Taking public policy as an example, the wars in Iraq and Vietnam generated behavioral commitment to continuing them even when doing so was clearly irrational. That is, continuing commitment of resources to both war efforts (both of which were clearly unwinnable) generated an even stronger commitment to further commitment of resources and concomitant minimization of risk to justify those decisions. Withdrawal (breaking the cycle of commitment) was difficult in both cases because these decisions were highly visible, volitional and important. They would also be admissions that the prior courses of action and commitment of resources had been a mistake perhaps leading to a public rebuke and even a loss of status or employment.

A case can be made that behavioral commitment operates in a similar manner in asset bubbles. Investors make highly visible, volitional and important (and often strategic) decisions to invest in certain assets with an expected return. Large initial investments generate behavioral commitment and studies have shown that preference for risk increases as behavioral commitment builds (Staw, Barsade & Koput 1997; Dennison 2009). Thus, investors are more likely to prefer their initial decisions to less risky and more rational alternatives.

It is not difficult to see how behavioral commitment can influence asset bubble development. The initial investment creates a commitment to a course of action and future investments in that same asset or asset class serve to reinforce that commitment. In the early phases of a bubble, these investments can produce excellent returns and valuations can appear to be in line with the intrinsic value of the underlying assets such as with the AOL Time Warner merger. As valuations get stretched and risk increases (and investors appetite for these assets should be diminishing), prior behavioral commitment leads to greater preference for the now overvalued assets and a commitment to higher levels of investment. This situation can be reinforced by analysts that previously recommended the investment and suspended tough analysis of questions concerning its continued quality as the analysts get captured and committed through their own success and greater visibility.

In the aggregate, this activity might be characterized as a mania or as extreme herding. However, from the point of view of individual market participants, it is simply a natural extension of a course of action. Although any one individual or institution might characterize the behavior or others are irrational, they are likely to see their behavior as a rational response to market conditions justified by their perceived greater knowledge and expertise.

Application of the Conceptual Framework

In order to assess the usefulness of the conceptual framework presented in Exhibit A, it is necessary to examine it empirically. As some of these concepts are new such as inverted legitimacy and others are derived from management theory not specifically geared toward explaining markets or asset bubbles, assessment of the framework is necessarily preliminary. Nonetheless, it is possible to explore whether these concepts have explanatory utility in relation to asset bubbles and if they provide new insights into signals that suggest that conditions are amenable for an asset bubble to develop or to have developed.

Methodology

Unlike most research in finance and economics, which is based on quantitative models, assessment of our conceptual framework will be done using qualitative methodologies. That statement alone is not very informative because there are many different approaches to qualitative research, each with its strengths and weaknesses. However, they all share a subjectivity that leads to an indeterminacy that can be troublesome to some researchers and practitioners (especially to those in finance). These concerns are not without merit, but as with any empirical testing procedure, critical issues revolve around the specificity of what is being tested and the degree to which the methods employed follow established research procedures.

Qualitative methodology was used here for two reasons. First, asset bubbles happen *in vivo* so that laboratory experiments or behavioral simulations cannot capture this phenomenon in a meaningful way. Second, the concepts included in the conceptual framework are not easily measured using questionnaires. For example, attempting to assess the notion of inverted legitimacy would require respondents to admit that they had little if any understanding of the innovations that they were selling or buying, and as a result had little regard for those who were buying or selling them. For obvious reasons, this concept is not well suited to being studied with quantitative survey methodologies, though Elliott Spitzer when he was NY Attorney General showed that in fact many Wall Street Analysts effectively adopted this behavioral framework.

Although comparatively sparse in number, there are studies in management research that use archival qualitative data to (re)-construct and gain insight into a specific event or to test and build management theory. For example, Ross & Staw (1993) studied the Shoreham power plant to test their model of behavioral commitment to a course of action. The power plant was never completed yet large sums of money were invested in it despite obvious obstacles to operating a nuclear power plant on the eastern end of Long Island. However, the behavioral commitment to the project led to persistence and increased investment despite growing, effective opposition to it. Similarly, Weick (1993) and Weick & Roberts (1993) have used this methodology to assess sense-making processes in organizations related to natural disasters and interrelationships among employees under difficult conditions where coordination was essential. A similar methodology is used here.

Exploring Institutional Context:

Asymmetric Information, Inverted Legitimacy, and Trust

The notion of inverted legitimacy has two components. First is firms investing or involved in an innovation have a limited understanding of it, yet are prepared to actively market assets tied to the innovation to investors. Thus, the innovation gives the firm legitimacy and not *vice versa*. The second component involves inculcating the belief that the institutions involved in marketing the innovation have a complete understanding of it including the capacity to assess and monitor the risks involved, both to themselves and to investors [Chapter 5].

Asymmetric information serves to exacerbate this problem because investors clearly do not have the same information base as those marketing the assets that ultimately become inflated when bubbles develop. Institutional theory suggests that these transactions occur in an institutional context where investors expect firms to properly and fully identify the risks associated with a given asset or asset class and represent them accurately. Since information is necessarily asymmetric, trust becomes a significant component of the institutional context. Abolofia (2010) implies that markets are self-immolating partly because of the inherent risks of asymmetric information, but this does not necessarily need to be the case if the sell side firms act responsibly [Chapters 5 and 7].

The financial crisis of 2008-2009 was driven by a meltdown of financial instruments called Collateralized Debt Obligations (CDO's) that were backed by home mortgages. The innovation behind CDO's was to combine prime and subprime mortgages into financial instruments using highly sophisticated quantitative models that would generate assets with AAA credit ratings. This outcome was accomplished by mixing prime and subprime mortgages into complex debt instruments, which included 30 or more tranches or "slices" with sophisticated algorithms so the net result was an AAA rating even though the components of the CDO were not based solely on prime mortgages.   Investors were, thus, supposedly offered better returns through higher yields with no additional risk_given the obligations' triple A ratings.

As the market for mortgage backed CDO's grew, the number of firms offering them also grew, as did the market for mortgages regardless of their risk of default. The first condition for a case of inverted legitimacy is this rapid expansion of the number of participants in the market as firms seek to establish their legitimacy and expertise. Of course, profits are not to be discounted as a reason to enter the market, but institutional theory suggests that legitimacy or me-too action is an important factor as well. Put simply, a firm requires an explanation as to why it would pass up the opportunity to offer leading edge, innovative products that sit at the center of its competencies and legitimacy.

Indeed, we saw this same behavior in the Internet bubble when many companies moved to e-marketing simply because they did not want to be left behind. (Of course, these large capital expenditures proved to be ill advised in many cases as the Internet bubble grew and then burst). The second condition for inverted legitimacy is a limited understanding of the innovation being offered.

In the case of CDO's, this lack of understanding is reflected in the confusion about how it is possible to use sophisticated mathematical formulae to mix assets of varying risk and produce a composite asset with a much lower level of risk. How is this possible given the risk of default remains based on the quality of the underlying loans? A recent quote by John Thain, former CEO of Merrill-Lynch presented in Exhibit B suggests it is not possible. In fact, the process was so complex that, in his view, it was not well understood by anyone, even those who were developing the formulae to manage the risk.

Thain thus suggests that the innovation largely responsible for the financial meltdown of 2008-2009 was not well understood by the firms that developed it. The complexity of the CDO's is highlighted by the fact that it took three hours of high speed computing to model one of the 30 tranches of one CDO and Thain goes on to suggest that firms that were selling them did not understand this product or the risks associated it.

Thus, a case can be that it was not the firms that were legitimizing these securities, but rather the securities that were legitimizing the firms because they presumably had the expertise to develop these complex instruments and then manage the risks associated with them and certainly many made this case in their marketing to investors [Chapters 5 and 7]. Indeed, the institutional context and its associated culture would lead an objective observer to reach the conclusion that firms marketing CDO's had invented a new, innovative security that they understood well when this clearly was not the case.

The marketing and public relations message that Wall Street investment banks were crafting was designed to reassure all other participants in the institutional context (investors, regulatory agencies, and the general public) that any risk was being managed effectively and that there was no need to be concerned about the financial innovations that were being developed or the leverage associated with them. As indicated in Exhibit C, which is taken from a *Business Week* article on Wall Street's culture of risk before the financial meltdown, the message conveyed was that the institutional culture (e.g., across firms) was vigilant when it came to risk management and that the expertise to accomplish this task was in place.

Exhibit B

Issue: Limited Understanding of Innovation Underlying Asset Bubble as a Key Component of Inverted Legitimacy

Source: Quote from John Thain, Former CEO, Merrill-Lynch

To model correctly one tranche of one CDO took about three hours on one of the fastest computers in the United States. There is no chance that pretty much anybody understood what they were doing with these securities. Creating things that you don't understand is really not a good idea no matter who owns it.

A critical aspect of the information presented in Exhibit C is it is cast in terms of institutional context. That is, risk is presented as managed at an inter-firm level as part of the "culture" of investment banking using methodologies that were propagated across firms. This institutional context is critical to establishing the efficacy of the displacements that evolve into bubbles and in establishing the legitimacy of the firms that develop and market them.

Asymmetric information embedded in the institutional context operates to exacerbate a situation where there is inverted legitimacy, which, in turn, increases the likelihood of an asset bubble. For example, while the public view of risk management was that it was being handled by the greatest mathematical minds in the world (see Exhibit B), the reality was that these great minds were struggling to model small pieces of very complex securities. Clearly, investors in these securities were not aware of the complexities involved in assembling them nor were they privy to the process of establishing their various credit ratings. If this information were more readily available, that is there was symmetry and transparency, it seems reasonable to conclude that investor appetite for CDO's would have been diminished greatly thereby reducing the magnitude of the ensuing bubble.

Exhibit C

Issue: Defining the Institutional Context to Justify Inverted Legitimacy

Source: Business Week, June 12, 2006. Inside Wall Street's Culture of Risk

We are in the business of risk management 24/7, 365 days a year. Lehman's Chief Operating Officer

Yet for all of the risks that they are taking on, banks insist that they are safer than ever. They've hired many of the greatest mathematical minds in the world to create impossibly complex risk models. They deal in so many markets that the chances of all of them going haywire simultaneously appear miniscule.
Article author's conclusion.

Understanding Investor Persistence:

Behavioral Commitment to a Course of Action

Asymmetrical information is not the only factor influencing investors' appetites for increasingly overvalued assets generated by bubbles. While notions such as irrational exuberance and manias can explain some of the late stage (and rapid) appreciation of assets near the top of a bubble, they are unlikely to explain the process of bubble formation and growth. This is because a bubble requires psychological and financial commitment to a course of action over a relatively extended period of time.

Research on the topic of behavioral commitment or escalation research is concerned with why individuals and organizations pursue losing courses of action; that is, the tendency to remain committed to losing courses of action. In finance, this outcome can be seen as a commitment to a course of action such as an investment that results in "throwing good money after bad" (Staw et al 1997).

This latter characterization is the essence of an asset bubble, and interestingly from the point of view of escalation research, the process is not seen as a craving for additional investments, but rather as a natural consequence of prior actions. Thus the underlying psychology is not seen as a suspension of reason, but rather as an attempt from the viewpoint of the decision-maker and/or investor to turnaround a difficult situation. Since escalation is derived from personal responsibility for a decision, those individuals directly involved are more likely to invest additional time, money and other resources to correct a poor decision (Staw et al 1997). Research has shown that those responsible for risky or unprofitable decisions are far more likely to seek information that supports their actions, and to distort or discount information that does not (Staw 1981), especially if worried about shareholder lawsuits.

Applying escalation theory to asset bubbles, thus, provides some insight into why they persist and grow over time. Investors (individuals and organizations) are likely to distort and discount objective information an asset might be greatly overvalued (this time it is different) in direct proportion to the magnitude of their investment in that asset. Further, as assets are increasingly overvalued and their appreciation moderates, investors are likely to increase their level of investment and do it more aggressively if losses are incurred (Colon & Wolf 1980; Chow, Harrison, Lindquist & Wu 1997; Dennison 2009).

Further, while much has been made of the comparative disadvantage of asymmetric information for investors from the viewpoint of institutional theory in forming bubbles, escalation research suggests the asymmetry is relevant only at the time of the initial investment. Once a substantial investment has been made, those responsible would likely distort any and all information not consistent with that decision so a more transparent institutional context would have little effect on subsequent decisions [AOL-Time Warner].

Escalation and the concomitant psychological processes are best understood by example. Much of this research has been in the areas of policy decisions (a commitment to unwinnable wars) but there are applications in a financial context too that are useful in understanding asset bubbles. A recent account of the use of currency and interest rate swaps to improve its ability to finance development by the city of Saint Etienne, France demonstrates the concept of escalation and the subsequent distortion of the actual risk assumed (*Bloomberg Business Week* 2010).

Banks throughout Europe pushed these financial instruments as a means to reduce costs on fixed rate loans without fully explaining the underlying risks to the buyers. Given an ambitious redevelopment plan, Saint Etienne's Mayor Michel Thiolliere, used credit and interest rate swaps to finance high profile projects such as a new streetcar line and a design center. The cash to finance these projects was made available with currency and interest rate swap contracts one of which hedged the US dollar against the Swiss franc until 2042. As might be expected, it was only a matter of time before these contracts blew up and the City of Saint Etienne faced enormous losses. Further, objective analysis indicated the savings the city generated were far less than the risks it assumed. Further since such long-term currency hedges almost always involve counterparties, the City should have inquired who they were and why they were taking the opposite position.

Although this might seem like a shocking outcome, it is consistent with predictions from escalation theory and escalation research. As indicated in Exhibit D, taking on continued risk was meant to mask prior risks and permit the Mayor's redevelopment agenda to continue.

Exhibit D

Issue: Escalating Commitment to a Course of Action

Source: Bloomberg Business Week, April 26, 2010

"It wasn't a race to keep the city hedged. It was a race to mask potential losses because the more risk that you take, the more potential losses you can hide.

It's a joke that we are in markets like this.

Cedric Grail, City of Saint Etienne's New Director of Finance

---

More specifically, the perceptions of the incoming Director of Finance, Monsieur Cedric Grail, clearly demonstrates the psychology of escalation of commitment to a specific course of action. As the potential for large losses loomed and the risk reward ratio became clearer, the prior administration took on additional, even riskier currency and interest rate swap contracts to allow their redevelopment agenda to continue (involving the commitment to a second course of action) and to mask potential losses. These notions in turn follow directly from and are predicted by escalation research.

Further, it is clear the risks the City was incurring were not clear to those entering the swap contracts. Exhibit E captures the viewpoint of the former Mayor who suggests these decisions were business as usual and no significant risks were taken. Again, this is consistent with escalation theory in terms of distortion of information and the need to justify unjustifiable decisions, commitment to a second course of action, and to mask potential losses. These notions in turn follow directly from and are predicted by escalation research.

Exhibit E

Issue: Distortion of Risk Due to Escalation

Source: *Bloomberg Business Week*, April 26, 2010

"I put myself in the context of ten years ago, I don't really see what I could reproach myself for. I made sure that I had a professional team, with a clear goal to lower debt, lower taxes, lower financial charges." "There are useful debts, ones that allow you to rebuild a city." "Managing a town is like running a company. It's taking risks daily."

Michel Thiolliere, Former Mayor of Saint Etienne

Application to Asset Bubbles

Most research focused on identifying asset bubbles is drawn from the finance and economics literature and is based on quantitative modeling. There is nothing to quarrel with regarding this research as illustrated in other chapters in this book nor is it our purpose to assess its value. Rather, using the concept of triangulation (Jick 1979) that is based on the premise of studying the same phenomenon using multiple methodologies, a behavioral perspective on asset bubbles is offered as another source of data derived from a different and extensive research tradition.

The conceptual framework presented in this study points to three areas in assessing the likelihood of asset bubbles. The first area concerns the nature of the displacement or innovation that has attracted investors and increased investment. The second concerns the level and likely consequences of information asymmetry in the marketplace. Finally, the last factor concerns the level of investment in the asset class and the associated ease of psychological withdrawal from past investment decisions.

Displacement or Innovation

As noted at the beginning of this chapter, for an asset bubble to form, there must be some displacement or innovation that generates a significant change in perception regarding the value of an asset. The change can be initially focused on financial markets or can be much broader depending on the nature of the displacement. For example, the Internet was a displacement that affected and continues to affect a wide range of human activity. In contrast, although they had far reaching consequences, the new financial instruments associated with the 2008-2009 economic crisis had smaller initial impacts relative to the disruptive innovation generated by the growth of the Internet.

Institutional theory and the concept of inverted legitimacy introduced in this chapter point to the importance of analyzing the nature of the displacement before investing in it. As has just been explained, it is reasonable to conclude most firms selling CDO's and related securities had a very limited understanding of the models and methods used to manage the associated risks. [See also Chapter 7 on SIVs.] Although trust is a significant component of the institutional context, serious questioning by investors would surely have raised questions about claims regarding the risk profile of these securities.

Put simply, a full and complete answer to the question "How can you assure us that these securities have a credit rating of AAA?" would have sounded something like this: "Well, we mix mortgages of different quality into an instrument comprised of 30 tranches or slices, each of which has its own optimal mix. Then, we alter the revenue streams from the various tranches so that prime mortgages or subprime mortgages make up a larger percentage of cash flow for part of the term of the security. This structure is modeled expertly on high speed computers using the most sophisticated mathematical models to manage risk and cash flow, and we have our assumptions reviewed by the major rating agencies, we can thus assure you that these securities are equivalent in quality to US Treasuries."

When viewed in these terms, these safe CDO's look considerably less safe. Further, and more importantly, the process behind the innovation should raise some concerns that this might be a case of inverted legitimacy. That is, there seems to be cause for concern that the firms devising and marketing this innovation did not understand it very well. Thus their assurances that risk was being effectively modeled were somewhat suspect despite the Rating Agencies' stamp of approval.

A similar case can be made for the Internet bubble. Although there is no question the Internet has had a profound effect on business and on everyday life, the business models for early Internet companies were highly suspect. The primary reason was the Internet as a business development tool was not well understood at the time. Thus, investors were asked to believe revenues and profits were not valid metrics for these "new economy" businesses. Rather, hits, page views and clicks were marketed as the indicators of business success and long-term profitability.

The Internet bubble appears to be another case of inverted legitimacy. In this instance, a group of "experts" provided this legitimacy even though they did not fully or even generally understand how this innovation was going to change societies and where the profits would be found as Internet companies sought capital from investors. As in the case with CDO's, several simple questions could have easily raised concerns this was a case of inverted legitimacy.

Asymmetric Information

The institutional context in which bubbles develop is based on institutional relationships defined by the prevailing institutional culture and the ensuing social networks. Information by definition is thus restricted based on patterns of social interaction where there are "insiders" and "outsiders." For example in the aftermath of the 2008-2009 financial crisis, it became public knowledge that Goldman Sachs was betting against many securities it sold to its customers. Only an insider not necessarily a Goldman Sachs employee would be aware at the time of this information.

Asymmetric information plays a role in inverted legitimacy. However as discussed above it is possible to gain insights into the extent to which this problem is present with proper due diligence. It is not possible, however, to assess the institutional context as an "outsider" so that any information that is gathered is likely to be in the form of rumors and gossip. In other words, it must be viewed as highly unreliable.

The best way to view asymmetric information is to understand it is a property of financial markets. One writer has suggested asymmetric information is a key factor in understanding why financial markets are self-immolating (Abolafia 2010). From this viewpoint of managing assets and risk, the fact outsiders may well be taking on a greater degree or risk than they appear to be must be kept in mind. [See Chapter 2 on Contracting Risk and Macro Aggregation Effects.] This distorted sense of risk can in turn influence the formation of asset bubbles as investors fail to realize the underlying instability of their investments.

Escalation

Escalation research demonstrates how risks are distorted as a commitment to an investment or a class of investments builds. Putting this in an institutional context, it is important to pay close attention to the history and tenure of executives in asset management firms. Research has shown the longer they have been in their positions, the more likely they are to discount the risks associated with assets in which they have large positions (Kanodia, Bushman & Dickhaut 1989). As such, they are less likely to spot or take action with respect to potential asset bubbles. Further any financial advice that might be given (and done so in good faith) must be viewed in light of the psychology of escalation and its implications for pursuing losing courses of action.

In addition, individual investors must also be aware of the tendency to distort risk when they have taken large positions in one asset. This commitment to a course of action is likely to lead to greater commitment of new money when asset prices fall under the guise of a buying opportunity. Importantly, from a psychological perspective, this additional commitment of funds is not associated with a mania or a compulsion to own a particular security at any price. Rather, it is experienced as a natural consequence of a perceived sound strategy expected to produce gains. For this reason investors easily discount the claims of assets being overvalued or problems with the risk-reward ratio of certain investment decisions. This point was evident in the mindset of Saint Etienne's administration when the huge additional risks they incurred were viewed as the part of the trade-off in running a city.

Escalation, thus, tends to camouflage bubbles in the minds of investors because of the distortion and thus misperception of risk and the need to justify past decisions in increasingly risky assets. For these reasons, bubbles are difficult to detect because the objective evidence that indicates they are forming is likely to be ignored or discounted by those with large positions in those risky assets. Further, investors who claim these assets are not overvalued are likely to have large positions in them, which might be seen as a source of comfort to other investors. In fact, it is more likely a cause for concern or even alarm_because once the reality is perceived a large number of investors will try to exit at once; that is, the bubble will burst dramatically, which is of course what usually happens.

Using Behavioral Theory to Help Identify Bubbles:

Five Key Questions

Exhibit F presents five questions derived from institutional and behavioral theory that can be useful in identifying asset bubbles. They can and should be used in conjunction with economic indicators, market metrics including technical and fundamental market analysis, advice from experts, and comparison with prior and known asset bubbles as all described in other chapters in this volume. The behavioral approach, though, differs from traditional, quantitative analyses in that it is more subjective, and to some degree, includes an element of introspection.

The underlying rationale for these questions has been covered in other parts of this chapter and need not be repeated here. Rather, the purpose is to examine if there is a consistency across these questions of poor understanding of the innovation, the large scope and relatively large capacity for disruption, the highly committed firms and employees on the sell side as defined by large financial and psychological investments in the asset, the troubling gaps in information, the fully committed investors in terms of financial and psychological resources, and the more than likely reality that an asset bubble is either forming or has formed. It is not possible to determine when the bubble will burst using behavioral theory, but these questions can lead investors to take a more cautious approach to specific asset classes in particular and to financial markets in general especially when sentiment is uniformly positive and overly optimistic.

The Issue of Ethics

The question of the ethics involved in asset bubbles is difficult to disentangle because it involves making judgments about the motivation and knowledge of the participants and such judgments are necessarily speculative. There is no question that there are scoundrels seeking to profit from asset bubbles, but there are scoundrels seeking profit from most human activity. Such individuals are clearly unethical, but their presence and behavior sheds no light on the ethical behavior of the primary participants associated with asset bubbles.

Rather than beginning with a focus on the behavior of the parties involved in asset bubbles, it seems better to begin with an analysis of the context and the conditions in which that behavior occurs. That context, in turn, refers to the institutional context that ultimately governs how markets and relationships are managed. This includes the legal and contractual arrangements examined in Chapter 2.

The primary source of difficulty with respect to the ethics of asset bubbles seems to revolve around the problem of information asymmetry. That is, it has been asserted that one party has access to information that others do not have and that this information has been used to the advantage of that party to the detriment of others including customers. [See Chapter 2.] Further, it has been suggested that had the "privileged" party been more open about the information that it had available, counterparties would not have been as eager to purchase the assets in question (Farzad & Dwyer 2010).

The question of information asymmetry is a thorny one because it suggests that the market might ultimately be "rigged" so that those firms who sell or value assets do so at the expense of those who purchase them. Recall, however, information asymmetry is a consequence of institutional structures and systems so it is embedded in well-established institutional cultures. As such, if information asymmetry is a characteristic of

---

Exhibit F

Five Issues to Consider in Identifying Asset Bubbles

1. How well understood is the displacement or innovation driving investment in the asset in question? Can it be explained simply and cogently? Does this explanation make sense?

2. How disruptive is the innovation or displacement in question? What is its scope and reach? How credible are the arguments that this innovation is truly transformative and is likely to persist?

3. How committed are the firms and individuals marketing the assets in question? How much does it affect their firms' profitability? How long have they been with the firm? What is the personal and professional cost of error on their part?

4. To what extent is there the impression that investors have not been told the whole story? That is, to what extent is there an asymmetry in information that is designed to make outsiders feel like insiders?

5. To what extent have investors made large bets on the assets in question? When the assets' value dip, do they make substantial additional investments thereby temporarily shoring up asset prices?

---

institutions and institutional structures, the question of ethics must be framed in terms of trust. Thus, a case can be made that firms have acted unethically if they have used information asymmetry knowingly and willingly to the detriment of clients who are counterparties.[55]

This ultimately is a thorny and difficult problem to address because it involves analyzing the behavior of those involved in asset bubbles on a case-by-case basis. Thus, broad labels such as a "culture of corruption" might make interesting news stories, but they do not do justice to the careful analysis that is necessary to objectively explore the questions of ethics in relation to the valuation and sale of assets.

Although it is very difficult to establish the motivation and exact knowledge of the parties involved in asset valuation with respect to asset bubbles, it is possible to examine aspects of the institutional context to gain insights into the prevailing values and perceived responsibilities of the firms and individuals who define and comprise the institutional culture.

The logical place to begin is with the network of inter-organizational relationships and networks that define the institutional system. Clearly, there are interdependencies among firms and actors and those actors help clarify prevailing values and practices. In so doing, it is possible to get a sense of how "things work" in relation to broader principles of ethics and fairness.

In this regard, while it is reasonable to argue that the institutional context and relationships are nuanced and might not

---

[55] Something along these lines seems to have occurred when Goldman Sachs allowed John Paulson to select the securities he would bet against and that Goldman then sold to other clients.

be fully understood by outsiders, it is not reasonable to argue these complexities preclude or vitiate an objective analysis of ethical conduct. Simply because something is complex and perhaps arcane does not mean it cannot be understood. Nor does the complexity undermine the application of ethical principles. Indeed, the argument we "did nothing wrong" based on long established and accepted practices can be used to_justify any behavior no matter how unethical or barbaric it might be, and simply is not an acceptable explanation for what might have happened during the formation and development of asset bubbles.

Each asset bubble has its own institutional context and characteristics. For example the Internet bubble involved venture capital and their associated networks while the 2008 financial crisis did not. Thus it is necessary to consider the ethics associated with asset bubbles on a case-by-case basis. However, it is possible to use institutional theory to guide such an analysis in identifying those aspects of the institutional context to analyze.

As noted earlier, the most logical place to begin is with the inter-organizational relationships that define the institutional context. If we use the 2008 financial crisis as an example, the asset bubble in mortgage backed securities was embedded in a series of inter-organizational relationships that involved writing mortgages, bundling them into new instruments (CDO's), evaluating the risk of those CDO's (Rating Agencies) and then selling them mostly to institutional investors.

In order for this market to function, it was necessary to have a steady supply of mortgages, an intermediary to bundle the mortgages into CDO's and sell them, and Rating Agencies to assess the credit quality of the CDO's and the homebuyers.

Strictly from the point of view of institutional efficiency, for this system to operate well, it was necessary for investment banks to build a series of relationships and/or open subsidiaries that provided the mortgages necessary to populate the CDO's. It was also necessary for the Ratings Agencies to certify that these new instruments were rated AAA because this was a necessary requirement for most institutional buyers (Chapter 7). Finally, an aggressive sales force was needed to move these new products (Chapter 5).

Looking at this situation from an operational perspective leads to the conclusion that a fairly effective institutional context evolved to devise and sell these new financial instruments. Such a statement is ethically neutral. So while it is arguably accurate, it misses elements of the institutional context that have a direct bearing on the ethical conduct of the firms and individuals involved. The first ethical issue concerns how CDO's were produced. For the institutional context to function, investment banks needed a regular and growing supply of mortgages. Since the banks that wrote the mortgages that were bundled into CDO's sold these mortgages, there was little incentive for them to do a proper credit analyses. Indeed, to do so would have delayed the process of supplying mortgages thereby limiting the profits of the parties writing and bundling mortgages.

As a result, there were significant breaches of commonly accepted practices associated with assessing credit risk. Perhaps the most ridiculous illustration is an $850,000 mortgage written by Washington Mutual to an individual who made his living as a member of a mariachi band. The bank took a photograph of this person in his mariachi costume as the sole verification of his occupation and income. When a junior loan officer objected, he was told not to worry because the bank was going to sell the mortgage anyway. Countless other examples of such behavior are available, and one would be hard pressed to argue these were not clear and undisputable breaches of ethics. However institutions chose to ignore their own standards of behavior to pursue short-term profit. In this way the self-regulating elements of the institutional context failed because immediate greed overshadowed ethics and the near certainty that the security would blow up in a couple of years.

Yet for this system to hold, it was necessary to provide evidence that these bundled mortgages were really low risk (AAA credit rating). The Wall Street firms insisted their quantitative models controlled for risk, but we now know this was not true. What the "quants" assembling these instruments knew at the time outsiders cannot know. But we do know that independent verification of their claims was required for the CDO's to be marketable and that three ratings agencies produced the required AAA ratings.

That these ratings were incorrect resulting in significant distortion of risk is not, in and of itself, an ethical breach. It could have been an honest mistake tied to the complexities of evaluating new financial instruments. There are, though, several elements within the institutional context that suggest otherwise. First, the CDO business was one of the most profitable for ratings agencies. Second, a rating lower than AAA would serve to shut down a much larger profit machine for Wall Street's leading investment banks. Third, as we have seen after the fact, firms assembling CDO's had little clue how to value them, raising questions about how an "independent" assessment could consistently result in a AAA rating. Indeed, why were tough questions not asked by the ratings agencies?

Rather a case can be made that the institutional context evolved so relationships among investments banks and the ratings agencies were more valuable than were the ratings agencies' responsibility to the buyers of the mortgage backed CDO's. Indeed, Goldman Sachs has argued the CDO and CMO buyers were sophisticated, institutional investors who were able to assess risk and should have done so with more care. The problem with the "buyer beware" argument, however, is that the very same institutions who are using it assembled a marketing machine to assure customers the CDO's that they were buying were low risk. [See also Chapter 5 on Marketing Bubbles.] Thus one cannot have it both ways in that a firm cannot expect buyers to conduct their own due diligence while at the same time assuring them there is no need to do so.

It is, therefore, reasonable to conclude that the institutional context in which assets are traded can evolve in ways that information asymmetry is no longer a source of relative advantage, but rather becomes a tool to deceive customers in order to support a profit stream. But because the institutional context is complex and dynamic, one cannot make a blanket statement that information asymmetry will always be exploited to a buyer's detriment. As seen with mortgage backed CDO's, though, a case can be made that it can and has been exploited in ways not consistent with accepted ethical principles despite the contrary protestations of those accused.

Conclusion

It is reasonable to argue asset bubbles are not fleeting events. Rather based on historical and institutional analysis they are characteristic of market economies. Still understanding their formation, growth and implosion requires sensitivity to the complexity of the forces that lead to asset bubbles. Financial conditions such as the availability of cheap and easy money as explained by Professor Aliber seem a necessary condition for forming an asset bubble as is some tangible displacement in markets.

Therefore these conditions are likely to be present in the future and are_likely to spawn new asset bubbles. Business, however, is ultimately a human activity and, as such, it is also affected by human nature and social structures both of which also influence asset bubbles. This chapter has focused on these areas and has offered a perspective that is intended to be complementary to more conventional research in the areas of finance and economies on asset bubbles covered in other Chapters in this book. Whether scanning the social and financial environments for markers of asset bubbles as suggested here will prove useful in identifying them remains to be seen, but such signals associated with prior bubbles as examined in this chapter indicate that they are certainly worth monitoring.

References

Abolafia, M 2005. *Markets* (Critical Studies in Economic Institutions), Edward Elgar Publishing, Aldershot, UK.

Abolafia, M. 2006. *Making Markets: Opportunism and Restraint on Wall Street.* Harvard University Press, Cambridge, MA.

Abolafia, M. 2010. "Can speculative bubbles be managed? An institutional approach", *Strategic Organization,* 8.

Abolafia, M. & Kilduff, M. 1988. "Enacting market crisis: The social construction of a speculative bubble", *Administrative Science Quarterly*, 33.

Akerlof, G. & Romer, P. 1993. "Looting: The economic underworld of bankruptcy for profit", *Brookings Papers on Economic Activity*, 2.

Arkes, H. & Blumer, C. 1985. "The psychology of sunk costs", *Organizational Behavior and Human Decision Processes,* 35.

Brockner, J. 1991. "The escalation to a failing course of action: Toward theoretical progress", *Academy of Management Review*, 17.

Chow, C., Harrison, T., Lindquist, T. & Wu, A. 1997. "Escalating commitment to unprofitable projects; Replication and cross-cultural extension", *Management Accounting Research*, 8.

Conlon, E. & Wolf, G. 1980. "The moderating effects of strategy, visibility, and involvement on allocation behavior: An extension of Staw's escalation paradigm", *Organizational Behavior and Human Performance*, 26.

Davis, G. 2010. "Not just a mortgage crisis: how finance maimed society", *Strategic Organization*, 8.

Dennison, C. 2009. "Real options and escalation of commitment: A behavioral analysis of capital investment decisions", *The Accounting Review*, 84.

Farzard, R. & Dwyer, P. 2010. "Not guilty, not one little bit", *Bloomberg Business Week*.

Flood, R. & Garber, P. 1980. "Market fundamentals versus price-level bubbles: the first tests", *Journal of Political Economy*, 88.

Flood, R. & Hodrick, R. 1990. "On testing speculative bubbles", *Journal of Economic Perspectives*, 4.

Ferguson, N. 2008. *The Ascent of Money*, Penguin Books, NY.

Garber, P. 1990. "Famous first bubbles", *Journal of Economic Perspectives*, 4.

Jick, T. 1979. "Mixing qualitative and quantitative methods: Triangulation in action", *Administrative Science Quarterly*, 24.

Hirsch, P. 1972. "Processing fads and fashion: An organization-set analysis of cultural industry systems", *The American Journal of Sociology*, 77.

Kanodia, C, Bushman, R. & Dickhaut, J. 1989. "Escalation errors and the sunk cost effect: An explanation based on reputation and information asymmetries", *Journal of Accounting Research*, 27.

Kindleberger, C. & Aliber, R. 2011. *Manias, Panics and Crashes*, op.cit.

Kotler, P. 2008. *Marketing Management*, Prentice-Hall, Englewood Cliffs, NJ.

Krugman, P. 2009. *The Return of Depression Economics and the Crisis of 2008*, WW Norton, NY.

Minsky, H. 1986. *Stabilizing an unstable economy*, Yale University Press, New Haven, CT.

Minsky, H. 1993. "The financial instability hypothesis", in Arestis, P. & Sawyer, M. eds. *Handbook of Radical Political Economy*, Edward Elgar, Aldershot, UK.

Palmer, D. & Maher, M. 2010. "The mortgage meltdown as accidental wrongdoing", *Strategic Organization*, 8.

Papadimitriou, D. & Wray, L. 2008. "Minsky's Stabilizing an Unstable Economy: Two Decades Later", in H. Minsky *Stabilizing an Unstable Economy*, McGraw-Hill, NY.

Posner, R. 2009. *A Failure of Capitalism: The Crisis of '08 and the Descent into Depression*, Harvard University Press, Cambridge, MA.

Powell, W. & DiMaggio, P. 1991. *The New Institutionalism in Organizational Analysis*, University of Chicago Press, Chicago, IL.

Scott, W. 1987. "The adolescence of institutional theory", *Administrative Science Quarterly*, 32.

Ross, J. & Staw, B. 1993. "Organizational escalation and exit: Lessons from the Shoreham nuclear power plant", *Academy of Management Journal*, 36.

Staw, B. 1976. "Knee-deep in the big muddy: A study of escalating commitment to a chosen course of action", *Organizational Behavior and Human Performance*, 16.

Staw, B. 1981. "The escalation of commitment to a course of action", *Academy of Management Review*, 6.

Staw, B., Barsade, S. & Koput, K. 1997. "Escalation at the credit window: A longitudinal study of bank executives' recognition and write-off of problem loans", *Journal of Applied Psychology*, 82.

Staw, B. & Ross, J. 1989. "Understanding behavior in escalation situations", *Science*, 246.

Stiglitz, J. 2002. "Globalism's discontents", *American Prospect*.

Weick, K. 1993. "The collapse of sensemaking in organizations: The Mann Gulch disaster", *Administrative Science Quarterly*, 38.

Weick, K. & Roberts, K. 1993. "Collective mind in organizations: Heedful interrelating on flight decks", *Administrative Science Quarterly*, 38.

West, K. 2002. "Bubbles, fads and stock price volatility tests: a partial evaluation", *International Library of Critical Writings in Economics*, 143.

CHAPTER FIVE

THE ROLE OF MARKETING IN CREATING BUBBLES

THE US HOUSING BUBBLE: AN ENVIRONMENTAL AND STRATEGIC MARKETING ANALYSIS

Here's the smell of the blood still: all the perfumes of Arabia will not sweeten this little hand.

D. Viola   W. Rapp   R. Mehta

Introduction

Often referred to by different titles, such as "The Great Recession," "The Financial Armageddon," and "The Financial Apocalypse," if there ever was another crisis that almost brought about a second depression and a catastrophic global economic downturn, that event, which captured collective imaginations was the "The Financial Crisis of 2008." In addition to the book by Morgenson and Rosner [2011] appropriately entitled, "Reckless Endangerment: How Outsized Ambition, Greed and Corruption Led to Economic Armageddon," an enormous amount of literature continues to emerge, which discusses the causes of the crisis and seeks to identify the "Reckless Masters Of 'Economic Armageddon'," [McEdwards 2011].

However, relative to the numerous articles on finance and experiments in creating exotic financial securities, the literature on the role played by marketing in creating the housing bubble is fragmented and sparse. Yet though largely ignored, and no matter what term is used to describe it, the 2008 subprime mortgage-lending crisis also arguably resulted from the ingenious marketing campaigns that shifted the notion of buying a home as a long-term investment into speculation in housing. As a consequence, housing prices, which kept increasing, were fed and fuelled by a mythical and overly optimistic belief that people could make astronomical returns by moving money from bank savings into buying and selling homes at a profit. Indeed the financial crisis was also the creation of several marketing campaigns in which banks knowingly and purposefully incentivized unqualified buyers into mortgages fully aware the majority of borrowers could not repay their loans.

Still, as discussed in prior chapters, current and past research readily reveals that these lenders had little concern given the securitization of mortgages and the creation of collateralized mortgage obligations (CMO), which brought them additional profit while simultaneously transferring the credit risk to others. Thus CMOs incentivized banks to finance as many mortgages as possible due to the lucrative returns. This led the banks to become very innovative in drafting the terms of a mortgage that was then securitized.

Purpose

The objective of this research is to document how the mortgage lending institutions crafted their marketing strategies for subprime loans around specific target markets. For example, many banks employed deceptive marketing techniques to lure in potential borrowers. [Also see Chapter 2, which describes how teaser rates and Adjustable Rate Mortgages (ARM) were used to support these marketing strategies and to exploit borrower optimism.] Moreover, this chapter will identify the demographic factors used in targeting mortgage customers as well as the characteristics common among debtors.

Scope

The housing market began rising rapidly in value in 2002 and peaked in 2006. Hence, the time frame covered by this research covers 2001 through 2007. As this chapter will show, most mortgage related marketing, advertising and promotion campaigns run during this period were specifically crafted to attract and exploit a particular demographic target market.

While the chapter focuses exclusively on the marketing of subprime mortgages and the channels used to reach the related target market during the US 2001 to 2007 housing bubble the authors believe further research will show that similar marketing techniques have been used in other bubbles such as the dot.com bubble. Each major bank used similar means to reach this target market, though the slogans, promotions and campaigns differed slightly. An analysis of each bank's direct advertisements can determine which banks were using deceptive marketing practices as well as those lending institutions "Reverse Redlining," that is specifically targeting the poor and minorities [Fisher 2009].

Organization

In this chapter the first section covers how the political-legal, economic, technological, socio-cultural, and competitive environments that influenced the real estate market helped develop the housing mania. The target market and market segmentation strategy is discussed in section two. In section three, a description is provided of the marketing strategy employed by mortgage banks. The final section offers conclusions and suggests avenues for future research on the role of marketing in bubble development.

The Recent Elements US Real Estate Market Environment

Leading up to the 2008 crisis, the US real estate market was valued at an historical high [Morrow 2011]. Meanwhile, banks and other lenders had very relaxed credit criteria regarding the borrower qualifications for home loans and mortgages especially for subprime mortgages. As a result, lending institutions had more freedom to design subprime mortgages to be seemingly affordable for many more Americans allowing them to purchase homes they could not afford.

Political and Legal Environment

While the blame for the collapse of the housing market can be pointed in many directions, one major reason for the real estate bubble can be attributed to deregulation by the government. After the Great Depression took its toll on the financial markets and the US economy in the 1930s, the Glass-Steagall Act [Legal Dictionary 2013] was passed to separate commercial and investment banks from common ownership. However, the Gramm–Leach–Bliley Act of 1999 reversed Glass-

Steagall and allowed commercial and investment institutions to merge. Some economists such as Stiglitz [2010] supported the Gramm-Leach-Bliley Act because they felt it tempered the downfall of the economy by allowing financial companies to merge and stay alive competitively.

On the other hand, Krugman [2008] and others have argued that this deregulation greatly contributed to the development of the subsequent financial crisis. This is because once the banks, investment banks and insurance companies could be merged together the collateralized mortgages could be sold and passed on through other related institutions without any indication of their true value. The ability of Bear Stearns, for example, to take loans from its mortgage bank, ECM, bundle them through their investment bank and sell them to one of their managed hedge funds clearly illustrates this problem. Similarly, Citicorp could originate subprime mortgages in Citibank securitize and bundle them through their investment bank, Solomon Smith Barney, and then sell them to a Citibank managed SIV. [See Chapter 6 for an extended discussion of this topic.]

Further influencing the financial environment for subprime housing loans was the passing of the Community Reinvestment Act 1977 [Federal Reserve Board 2011], which the Federal Reserve Bank (FRB) used to encourage financial institutions to grant loans to low-income communities and made regulatory exceptions for such borrowers to get loans [FRB 2011]. Although, it is reported these government mandated loans were only a minimal percentage of those involved in the housing crisis, it is still a heavily debated aspect of the collapse.

Another government program similar to the Community Reinvestment Act are loans administered through the Department of Housing and Urban Development (HUD), whose mission is to create affordable US home ownership [HUD 2013]. While this is a potentially great idea that can help to increase the standard of living for all citizens, it poses a threat to the lending system and creates tension for mortgage institutions that are pressured to lend money to people that may not be able to repay the loans. Indeed before the rise of the housing market, bank establishments were skeptical about loaning money to low-income families predominately consisting of various minorities. However, as the housing market began to boom in 2002, lending institutions became eager to target these same minorities and low-income individuals to borrow using subprime mortgages because as explained in prior chapters in addition to high fee income they optimistically believed rising home prices would assure repayment even if the low-income borrowers defaulted.

The Federal National Mortgage Association (Fannie Mae 2013), a government backed agency created to help families have access to mortgage loans that are within their means through buying or insuring such loans, also contributed to the process by buying or guaranteeing pools of these subprime loans. This was also true of the Federal Home Loan Mortgage Corporation (Freddie Mac 2013), which was created in 1970 to ensure that financial institutions had the capital to lend while making it easier for consumers to afford owning a home. It is for this reason many people blame Fannie Mae and Freddie Mac for the 2008 collapse given that they had insured around 24% to 48% of the mortgages that failed between 2002 and 2006 [Goldstein & Hall 2008].

These agencies were designed to help lower income families. However they felt pressured by the changed environment that developed once commercial banks merged with investment banks and could easily originate and collateralize mortgage debt that they then securitized and bundled for purchase by investors. This was because Fannie Mae and Freddie Mac lost market share and were no longer the major buyers of mortgage-backed securities, though this switched back after the 2008 subprime mortgage Collapse and the Great Recession began.

Another government contribution to the housing bubble was the Alternative Mortgage Transaction Parity Act that before its reformation in 2011 allowed non-federally chartered housing creditors to write adjustable-rate mortgages [Investopedia 2013]. Traditional fixed-rate amortizing loans reduce the credit risks associated with lending money and allow for a weighted average payment with smaller interest payments in the future. However ARMs permit the resetting of interest after few years and thus can substantially increase monthly payments which is why they were the most commonly failed subprime mortgages in 2008 as well as the ones most exploitive of borrowers.

Indeed, banks and mortgage brokers actively sought and

approved home loans to applicants that had "No Income, No Jobs, No Assets," which gave rise to an oft-used acronym: NINJA loans that like their Japanese namesakes can easily disappear. What's more, banks and mortgage brokers also gave "No Doc" and "Liar's Loans" [Foote, Gerardi & Willen 2012 and Timiraos 2012], where borrowers did not have to provide any supporting documentation, which resulted in many applicants lying about their employment income and assets. Since many lenders did not check their credentials, it was not surprising borrowers would be able to temporarily afford their home mortgage until the end of the low interest rate or "teaser" period. However, after interest rates were reset and increased, borrowers would be unable to meet their mortgage payments, culminating in the loss of their homes through foreclosure.

Starting in 2003 and culminating in 2005, the FRB [Federal Reserve Board] lowered interest rates to an all-time historic low last seen in 1958 [Ifill & Jones 2003], to spur spending, thus fostering economic growth after the Dotcom collapse and the terrorist attacks of September 11, 2001 (See: Exhibit 1). But after interest rates were lowered in this way, the Fed started to raise rates in 2005 driving many prime borrowers who had been refinancing from the market.[56] Many lending institutions wanting to continue their profitable securitization business then promoted

---

[56] The target Fed Funds rate reached a 1% low in July 2003 and stayed there until June 2004. It then began to rise hitting a 4% high in 2005 and a 5.25% high in 2006 that lasted until September 2007. See http://www.moneycafe.com/library/fedfundsrate.htm.

subprime mortgages with variable interest rates [Investopedia #2 2013] where the interest rate on the mortgage loan after 2 to 5 years changed to reflect the prevailing market interest rate. The result could be a large increase or decrease in the monthly payments depending on market conditions. But given rising market rates combined with the fact the initial teaser rates were below market the actual monthly payment was bound to rise sharply.

At first when interest rates were low and lending institutions had fewer restrictions regarding such loans, there was a surge in the subprime mortgage market. Although many could ill-afford them, many borrowers who were making monthly payments were now at the mercy of changes in market interest rates. So once the FRB started tightening interest rates in 2005, many borrowers were forced into foreclosure due to the drastic increases in their monthly payments.

Yet, the exit strategy did not prove as easy as many lenders had optimistically assumed. Because financial institutions had collateralized these mortgage obligations and separated them into different tranches with different terms, managing the dramatic increases in foreclosures became a nightmare that has haunted many and bankrupted others—a condition that has continued through 2013.

Still, at that time despite the obvious risks for many banks an AAA-rated tranche of subprime collateralized debt obligations (CDO) had advantages. Higher upfront and refinancing fees and premiums meant higher profits while securitization reduced capital requirements [Investopedia #3 2013]. The combination significantly increased return on equity and often led to higher stock prices and thus lucrative increases in executive compensation. Further, many investors decided that the real risk existed only if several mortgages defaulted at the same time or there was a sharp economic downturn. More specifically many investors chose to buy CDOs due to what they optimistically perceived as a relatively low risk because they had first claim on any interest income from the mortgage pool. (See: Exhibit 2 for AAA subprime Tranche prices during 2007-2008.)

In reality, though, the risks associated with CMOs and CDOs were unknown. Credit-rating agencies often relied on information provided by the investment banks distributing the securities while the agencies' evaluation models were historically based and did not actually reflect the current situation [Kindleberger & Aliber 2011]. As explained in other chapters, the risks associated with these securities were underrated due to their complexity and the poor credit of the underlying mortgage where lenders had not been concerned with a borrower's ability to repay because the securities were rapidly passed along to other institutions. There was also the unrealistically assumed foreclosure exit strategy at rising prices.

The disassociation of the risk related to CDOs and CMOs were made apparent once mortgage defaults increased, and real estate prices declined sharply due to both decreased demand and the increased supply from foreclosures. The resulting increased number of lawsuits also proved very costly. Further because the value of the CDOs and CMOs could not be easily determined, they became difficult to sell and the investment banks began to incur losses on their mortgage pipeline and in their managed assets. [See Chapter 7: For an extended discussion on CMOs and CDOs.]

Economic Environment

It is generally accepted that historically the US economy witnessed its long recent sustained growth over the eight years under the leadership of President Bill Clinton. However, when President George H. W. Bush entered office in 2001 he had inherited an economy teetering on the verge of recession due to the dot-com bubble and Internet bust that collapsed in 2000 and pressured the FRB to decrease interest rates to sustain economic growth and price stability [FRB 2013]. This pressure was compounded by the terrorist attacks of 9/11 that were seen as creating a "double-whammy" effect on top of the dot.com bust that pushed the economy into a recession. As a result, the FRB reduced interest rates even more to calm the economy and the country [Gandel 2011].

This decrease in rates allowed banks to tailor mortgages to seem more affordable and easier to attain for low-income borrowers through low initial cost teaser rates that covered the banks' funding costs if not their true risk. From 2004 onward, though, the FRB as noted above increased interest rates a record 17 times from a low of 1% in 2003 to a 5.25% high in 2006. This forced homeowners to make larger monthly payments on their adjustable rate mortgages as teaser rates lapsed. This was the first sign many homeowners were going to default on their mortgages, initiating with severe systemic consequences the subprime and housing market collapse.

In this way the increase in property values and the boom in the housing market had lured people to begin investing in real estate and homeownership. Yet while the overall US housing market was increasing, some areas experienced truly explosive bubble surges in value while others only saw minimal increases. Exhibit 3 shows housing markets in California, Nevada, Arizona and Florida almost tripled in value while those such as Cleveland only increased slightly.

Still as the values in the surging areas kept rapidly increasing many people did not want to miss the opportunity of seizing a piece of the housing market. However, when the collapse of the bubble began in 2007-2008 many people who had borrowed traditional prime loans were left holding mortgages worth more than their homes, while subprime borrowers were generally even less fortunate. Due to the skewed market, potential applicants with poor or no credit had been eager to finally purchase a home and had borrowed at what turned out to be predatory rates. Then after the collapse they were not able to refinance due to lower property values.

The popularity of low or no down payment mortgages had made it easy for more low income people to have access to home ownership opportunities. Further as explained above the relaxed government regulation of bank lending allowed such mortgage distribution to take place at a faster pace than previously. With relaxed lending regulations, many banks could distribute subprime mortgages and make quick profits by collecting high origination fees, then selling the mortgage-backed securities to other institutions while continuing lucrative service contracts. This process depended though on a continued mortgage flow despite the changed economic and lending environment once the FRB started increasing interest rates. So subprime lending continued and grew far longer than should have been allowed.

While some promotion campaigns to assure this flow focused on people buying a new home, other marketing tactics encouraged people to build homes and acquire properties. As a result, some areas were impacted by both the purchase of existing homes and the construction of new ones. As property values increased, construction projects rose sharply. This was the mania phase of the housing market boom where the purchase of the property and the loan for building homes would eventually be considerably more than its market value after the 2008 housing market bust.

That dramatic decrease in value would eventually lead to an explosion of defaulted loans and increased urgency by both borrowers and lenders to sell the property to avoid a greater loss. Robert Shiller has argued that in this way irrational exuberance was shifted from the falling stock market of 2000 to the housing market in 2008. He states: "Once stocks fell, real estate became the primary outlet for the speculative frenzy that the stock market had unleashed" [Taylor & Francis 2013].

The above noted economic conditions can be summarized by Gandel [2011], who succinctly asserts:

> "Right after 9/11, the Federal Reserve lowered interest rates in order to boost the economy in the wake of the terrorist attack. In a search for higher yields investors began to buy up subprime mortgage bonds. In order to create more high-yield bonds, lenders made loans to riskier and riskier borrowers, who drove up housing prices and created the bubble. Eventually, many of those borrowers couldn't pay their loans. The bonds start to go bad. Lehman goes belly up. Financial crisis on."

Technological Environment

Technology, in general, and the wide extension of the Internet, in particular, propelled the dissemination of information relative to the housing market and thus facilitated the bubble. More specifically, technological advancements that contributed to the housing crisis were rapid communication and the widespread adoption of the Internet. As more people became familiar with e-mail and Internet searching, this impacted how potential home buyers and mortgage borrowers could be reached for sales promotions and marketing campaigns. It also speeded up the application, processing and bundling of loans. Indeed the Internet provided banks a window to affordably reach more people over a wider geographic area with home buying and mortgage opportunities. Additionally, it provided consumers an easier way to find a home and be approved for a mortgage. Each mortgage lender has a website with easy ways to apply online for a mortgage at anytime from anywhere in the country.

Bank of America offered customers this service (See Exhibit 4). Once approved for a certain mortgage amount people could surf the web on websites such as Truilia [2013] and Zillow [2013] to find homes for sale anywhere in the US. These Internet portals allowed homebuyers from anywhere to purchase a home in a growing area or city where the housing boom was most prevalent.

The escalation in selling mortgages also began to create more career options for sales associates, "mortgage specialists," and mortgage brokers to act as a liaison for banks and lending institutions to reach more consumers. With the surge in demand for mortgages, the increased values in the housing market, and the request for more mortgage related securities, many banks hired and created middlemen to help reach out to more potential customers. These intermediary mortgage brokers could then use the Internet to get more information and reach more consumers that were targeted for these loans.

In turn, companies were created with the purpose of determining a product's target market and the distribution channels most likely to reach the targeted consumers. Banks often used companies like Claritas [Neilsen 2013] and In Touch Today

[Mortgage Company Marketing Tool 2008] to reach the target subprime mortgage market. Without the Internet many companies could not have achieved the volume and in turn the perceived successes created by the housing bubble.

At the same time the many financial innovations in banking and lending [such as the SIVs described in Chapter 7], the complexity of tranched financial products, and the development of exotic derivatives for hedging, all created greater market uncertainty and increased the probability of risk assessment error. Indeed computer modeling of default risk and portfolio management may have created a false sense of security as to what could happen if there were massive defaults and foreclosures. This is indicated by the fact that the development of tranched mortgage backed securities combined with adjustable rate mortgages with teaser rates and balloon payments, CDOs, credit default swaps, and loans using derivatives made the crisis more widespread once it began. This is because it allowed more people to be a part of the housing market boom, while simultaneously adding to the complexity of managing the aftermath of the bust.

In sum, when compared to other bubbles, it is evident that the housing mania and bull market probably inflated more rapidly and was more widespread due to the many technological advances that allowed buyers, borrowers, lenders, investors, asset managers, lawyers, government regulators and developers to interact, communicate and transact much more quickly and on a global scale.

Socio-Cultural Environment

Reflecting the norms, values, customs and traditions of a group of people, culture also directly influenced the creation of the bull housing market. Owning a "home with white picket fences" and "living the American dream" are widely known to be sentiments and values that are deeply ingrained in the US population. Yet instead of thinking of it as a place of refuge, home ownership during the boom was also marketed as an investment opportunity not to be missed and a method of creating wealth adding another US ideal that is highly valued. In this way cultural values contributed to the housing market craze since no one wanted to miss out on the opportunity to both own a home and increase wealth. Many marketing tactics and promotion campaigns were therefore geared to reach the particular audiences that were most vulnerable to being persuaded to buy a home.

Typically these targeted groups were lower-middle class families and minorities including those with little English or legal sophistication. They were usually financially illiterate but still focused on achieving the American dream since they were frequently first and second generation Americans [Fisher 2009]. The sentiments associated with living the American dream would often drive borrowers to stretch or fabricate their incomes. Since this target market had little understanding of finance and the economy, many ads and popular books were published as a one-dimensional way to try and make them knowledgeable enough.

However, seemingly bad advice steered many in the wrong direction. For example, Lereah [2005] brags about the stabilization of the housing market in his popular book entitled "Are You Missing the Real Estate Boom? Why Home Values and Other Real Estate Investments Will Climb Through The End of The Decade—And How to Profit From Them." What's more, books, television shows, advertisements, e-mail ads, and billboards were all targeted to reach specific cultures to show how appealing was this home buying opportunity. People were surrounded with the temptation to take out a loan and buy the home they could not afford. In many cases the borrowers were misled by the innovative financial lending strategies offered by banks using low initial teaser rates. Other borrowers were encouraged to misstate income and assets since with lax regulations and credit processes they were not caught and got loan approval. Such predatory lending was a common tactic among mortgage brokers and loan officers because it created easy marketing strategies that worked and for which they were paid attractive upfront commissions. The ads and promotions, thus, created a sense of urgency and competitive pressure to convert any consumer hesitation into action.

Competitive Environment

The competitive environment in the US is usually intensely competitive in almost all industries. This is especially true in real estate and financial services. The financial industry during this period had many players such as Citigroup, HSBC, Countrywide,

Washington Mutual [WaMu], Provident, Wells Fargo, and Bank of America. All were fiercely competing to increase market share, profits and compensation.

A national mortgage market had evolved since World War II and especially since the development of mortgage-backed securities in the 1970s to serve traditional customers with good credit and to also provide loans for customers with poor credit through the Federal Housing Administration. However securitization altered the identity of banks with their customers since the banks were now merely intermediaries between investors and borrowers replacing the prior relationship of depositors and borrowers [Kindleberger & Aliber 2011].

The growth of mortgage-backed securitization, which was flourishing in early 2002, created a fiercely competitive environment for prime and non-prime loans. Once banks had sold the mortgages to the borrowers they then packaged them and marketed them to investors for a profit and generated the cash flow to make new mortgages. CMOs and the securitization of mortgages allowed the banks to have more money to make more loans and mortgages and to generate continuing servicing revenues. As a result, the value of US residential real estate increased from 110 percent of US GDP to 150 percent between 2002 and 2006 [Kindleberger & Aliber 2011].

This increase in property values created a bubble frenzy where everyone wanted to participate. Because banks had more money to lend and the housing market was at an all-time high, subprime mortgages satisfied the new homeowner's dream and the banks' business need to securitize and sell more and more mortgages. Furthermore, these were mostly interest only or adjustable rate loans that were inherently high-risk [Laing 2005]. Thus, lenders needed to target the demographic groups with questionable credit histories that would commit to this type of mortgage since prime borrowers would not borrow on such a basis. Yet since the lending institutions almost never kept these loans in their own portfolios, there was no incentive for the banks to check the validity of an applicant's credit history or proof of income. This was a decision some financial institutions, such as WaMu or Lehman Brothers, lived to regret when they became saddled with large inventories of loans to be securitized as the market suddenly collapsed around them in the summer of 2008.

In sum, after the prime loan refinancing market dried up around 2003 to 2004 as the Fed raised interest rates, competition still continued to intensify in the mortgage market among both local and national banks due to the large perceived profits. However it took a new form as lenders needed to create new products in the form of subprime mortgage loans if they were going to profitably appeal to a new and relatively untapped class of homebuyers. This shift also required using an innovative target marketing strategy as described in the following section.

Target Market and Market Segmentation Strategy

In an extremely low interest rate environment, making higher profits in financial services from traditional lending is increasingly difficult. Thus these firms in general, and mortgage companies, in particular, developed a new, more innovative way to increase profits by offering subprime loans to a new target market, which refers to the specific segment of consumers most likely to purchase this particular product or service. That is, using a market development strategy where firms offer tailored products and services to a new target market can be effective in increasing profits. More specifically, in the financial services industry, mortgage firms could increase their customer base by offering attractive mortgages with low initial interest rates to those individuals who were currently renters. In essence, even individuals who had no income, no jobs and even no assets (the NINJA segment) could become the new source of profits.

Marketing practices have been developed and perfected over the years by obtaining more information on a targeted consumer group using market segmentation. This refers to methods and process of dividing a total product or service market into smaller, relatively homogeneous consumer groups [Boone & Kurtz 2013]. The group connections can include psychographic, geographic and benefit (e.g., usage rates) factors. Demographic segmentation or the method of classifying customers into a homogeneous group using factors, such as household income, age, employment, zip code, credit cards, past purchases and other useful character traits, are also a commonly used targeting strategy. Armed with this information, marketers can determine which consumers are more likely to purchase a particular product or service, in this case subprime mortgages.

As noted above, once lenders sifted their focus around 2004-2005 they targeted borrowers for subprime loans who had never purchased a home and were under qualified. Many banks used P$YCLE [Claritas P$YCLE Segmentations System], which divides people into 58 different segments using demographic markers. One popular targeted category was "Urban Essentials" that includes individuals characterized as having low-income, low to no assets, low to nonexistent savings, and typically renters [Claritas].

Thus many mortgage brokers were not concerned about the ability of these borrowers to repay because the credit risk would be transferred to others in the credit distribution pipeline or they assumed that rising home prices would cover the loans through foreclosure [Kindleberger & Aliber 2011]. Rather these lenders were primarily concerned with signing more mortgages to generate more collateralized mortgage products, collect more high upfront fees and enlarge their lucrative servicing business.

Having made the decision to keep peddling this financial bicycle, lenders also targeted people that were considered financially uneducated, thus highly vulnerable to optimistically agreeing to this type of high-risk loan. This included customers with poor credit and multiple credit cards. In fact, last minute bait and switch tactics were often employed to convince some creditworthy borrowers to accept a higher cost subprime loan when they could have qualified for a prime loan [Carr & Kolluri

2001]. Usually, low-income communities consisted of more uneducated people and minorities. Banks could use their own data systems to determine which customers had poor credit and multiple credit cards as well as their age. More specifically, Carr and Kolluri [2001] report research conducted by Freddie Mac and Fannie Mae that suggests even early on 35% to even 50% of subprime borrowers could have qualified for prime market loans. Further, banks even targeted borrowers that were already in financial anguish by persuading them to refinance using these high cost subprime products.

Banks also found target markets for subprime mortgages through zip codes [Peterson & Krivo 2009]. Many targeted minorities and non-English speakers and advertised in these communities by sending ads and flyers to a zip code that was primarily low-income or minority, though this was not always intentionally racist since many white families also lived in these neighborhoods. As property values increased in some areas, surrounding low-income areas were targeted for loans. This also led to "flipping" homes to make a profit in areas such as Florida.

Although this target market should have been unable to purchase a home due to low-income and poor credit, lenders used psychographic segmentation or the process of dividing a target market into homogeneous groups based on similar attitudes, opinions, and value systems to get them to consider borrowing. Being offered a subprime mortgage gave them the opportunity to become homeowners, thus fulfilling the traditionally much valued dream of having their own piece of Americana. Because of the emotional aspects of homeownership, these borrowers were frequently not afraid to inflate income and job security on their loan applications, giving lenders incentives to approve more loans that would never actually be repaid. In some cases, loan officers created these profiles without the borrower's knowledge in order to meet sales quotas. Thus based on fraudulent data, mortgages were approved, which created the existence of liar loans [Farlex 2013]. As the lenders were under-regulated, liar loans were approved and because the lenders did not know the borrowers preexisting spending habits borrowers were not given any financial guidance, leading many to default even more quickly on their mortgages.

Marketing Strategy

The broad principles used to achieve marketing goals and objectives comprise four elements including product, promotion, pricing and distribution. Examples of how financial institutions used each of these elements in marketing mortgages are described next.

Product Strategy

Comprising a cornerstone of a firm's marketing program, product strategy refers to the element of marketing decision-making comprising activities involved in developing the right goods or services for customers[Boone & Kurtz 2013]. Once banks had identified their target market, they created financial products that would almost guarantee success. In addition to traditional mortgages, banks could tailor a mortgage according to the homebuyer's situation. The bait was that there was no or a low down payment on the home. Typically, targeted subprime borrowers had never owned a home nor had any financial assets (cash) to make a substantial down payment.

The other contributing factor to this product's success was that the lending institution never carefully obtained, analyzed, nor checked the borrower's credit history or proof of income. That is there was virtually no risk assessment, partly due to the quick securitization. In addition, the sales pitch highlighted that the adjustable rate and interest only loan meant low, affordable payments during the first few years, while glossing over the fact after the initial years the monthly payment could sky rocket leaving many homeowners in even greater financial distress than before. Also many borrowers wishfully hoped after the higher payments began they would be making more money or could refinance.

"Liar loans" also gave borrowers an even greater chance to obtain a loan for which they did not really qualify since little or no documentation was needed to get an approval. Thus, lenders were guilty of making loans on which most borrowers were expected to default. Taxpayers or shareholders would, ultimately, cover this cost [Nocera 2010]. The basic product strategy was, thus, to make the subprime loan with borrowers able to cover payments for the first few years due to the low teaser rates. During this period the bank could fully securitize the loan, package it, and then market it to investor institutions. When the low-interest rate initial incentive years were over and the borrower could not continue making payments the mortgage was already out of the bank's portfolio and became some other institution's problem, though numerous lawsuits and large settlements after the market collapse would bring this assumption into question.

Another financial product mortgage banks "sold" to borrowers was the notion of "investing." That is, purchasing a home or apartment as an investment could generate rental income that helped persuade target borrowers into accepting the skewed market values that would eventually implode. Most of the time the people that tried to "flip" homes were not educated on the financial aspects of flipping. Instead the lenders treated this phenomenon as an opportunity to persuade everyone that they could get rich and that housing prices would continue to escalate due to increasing demand. Unfortunately, this situation often led to mortgage defaults on rental apartments and houses by the investor-landlords with tenants ultimately facing the consequences of eviction.

As noted above, banks and other lending institutions were experiencing intense competition to sell subprime mortgages due to the profitable securitization process while the strategy to sell these products succeeded because the target market was comprised of low-income families that had never previously owned a home nor qualified for a mortgage. Banks used the notion of fulfilling the "American Dream" as their marketing ploy, even though the banks' target market customers had been unable to own a home due to poor credit. However, with their relaxed loan policies lenders could expand their product distribution by assuring these customers credit history was no longer important.

Instead, attention was focused on the income that many lied about with lender complicity. These factors passed the mortgage loan product along with few refusals. Banks were making huge reported profits from subprime mortgages and many people could now seemingly afford homes they normally never would. This Ponzi finance-based and too-good-to-be-true world had, indeed, become reality until a different reality emerged .

Pricing Strategy

A key aspect in baiting customers into signing subprime mortgages was devising a pricing strategy or the element of marketing decision making comprising methods of setting profitable and justifiable prices [Boone & Kurtz 2013]. Lenders therefore priced their mortgages by offering an attractive initial interest rate. Offering low interest rates on a mortgage for the first few years gave applicants a false hope of security. Realistically, however, even if a subprime borrower could afford the initial payments, the hope of eventually being "in a better place" to afford the home vanished. That is, once the mortgage payments increased due to the interest rate increases, this illusion evaporated into thin air.

Essentially, this set-up was a time bomb waiting to explode in the borrowers face since most subprime borrowers knew eventually they would not be able to pay back their loans. However, they hoped that they might win the lottery, get a promotion, or more importantly that housing prices would continue rising, so they could refinance or sell at a profit. Yet it all worked for lenders such as WaMu and is why they continued lending to borrowers without proper documentation that were only working temporarily or not at all so they could buy a $250,000 home they could not afford in the first place. This was done through pricing these loans so customers could actually afford to pay the first few years, but once the market rate began increasing most borrowers had a surge in their monthly payment and many had no choice but to default and be foreclosed.

This was done knowingly since customers were targeted based on credit histories that told banks exactly what these targeted borrowers could temporarily afford. Technically, the banks considered these subprime loans as helpful in getting more Americans inside a home even if the borrowers could afford it only temporarily. This view gave customers the opportunity to purchase the home using a subprime loan with the hope that even "flipping" the house or refinancing would become an option given increasing housing prices. Many banks used these ideas as a strategy to get people to borrow and invest.

Banks were very creative with their promotional strategies, which refer to the element of marketing that involves determining the appropriate activities to communicate effectively with the target market [Boone & Kurtz 2013]. This was exemplified by the use of several different mediums, such as e-mail, flyers, commercials, telemarketing, and sales associates. The promotion strategy elements that are discussed next thus comprised advertising, sales promotion, personal selling, direct marketing, public relations and publicity.

Advertising strategy entails the use of paid, non-personal communication by an identified sponsor employing broadcast, print or interactive media. Citigroup ran the "Live Richly" campaign that advertised borrowing against the roof over your head as a means of entitlement [Story 2008]. Other promotional slogans, such as "Is your mortgage squeezing your wallet? Squeeze Back!!" [Story 2008] was employed by Fleet Bank that is now part of Bank of America. These promotions tried to get people to refinance their homes. However, the primary moneymaker for financial institutions remained new homeowners.

The promotional strategy for these customers was to have them feel time pressure due to increasing housing prices. Thus, the objective was to use fear to appeal to potential applicants that they would be missing-out on a terrific opportunity to own a home or make a tidy profit by investing as home prices and interest rates would be increasing shortly. Across the US, publicity was a-buzz about the new opportunities for homebuyers, but there was urgency to act fast before prices and/or interest rates rose further. Many people found that the promotions helped them to emotionally connect with the "American Dream" of owning a home. Indeed the media made these opportunities seem as though it was the best time ever to buy a home. This combined with the teaser rate loan pricing strategy to make these loans seem affordable and bait borrowers into signing and buying.

FinishRich Media and Wells Fargo's Home Mortgage teamed-up to launch the "Great American Homeowner Challenge" campaign that promoted home ownership and how investing and owning a home would provide long term financial stability and even long term financial success. Exhibit 5 shows this particular advertisement that was sent via email to the target market.

As noted above typically minorities were targeted due to their emotional attachment to success and building a life in the US for their families combined with the fact they generally could not understand the documents they were signing or the financial obligations they were actually assuming. The American dream baited these people to this country and now that same premise would bait them into a subprime mortgage [Friar, Abromowitz, Bodaken, Egan, Green, Halliday, & Kelley 2011]. Other promotional strategies lenders employed included the initial competitive rates that were never before offered to such borrowers. This group had never before had the opportunity to obtain a home loan and by offering it at a special low initial APR with 3 to 5 years of low payments, many people fell prey to these deceiving promotions.

"Seize Your Someday" was Wells Fargo's advertising campaign designed to encourage people to own a home [Chubak, Kaminski, & O'Connell 2007]. These advertising strategies were created to help the target market associate borrowing with their emotions and dreams of owning a home. Many banks even linked the "American Dream" slogan with their increasingly easy ways for borrowers to apply and be approved for a loan. These slogans made the target market feel like owning a home was easy and affordable through promoting low or no down payment plans with very low initial payments.

JPMorgan Chase ran an ad that promoted "sign and simple" as a way to be approved quickly. The ad [Exhibit 6] made people think the only difference between renting and owning a home was paper work and a signature. This fallacy baited borrowers over and over again. The American dream home with a white picket fence and a wicker doormat were pictured in many different campaigns. This particular JPMorgan Chase advertisement pictures the mortgage broker with a brick home with white windows and shrubbery behind him. Unfortunately, these types of ads targeted the low-income and minimally educated individuals with poor credit. "Remember way back in kindergarten when you learned to write your name? It's payoff time!" This ad indicates that the target audience only needed a primary school education. It clearly does not say "Put your algebra skills to the test" or indicate a high school or college education was required.

Also, notice the phrase "Sign your name and let us do the rest" reassures potential borrowers they can trust the bank and do not need to know what they are signing. Rather the result will be making payments to own a home. Further, "low-documentation" reassures borrowers that if even if one has poor credit or a low-income there is a good chance it will be overlooked. This is printed on the advertisement to alleviate any hesitation people might have for not being approved and wasting their time. This ad was sent to the target market by flyers, e-mail and snail mail.

Bank of America ran an ad [Exhibit 7] called "Save This Tree." It simply states, "Get a mortgage with 80% less paperwork." Again, the idea was to encourage customers in the bank's target market that were financially illiterate that home borrowing was very easy.

Another ad [Exhibit 8] indicates that buying a new home is so easy one only needs give up the daily cup of coffee. By conveying the message to borrowers that owning a home will only take a small sacrifice is of course deceiving and was created for the same minority, financially illiterate target mortgage market. The coffee cup, in fine print, reads "low interest rate and low money down." Given this promotional assault, it was only natural that many potential borrowers began to believe owning a home really was very easy and only required minimal monthly payments especially if others in the community were doing it.

Ads such as these made the target market believe owning a

home and finally living the American dream was very attainable. It also stimulated demand that kept prices rising adding to the home owning incentives. Despite a poor past credit history and low-income brackets many felt those factors could finally be overlooked. Logical reasoning disappeared [indicating a bubble] and many borrowers signed mortgages without knowing anything about what they had just done. Being able to move into a new home was an emotional high and the heartrending nightmare of foreclosure was never considered.

Sales Promotion Strategies are marketing incentives that are provided to ultimate buyers on a short-term basis for stimulating quick purchases. Borrowers were therefore given promotional incentives to get them to act quickly such as an e-mail that Bank of America sent to customers fitting the target market for subprime loans: Congratulations! You have been selected and pre-approved for a housing loan. To inquire please call 1800******* or click the link below to set up an appointment with a Bank of America Mortgage specialist [Friar, Abromowitz, Bodaken, Egan, Green, Halliday, & Kelley 2011].

Such e-mail promotions created many mortgage sales because these borrowers were already Bank of America customers. Research found customers trusted their current financial institution more compared to ads and promotions from other institutions [Coulton, Chan, Schramm, & Mikelbank 2008]. Also, lending institutions would offer sales incentives like no or low interest payments or additional discounts such as lower or no closing costs if the borrower mentioned the ad when they went to sign for the mortgage.

JPMorgan Chase had a similar approach calling their customers that had a credit card and were within the target market demographics. JPMorgan Chase representatives would particularly call customers who made a recent full payment on their credit card [Fisher 2009]. They then would congratulate them for becoming more financially stable and offer them the opportunity to be approved for a mortgage or set-up an appointment for the customer to get more information.

These promotions made consumers feel as though their bank was monitoring their credit history and, therefore, the consumers felt that if the bank was offering this opportunity then they deserved it. Many consumers signed on the premise their own bank would not offer them this opportunity if the bank did not believe they could afford it.

A Personal Selling Strategy is when a seller's promotional presentation is conducted through a personal contact with the buyer. Such personal selling played a key role in marketing subprime mortgages. For instance, playing the role of missionary salespeople, tellers at the bank counter would flag customers for selling a mortgage. On routine visits tellers could identify these target market customers and would refer them to a mortgage specialist for further consultation and promotion. During these meetings with customers, mortgage specialists would then use the fear appeals described earlier that would evoke a sense of urgency to buy a home given that market values were still increasing. This gave many applicants the belief that there were limited opportunities for wealth creation. Thus refinancing in addition to homeownership should be considered. Further, these scare tactics reminded potential applicants that they should make a quick decision lest they miss this one-time, limited opportunity of profiting by procuring a low-cost loan.

Interestingly even though the boom in the housing market created a frenzy that was contagious, many borrowers were still reluctant to commit to a loan. Mostly this reluctance was due to a lack of financial education and a sense of intimidation owing to the financial jargon that mortgage specialists were using. To alleviate these borrower concerns, many banks would have mortgages brokers make deals for these borrowers and complete the paperwork because the banks themselves were not always sure exactly what they were selling. The opportunities for fraud and abuse were thus magnified.

A Direct Marketing Strategy uses promotion activities aimed at obtaining a direct response and was most commonly tried on a location and demographic basis. Some banks even purchased telemarketing scripts to call customers and ease them into understanding what the promotions were about and how easy it would be for them to attain a mortgage [Exhibit 9]. Best Rate Referrals is a company that sold the banks telemarketing scripts for the telemarketers to pitch targeted loans [Mazzagetti 1997]. These telemarketing scripts helped to target specific customers for specific loans. The telemarketer had a list of frequently asked questions and answers that were rehearsed to assure the customer felt knowledgeable about the product by the end of the conversation. The call was made to people regarding whom the lender already had information such as name, age, residence/address, phone number and spending patterns. This data was then used to help decide which scripts would be most appropriate.

By using this personal information, the telemarketer made the customer feel as though they were being monitored and the bank would like to offer them a unique opportunity based on their credit history or lack thereof.

Other customers fell prey to the incentives and promotions offered by the different banks and advertised through the Internet, direct mail, telemarketing, e-mail, as well as door-to-door sales. In a similar vein, JPMorgan Chase had a promotion where customers could bring a flyer or ad from another bank that they would match [Mazzagetti 1997]. The banks were quite knowledgeable on which approaches were most likely to reach their consumers. As previously noted, to aggressively market subprime loans, consumers were often phone-called, were visited by salespeople or were approached by a mortgage specialist during a routine bank visit. Aside from advertising in newsprint and magazines, these people needed to be assured their poor credit and low incomes would not be an obstacle to getting a loan.

This is because unless the ad indicated minimal paperwork

as shown in Exhibit 6 many would just assume they could not be approved for a mortgage and would ignore the e-mails and flyers.

The lenders' Public Relations Strategies were communications meant to generate goodwill and confidence among their various stakeholders (customers, community, resellers, investors, government, shareholders, regulators and employees). They can be effective in generating firm promotion. Leading public relations firms also helped promote the American dream through getting a mortgage. "All Americans have the right to own a home" [Coulton, Chan, Schramm, & Mikelbank 2008] these companies touted. The low-income and financially uneducated identified with these statements since they had been studied and were determined to have an emotional connection to owning their own home [Coulton, Chan, Schramm, & Mikelbank 2008]. Factors that contributed to this emotional response were exploited to encourage prospective homebuyers to be unconcerned with the financial aspects and to only worry about meeting the low initial monthly payment obligation. But when the monthly payment increased and people could no longer afford their home then the crisis began with the lenders' servicing arms becoming aggressive and unsympathetic and thus starting the foreclosure crisis.

However, before this reality took hold, public relations groups portrayed their principal banks as being benevolent and altruistic by using innovative financial products to help people afford their own homes. However, after a customer assumed a loan, the lender would profit not only from the high upfront fees on the subprime mortgages, but would package and securitize them and then sell the pool to investors for a quick profit, effectively deceiving both sides of the transaction. Borrowers believed banks would not give them a mortgage that they could not afford and investors were uncertain of the risks associated with the CMOs due to their complexity. Yet, after the CMOs were sold to other institutions, the risk was seemingly gone for the banks and they could continue to market more mortgages, increasing profits and executive pay. However the true risks remained and grew in the system [Chapter 7] for which the regulators were ultimately responsible.

During the boom Publicity and local public relations regarding the housing market were mostly positive. Banks were praised for helping more Americans to own a home. Further shareholders were happy because the banks appeared to be profiting from the CMO sales. Indeed everyone in the homebuyer mortgage creation chain was competing to get a piece of the pie or to expand what they already had.

Like Lereah [2005], who helped increase the publicity for the profit–making opportunity from real estate with his popular book "Are You Missing The Real Estate Boom?", many other financial gurus similarly provided free publicity for mortgage institutions by exhorting that more people could become wealthy if they invested in and took advantage of the increases in housing values.

Financial gurus on talk shows, news programs, and financial news programs, claimed this was the time to buy a home. Thus, owing to this positive publicity many people's fear of failure was alleviated. Without the public doing any due diligence regarding mortgages or mortgage based securities, it seemed as if the housing market was a sure bet, a clear signal of the developing bubble.

Distribution Strategy

This strategy is the element of the marketing decision making process comprising the firm's activities plus the reselling institutions that are involved in getting products or services to the firm's target market. It thus plays a pivotal role in organizational success. It comprises intermediaries organized and managed by the firm such as retailers, agents, and brokers, while the marketing channel refers to the route, path or conduit through which the goods or services flow as they move from the manufacturer to the ultimate user of the product or service [Rosenbloom, Larsen & Mehta 1997 and Rosenbloom 2012].

Each lending firm differed in its mortgage lending strategy. Some chose to make loans directly while others went through brokers and intermediaries. Some used both in order to maximize securitization throughput. Bank of America, for example, had their own direct marketing channel that used their own internal data-bases to identify customers to whom subprime loans would be marketed that had low-income, high risk credit card spending, plus monthly payments on cars, but were renting apartments

[Fisher 2009]. Once customers most likely to enter a subprime loan were identified, Bank of America then sent e-mails to them with mortgage application incentives, such as low or no down payment and no interest for the first few months as a promotion for a loan. The e-mails would contain catchy subject lines that would get people to open the message and read more. Other lenders used similar approaches since it was easy to trace customer interest by discerning whether the e-mail was opened or deleted. Exhibit 5 shows an ad from Wells Fargo that contains many catchy slogans and incentives to encourage people to apply for a mortgage and buy a home.

Pay per click marketing research was also conducted to determine which websites the target market used most frequently. Then banks would advertise on those websites that would likely yield the best results. This direct distribution strategy helped save costs and targeted the customers most likely to assume such mortgages. To expand their reach, lending institutions also indirectly marketed their sub-prime loans through reseller intermediaries, such as agents and brokers, who were well educated and well versed on the product and service they were selling.

These intermediaries facilitated loans between borrowers and banks and helped to increase the system's lending capacity. Peoples Mortgage (www.peoplesmortgage.com), for example, is a company that finds all the different loan options for which a person qualifies and then helps them to decide which offer best suits the customer. Such intermediaries were able to persuade many potential customers to sign a mortgage using incentives like "No down payment."

Some door-to-door salesmen would even ask the family "What can you afford to pay?" and would then try to tailor a mortgage plan to fit the family's needs for the first few months [Fisher 2009]. When Hispanics were the target market the brokers spoke Spanish. Thus, many potential customers grew relaxed with the idea of someone meeting them to discuss borrowing and buying a home and putting to rest their uncertainties.

Reseller intermediaries were also equipped with scripts of what questions to ask as well as how to answer customer questions. Exhibit 9 shows how conversations were scripted for telemarketers contacting potential borrowers. Questions customers might ask were anticipated and then were answered via the script. In this way reseller institutions were able to indirectly make subprime loans and profit from the boom.

In addition to using the Internet and telemarketing to call particular groups, other strategies were devised on how to best reach them. Low-income families did not always have access to e-mail marketing or advertising. Therefore, some banks chose to send a mortgage broker to their residence for a door-to-door promotion. The personal interaction with a broker or agent helped make people feel more comfortable in signing a mortgage. What's more, many banks used such agents and brokers to work within the bank to make offers to customers when they visited the bank for other business.

In this way, companies of all types surfaced and tried to reap financial success while also contributing to the housing mania. Facilitating companies, such as Claritas and Best Rate Referrals, would sell mortgage brokers telemarketing scripts [Fisher 2009]. They also sold prospective customer lists, which contained data on recent home sales, dates of sale, current market values, loan amounts, interest rates, credit scores, foreclosure status, customer names, and addresses including email. Banks would then give this information to their internal salespersons for marketing mortgage loans.

Still the Internet strongly contributed to the initial success in subprime mortgage lending. Pay per click, social media marketing, display advertising, email marketing, and online banking ads were the most commonly used Internet marketing tactics. Lenders and intermediaries, alike, were well aware of social media outlets that could help create a buzz and help sell sub-prime mortgages. Exhibits 7 and 10 show examples of Bank of America and HSBC's advertisements that appeared on Facebook and other social media sites.

Conclusion

The immense marketing campaign launched by lenders played a large part in the subprime mortgage boom and subsequent meltdown. The target market included people with low-incomes that were financially uneducated and had a poor or no credit history. It typically consisted of many minorities eager for a mortgage since traditionally they did not have assets and would not be approved for a traditional prime mortgage. Yet, CMOs enabled banks to profit enormously from such lending, at least in the short run.

Once a bank loaned the money they could bundle and sell the obligations to other institutions and seemingly avoid the associated but unidentified risks. Over this time period the banks seemed to profit greatly and more Americans owned homes than ever before. Evidently the banks and other mortgage institutions were successful in employing ingenious marketing tools to continue this profitable activity. But eventually the absence of borrower background checks began to show through increasing defaults and foreclosures. This culminated in the collapse of the housing bubble during which home values began to plummet and many mortgage-holders who did not default on loans fell underwater as their home-asset was worth less than they owed.

Many blame these misleading marketing campaigns for the housing and subprime mortgage boom and bust while others blame borrowers who should never have been persuaded to take on a mortgage in the first place. Yet the marketing campaigns by lenders prior to the 2008 crisis were truly remarkable and bear many similarities to how other bubble assets have been marketed during other boom periods including Japanese real estate in the 1980s, Internet stocks in the 1990s, trust units in the 1920s, shares in the South Sea Company in 1720 or tulips in the 1630.

Therefore these all represent interesting areas for potential future research on the role marketing plays in such phenomena.

Exhibits

EXHIBIT 1 - Fed Funds Rate From 2004 to 2008

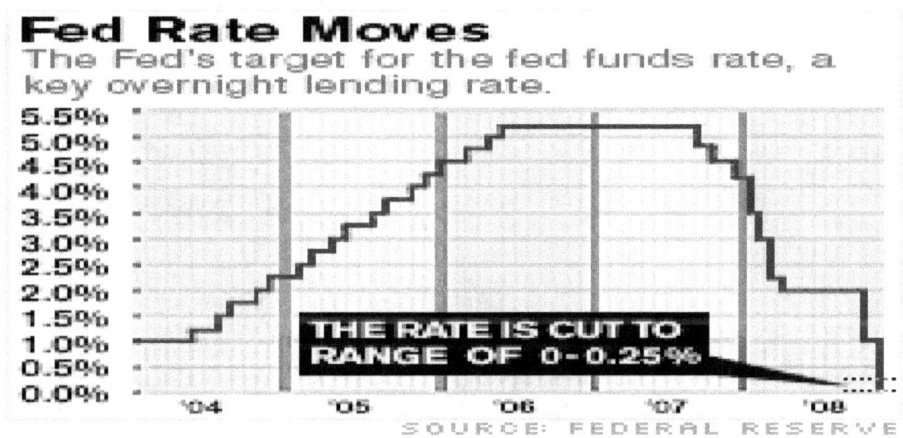

Source: Isidore, C. 2008. "Fed Slashes Key Rate to Near Zero" http://money.cnn.com/2008/12/16/news/economy/fed_decision/index.htm? postversion=2008121614.

EXHIBIT 2 - AAA Subprime Tranche Prices in 2007 and 2008

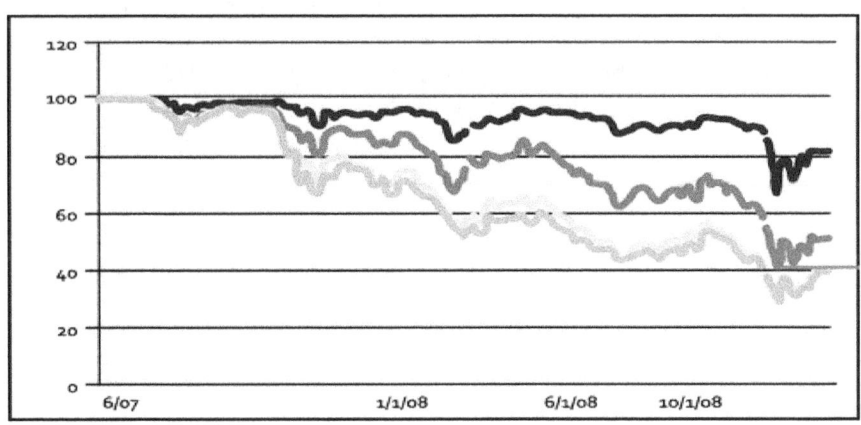

Note: Tranche prices declined severely from January 1 to October 1, 2008.
Source: Acharya, V. & Richardson, M. 2009. *Restoring Financial Stability: How to Repair a Failed System*, John Wiley & Sons, Hoboken, NJ.

EXHIBIT 3 - Comparison Calgary (Canada) and US Housing

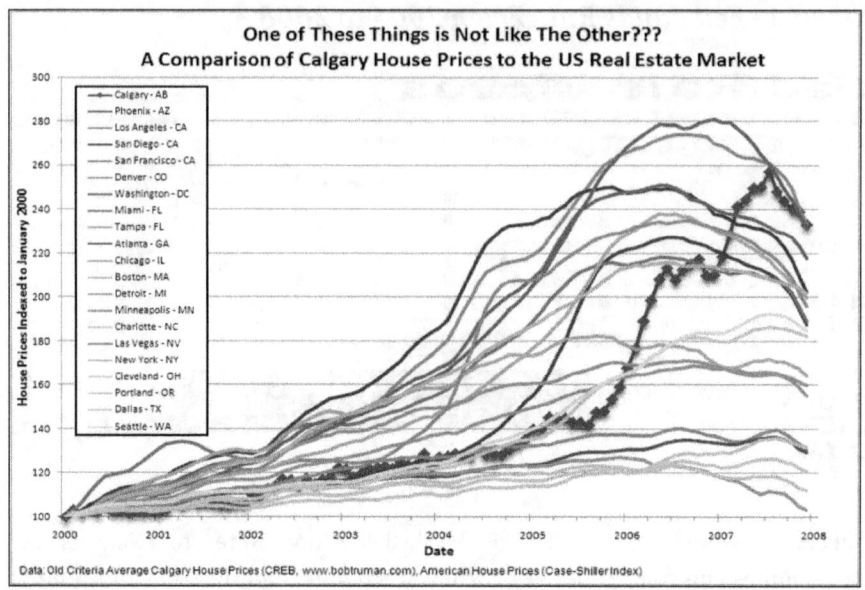

One of These Things is Not Like The Other???
A Comparison of Calgary House Prices to the US Real Estate Market

Legend:
- Calgary - AB
- Phoenix - AZ
- Los Angeles - CA
- San Diego - CA
- San Francisco - CA
- Denver - CO
- Washington - DC
- Miami - FL
- Tampa - FL
- Atlanta - GA
- Chicago - IL
- Boston - MA
- Detroit - MI
- Minneapolis - MN
- Charlotte - NC
- Las Vegas - NV
- New York - NY
- Cleveland - OH
- Portland - OR
- Dallas - TX
- Seattle - WA

Y-axis: House Prices Indexed to January 2000 (100 to 300)
X-axis: Date (2000 to 2008)

Data: Old Criteria Average Calgary House Prices (CREB, www.bobtruman.com), American House Prices (Case-Shiller Index)

Markets

Note: Although this graph compares the Calgary (Canada) housing market to the US, it is useful to see which US markets increased rapidly and those that only saw minimal increases.

Source: Jay, D. 2008. "A Comparison of Calgary House Prices to the US Real Estate Market," http://calgaryrealestatemarketblog.wordpress.com/2008/02/27/a-comparison-of-calgary-house-prices-to-the-us-real-estate-market/.

EXHIBIT 4 -Bank of America's

Logoff Marketing Offer for Home Mortgages

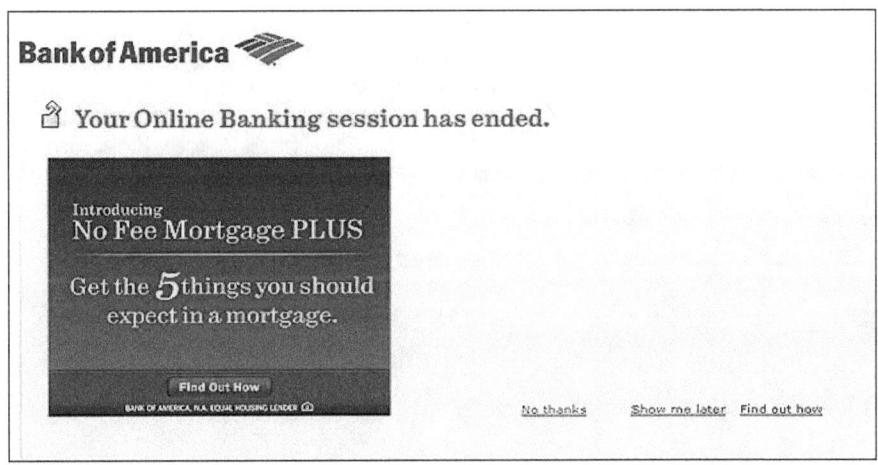

Note: As shown above, once a customer logs out of the online banking an advertisement appears with "No Fee Mortgage" and gives a link to customers to "Find out How." Also known as a logoff marketing offer, this link sends a trigger to market analysts to know which customers clicked and which did not. Using this approach, the bank can identify customers that are somewhat interested in a mortgage.
Source: Bruene, J. 2012. "Bank of America Pitches Mortgage Refi Upon Logout," http://www.netbanker.com/loginlogoff_marketing/.

Exhibit 5 – Example of Wells Fargo Bank's "Great American Homeowner Challenge" Advertisement Campaign

Wells Fargo Home Mortgage

FinishRich Media and Wells Fargo Home Mortgage have come together to launch a financial literacy campaign to educate millions of Americans about the lifelong benefits of homeownership. In March 2006, FinishRich released David Bach's newest book, The Automatic Millionaire Homeowner and launched The Great American Homeowner Challenge™. This multi-faceted, 3-year initiative is designed to help more Americans become homeowners, own investment properties and learn how to manage the equity in their home as an asset they can use to achieve their long-term financial goals. Click here for more info.

Note: Wells Fargo's e-mail advertising slogan used prior to the housing collapse used the sound-bite "Automatic Millionaire Homeowner," which also appeared on Facebook, a social media website.

Source: Levine, Y. 2012. "Recovered History: Wall Street-Funded Self Help Propaganda Greased the Real Estate Bubble," http://shameproject.com /report/recovered-history-selfhelp-propaganda-helped-banks-grease-real-estate-bubble/.

EXHIBIT 6 - An Example of a JPMorgan Chase Advertisement for Home Mortgages

Note: The ad above demonstrates how many banks would deceive customers into believing that signing for a mortgage was very easy. "Minimal paperwork," and "Simply sign by stopping in" are buzz words used to give people a sense of quickness and ease to go along with the competitive housing market and time being critical to owning a home while the market value is still increasing.
Source: O'Dell, J. 2009. "Want a Bank Loan, Just Sign Here!," http://www.nevadacounty.com/want-a-bank-loan-just-sign-here/.

Exhibit 7 – An Example of Bank of America's "Save this Tree" Advertisement Campaign

Note: Bank of America used ecological appeals in marketing home loans by adopting the sound-bite "Save This Tree."
Source: http://www.facebook.com/

EXHIBIT 8 - Example of An Advertisement For Quadrant Homes

Note: The advertisement for Quadrant homes uses the "Use your coffee budget to move into a new home," which shows the target market how easy and inexpensive it is to own a home.

Source: Timiraos, N. 2008. "U.S.-Backed Mortgage Program Fuels Risks: FHA Struggles To Eliminate Loans For Zero Down," http://online.wsj.com/article /SB12142668167 8998589.html

Exhibit 9 *An Example Of A Telemarketing Script Used For Selling Mortgages*

"Hello Mr. _____:

My name is _____ and I am calling from "Name of <u>Lending Institution</u>."

We would like to extend you an opportunity to be a part of our bank and offer you a mortgage with no money down.

Are you still at _____ address<u>?</u>

Have you ever explored the opportunity of owning a home?

What are your main concerns?

Can we send a representative to your current residence to go over a potential new residence for you to own?

Source: "Telemarketing Mortgage Scripts" http://www. bestratereferrals. com/consulting.html.

EXHIBIT 10 - Example HBSC Bank's Home Loan Advertisement

Source: "17 Banks Being Sued By The FHFA Over Shoddy Mortgages" http://www.forbes.com/ pictures/ffdj45egki/hsbc-north-america/.

EXHIBIT 11 - A Mortgage Now Advertisement, Yes Guaranteed!

References

Board of Governors of the Federal Reserve System. 2011. "Community Reinvestment Act," http://www.federalreserve.gov/communitydev/cra_about.htm.

Board of Governors of the Federal Reserve System. 2013. "Open Market Operations," http://www.federalreserve.gov/monetarypolicy/openmarket.htm.

Boone, L. & Kurtz, D. *Contemporary Marketing,* 16th Edition (South-Western/ CENGAGE Learning 2013).

Carr, J. and Kolluri, L. 2001. "Predatory Lending: An Overview." Fannie Mae Foundation. Washington, DC; http://www.knowledgeplex.org/kp/text_document_summary/article/relfiles/hot_topics/Carr-Kolluri.pdf.

Chubak, D., Kaminski, P., & O'Connell, S. 2007. "Surviving-and Prevailing- in the US Subprime-Mortgage Market," http://www.mckinseyquarterly.com/Survivingand_prevailingin_the_US_subprime-mortgage_market_2014.

Claritas P$YCLE Segmentations System. http://www.claritas.com/MyBestSegments/Default.jsp?ID=80&pageName=Learn%2B More&menuOption=learnmore.

Coulton, C., Chan, T., Schramm, M., & Mikelbank, K. 2008. "Pathways to Foreclosure: A Longitudinal Study of Mortgage Loans, Cleveland and Cuyahoga County, 2005-2008," http://www.neighborhoodindicators.com/sites/default/files/publications /coulton_-_pathways_to_foreclosure_6_23.pdf.

Farlex, Free Dictionary. 2013. "Definition of Liar Loan" http://financial-dictionary.thefreedictionary.com/Liar+Loan.

Fannie Mae. 2013."Company Overview," http://www.fanniemae.com/portal/about-us/company-overview/about-fm.html.

Fisher, L. 2009. "Target Marketing of Subprime Loans: Racialized Consumer Fraud, and Reverse Redlining," *Journal of Law and Policy*, 18 (1), 121-156; http://www.brooklaw.edu/~/media/PDF/LawJournals/JLP_PDF/jlp_vol18i.ashx.

Foote, C., Gerardi, K. & Willen, P. 2012. "Why Did So Many People Make So Many Ex Post Bad Decisions? The Causes of the Foreclosure Crisis," *Public Policy Discussion Papers*, Federal Reserve Bank of Boston, 12 (2), 1-61, http://www.bostonfed.org/economic/ppdp/2012/ppdp 1202.pdf.

Freddie Mac. 2013. "Company Overview," http://www.freddiemac.com/corporate/company_profile/our_business/index.html.

Friar, M., Abromowitz, D., Bodaken, M., Egan, C., Green, R., Halliday, T., & Kelley, B. 2011. "A Responsible Market for Housing Finance: A Progressive Plan to Reform the U.S. Secondary Market for Residential Mortgages," http://www.americanprogress.org/issues/housing/report/2011/01/27/8929/a-responsible-market-for-housing-finance/.

Gandel, S. 2011. "How Much Has Osama bin Laden Cost the US?," http://curiouscapitalist. blogs.time.com/2011/05/03/how-much-has-osama-bin-laden-cost-the-us/.

Goldstein, D. & Hall, K. 2008. "Private Sector Loans, Not Fannie or Freddie, Triggered Crisis," http://www.mcclatchydc.com/2008/10/12/53802/private-sector-loans-not-fannie.html#ixzz12xTyWY91A.

Ifill, G. & Jones, D. 2003. "Federal Reserve Rate Cut," *PBS Newshour Transcript*, http://www.pbs.org/newshour/bb/business/jan-june03/fed_06-25.html.

Investopedia. 2013. "Alternative Mortgage Transaction Parity Act," http://www. investopedia.com/terms/a/alternative-mortgage-transaction-parity-act-amtpa.asp.

Investopedia #2. 2013. "Comparing a Fixed Rate With a Variable Rate Loan," http://www.investopedia.com/ask/answers/07/fixed-variable.asp#axzz2CdLkqQ4Y.

Investopedia #3. 2013. "Who is to Blame for the Subprime Crisis?," http://www.investopedia.com/articles/07/subprime-blame.asp.

Kindleberger, C. & Aliber, R. 2011. *Manias, Panics and Crashes*, op. cit.

Krugman, P. 2008. "Financial Crisis Should Be at Center of Election Debate," https://www.spiegel.de/international/0,1518,543074,00.html.

Laing, J. 2005. "The Bubble's New Home," http://online.barrons.com/article/SB111905372884363176.html.

Legal Dictionary. 2013. "The Glass-Steagall Act," http://legaldictionary. thefreedictionary .com/Glass-Steagall+Act.

Lereah, D. 2005. Are You Missing the Real Estate Boom? Why Home Values and Other Real Estate Investments Will Climb Through The End of The Decade—And How to Profit From Them. Currency, Doubleday, Random House, Inc., NYC, NY.

Mazzagetti, D. 1997. "Dealing with Mortgage Loan Brokers: Legal and Practical Issues," *Banking Law Journal*, Thompson Media Group, Austin, TX.

McEdwards, C. 2011. "The Reckless Masters Of 'Economic Armageddon'?," http://business.blogs.cnn.com/2011 /05/27/reckless-masters-of-economic-armageddon/ ?iref=obinsite.

Morgenson, G. & Rosner, J. 2011. *Reckless Endangerment: How Outsized Ambition, Greed and Corruption Led to Economic Armageddon*, Times Books: Henry Holt and Company, LLC.

Morrow, R. 2011. "A Critical Analysis of the U.S Causes of the Global Financial Crisis 200-2008," www.politicalaffairs.net/a-critical-analysis-of-the-u-s-causes-of-the-global-financial-crisis-of-2007-200/, accessed March 26, 2013.

Mortgage Company Marketing Tool. 2008. http://www.intouchtoday.com/mortgage/mortgage-company-marketing-tool.php.

Neilsen. 2013. "Site Reports," http://www.claritas.com/ sitereports/Default.jsp.

Nocera, J. 2010. "The Give and Take of Liar Loans," *New York Times*, http://www.nytimes.com/2010/11/27/business/27nocera.h tml?pagewanted=all.

Peterson, R. & Krivo, L. 2009. *Race, Residence and Violent Crime: A Structure of Inequality*, University of Kansas.

Rosebloom, B., Larsen, T. & Mehta, R. 1997. "Global Marketing Channels and the Standardization Controversy," *Journal of Global Marketing*, 1997, 11.

Rosenbloom, B. 2012. *Marketing Channels: A Management View*, 8th Edition, Thomson/Southwestern, NY.

Stiglitz, J. 2010. "Build Strong Rules for Finance System," http://www.politico.com/news/ stories/0410/35636.html.

Story, L. 2008. "Home Equity Frenzy Was a Bank Ad Come True," *New York Times*, http://www.nytimes.com/2008/08/15/business/15sell.html?pagewanted=all&_r=0#.

Taylor & Francis Online. 2013. Subprime AAA Tranche. http://www. tandfonline.com/action/showPopup?citid=citart1&id=F0004&doi=10.1080/ 08913810902952903.

Timiraos, N. 2012. "Twelve Facts That May Surprise You About the Housing Bust," http://blogs.wsj.com/developments /2012/05/04/twelve-facts-that-may-surprise-you-about-the-housing-bust/.

Trulia. 2013. http://www.trulia.com/.

U.S. Department of Housing and Urban Development. 2013. "Mission," http://portal.hud.gov/hudportal/HUD?src= /about/mission.

Zillow. 2013. http://www.zillow.com/.

CHAPTER SIX

FINANCIAL ENGINEERING: EARNINGS - BALANCE SHEET MANIPULATION
EVALUATING THE RELATIONSHIP BETWEEN EARNINGS MANAGEMENT AND FINANCIAL BUBBLES

Out, damned spot! out, I say!

W. Xu   M. Ehrlich

Introduction

When Supreme Court Justice Potter Stewart was confronted with the challenge of ruling on a 1964 obscenity case, he conceded an objective definition of pornography was hard to produce, but "I know it when I see it".   Economists and academicians have treated financial bubbles the same way for most of recent history. Charles Kindleberger and Robert Aliber in their seminal work, *Manias, Panics, and Crashes: a History of Financial Crises* [2011], first published in 1978, define a bubble as "an upward price movement over an extended range that then implodes".

While the Kindleberger-Aliber definition relies on price movements that accelerate unsustainably to identify financial bubbles, this definition ignores traditional pricing theory that suggests prices are based on the present value of expected future cash flows, also known as intrinsic value.   This suggests an alternative definition that a financial bubble exists when the price of an asset exceeds its intrinsic value as determined by market fundamentals. However, financial bubbles seem to have relatively long lives and the market fundamentals that determine equilibrium pricing are unobservable.

For the analysis presented in this chapter, the two definitions are consolidated by recognizing that financial bubbles are characterized by a period of rapid and steady asset price increases followed by a sudden and sharp collapse in prices. Since asset bubbles may be based on excessive optimism, the price collapse would be consistent with a sudden updating of information that reduced expected future cash flows. In this chapter, the problem of unobservable fundamentals is side stepped by recognizing an observable financial behavior that is related to a financial manager's assessment of expected future cash flows and the market fundamentals, earnings management.

Another and even more challenging problem than recognizing a bubble through one of the above definitions but of paramount importance to market participants are the questions of "Are we in a bubble now?" and if so "What should I be doing with my financial assets?" To address these critical questions, the chapter will attempt to examine the link between earnings management and the cycle of financial bubble development.

More particularly this study aims to investigate if the discretionary accounting behavior of financial managers called earnings management is related to the bubble's cyclical development. Specifically, it investigates the dotcom bubble during three phases of the bubble cycle; the bubble up phase, the crash phase, and the post-crash normalization phase. It examines whether the behavior of financial managers as observed by their earnings management practices can provide a signal about when the market overestimates stock market growth and underestimates stock market risk during the bubble up phase; and whether companies will manipulate earnings again to buffer the shocks when a bubble bursts. It also examines if different industry sectors behave differently. Though numerous studies have been done in the distinct areas of earnings management (earnings quality) and stock market crisis, very few have explored the relationship between earnings management and financial bubbles and crashes.

Literature Review

Kwon et al (2006) empirically compared the levels of accounting conservatism between high-tech and low-tech sectors. By contrasting 2,728 high-tech firms and 984 low-tech firms during the period of 1990 to 1998, they found high-tech firms are more conservative across all their evaluation measures. However, as they also pointed out, their sample did not cover the market crash. Thus whether managements will manipulate accounting numbers to smooth earnings and to buffer earnings shocks during bad economic situations becomes an important research question.

In addition, by contrasting U.S. and Chinese IT industries during the period from 1999 through 2006, Xuand Yan [2011] found there is no sign of earnings smoothing for the US IT firms at the time of market collapse. In fact, the US IT firms tended to be more conservative, or, to take a big bath when confronting financial difficulties. However, due to data availability, this work could not able cover the pre-bubble period, and thus was unable to explore if earnings management contributed to the build up of the bubble. However, their findings do make it significant to examine whether such results can be extended to the entire range of US high-tech industries, and how the low-tech sector would react when the stock market collapses.

Several other studies have established that firms manage reported earnings to avoid earnings decreases or losses [Burgstahler & Dichev 1997]. Accounting values such as inventory costs, working capital usage, and other accruals are hard to estimate and therefore are easy to manipulate to smooth earnings so that a steady stream of small gains can be reported with no reported losses. Another study by Rangan [1998] has linked earnings management to stock price movements. In his study of seasoned equity offerings, he found that earnings management could lead the stock market to temporarily overvalue firms. In this chapter, Rangan's study is extended by developing a new link between earnings management and the evolution of financial bubbles.

Hypotheses Development

During the dot.com bubble as with earlier bubbles in Biotechnology, Computer Technology and even Railroads, the financial bubble developed most strongly in a new technology sector. This is because new technology sectors are where development of excessive optimism, market disruptions and updating of future expectations are most vulnerable. So as with previous work, this chapter's examination of bubbles and earnings management differentiates between two types of firms that are classified as either new technology (high-tech) or old technology (low-tech).

At the beginning of a financial bubble, some market participants correctly recognize the importance of the new technology and develop expectations for improving future earnings and cash flows. This leads to increasing prices and higher Price to Earnings ratios for the new technology sector's stocks. Since these firms are investing intensively in their new technology, they often adopt compensation structures that are more likely to include non-cash compensation in the form of equity grants and option participation for their management and even regular employees. This gives their executives a greater incentive to actively manage the firm's earnings because they will be rewarded by stock price increases for actions that improve earnings.

Another observed behavior of firms that have awarded large stock option compensation to management is that during the crash phase of a bubble, they will often take extreme efforts to retain management who have just discovered that compensation from previously awarded options have become worthless. The firms then frequently offer new "make up" awards of stock options at the new lower market prices and/or re-price the existing options to reduce the strike price to reflect the lower market price of the stock. Both these approaches have the perverse incentive of encouraging management to manage earnings with a downward bias once stock prices have fallen but before the option strike prices are reset since this will magnify the upside compensation benefit of any recovery.

This has been characterized as firms choosing to "take a bath" and report all of their bad news during a time when stock prices have fallen. Furthermore in calculating option prices using complex formulae increasing volatility increases the value of the options, so managers of hi-tech firms that receive large amounts of compensation in the form of stock options may actually be volatility lovers.

The management of low-tech firms will be less susceptible to such incentives to manipulate firm earnings by managing their discretionary accruals due to both their lower Price to Earnings ratio that reduces the price impact for a given level of manipulation and the reduced likelihood that management has received a large part of their compensation in the form of stock options. Reinforcing this perception there are several recent examples of hi-tech firms that have manipulated earnings to benefit management including Adelphia, Tyco International, and Worldcom and this could be a problem with "conceivably, many young fast growing" firms [Kwon et al. 2006].

From these observations the statistical study presented in this chapter consists of hypotheses for observable earnings management behaviors that are related to financial managers' recognition of the bubble phase in which the firm is operating. It also differentiates between the observable behavior of hi-tech and low-tech firms in their earnings management behavior.

H1: During the "Bubble Up Phase" firms should exhibit positive discretionary accruals that will increase reported earnings and upwardly bias stock prices.

H1A: The positive discretionary accruals during the "Bubble Up Phase" should be greater for hi-tech firms than for low-tech firms.

H2: During the "Crash Phase" firms should exhibit negative discretionary accruals that will reduce reported earnings and downwardly bias stock prices.

H2A: The negative discretionary accruals during the "Crash Phase" should be greater (more negative) for hi-tech firms than for low-tech firms.

H3: During the period where markets are behaving normally, the "Post Crash Normalization Phase", the discretionary accruals should be zero.

H4: Overall low-tech firms should be more conservative with respect to discretionary accounting accruals that will affect reported earnings than hi-tech firms.

Research Methodology and Data

To explore these research questions, discretionary accounting accruals re use as the primary earnings management measure. It is a classic measure of earnings management in the accounting literature because they are fully subject to management's decision making authority and thus can legitimately be used to manipulate accounting numbers without exposing the CEO or CFO to shareholder liability. The method used estimates discretionary accounting accruals using both a modified Jones model [Dechow et al 1995] and a modified Jones model that controls for asymmetrically timely loss recognition proxied by using the negative change in cash flows like Ball and Shivakumar [2006]. In particular, these are estimated using the following regression models by industry to calculate discretionary accruals for each of the three sub-sample periods:

Model (1)

$$TACC_{it}/TA_{it} = \alpha_1(1/TA_{it}) + \alpha_2(\Delta REV_{it} - \Delta REC_{it})/TA_{it} + \alpha_3 PPE_{it}/TA_{it} + \varepsilon\text{-}DA_{it}$$

Model (2)

$$TACC_{it}/TA_{it} = \alpha_1(1/TA_{it}) + \alpha_2(\Delta REV_{it} - \Delta REC_{it})/TA_{it} + \alpha_3 PPE_{it}/TA_{it} + \alpha_4 \Delta CFO_{it}/TA_{it} + \alpha_5 D_{LOSS} + \alpha_6 D_{LOSS}*\Delta CFO_{it}/TA_{it} + \varepsilon\text{-}DA_{it}$$

Where $TACC_{it}$ is the total accounting accruals; ΔREV_{it} is the change in sales revenues; ΔREC_{it} is the change in total accounts receivables; PPE_{it} is the total property plant equipments; ΔCFO_{it} is the change in operating cash flows; D_{LOSS} is a dummy variable that equals 1 if the change in operating cash flows is negative, 0 otherwise; and $D_{LOSS}*\Delta CFO_{it}$ is an interaction term. $\varepsilon\text{-}DA_{it}$ is the residual term of this regression, representing the estimated discretionary accounting accruals over the periods measured.

To carry out the tests, the study uses a long sample period from year 1995 through 2007 so as to include the entire dotcom bubble cycle involving the bubble up phase (period 1995-1999), crash phase (2000 to 2002), and post crash normalization phase (2003 to 2007). Furthermore, to compare the earnings management practices of high technology versus low technology firms, the study relies on the GICS classification of Standard and Poors and MSCI in preference to the more traditional measures of SIC or NAICS codes to differentiate hi-tech and low-tech firms since recent work has shown that GICS classifications are significantly better at explaining stock return co-movements [Bhojraj et al 2003].

For the purpose of this study, the high-tech (HT) sample is composed of firms within GICS economic sectors 45 (Information Technology) and 50 (Telecommunication Services). The low-tech (LT) sample is composed of firms with GICS economic sectors of 15 (Materials), 20 (Industrials), 25 (Consumer Discretionary), 30 (Consumer Staples), and 55 (Utilities).

All necessary data comes from Compustat Research Insight. The beginning sample, with 65,728 firm-year observations, then deletes all observations with incomplete data, zero assets or negative sales. The final sample is composed of 42,281 firm-year observations. The test variables are further winsorized at 1% with 0.5% on each tail. The sample distribution and descriptive statistics of selective variables are summarized in Table 1 and Figure 1.

The results from both regression models are presented in Table 1. The estimated coefficients are similar, but consistent with Ball and Shivakumar's [2006] argument, the explanation power from Model (2) is higher than the modified Jones model, Model (1), after adjusting for the asymmetrically timely loss recognition.

As shown in Table 2 and Figures 1 and 2, the observations show dramatically different earnings management patterns between HT and LT sectors during the three sub-sample periods.

The results therefore support hypotheses H1 and H1A because they show that the sample of hi-tech firms exhibits significantly positive accruals during the Bubble Up Phase and that the accruals of hi-tech firms are significantly greater than for low-tech firms.

The results also support hypotheses H2 and H2A because they show the sample of hi-tech firms exhibits significant negative accruals during the Crash Phase and that the accruals of hi-tech firms are significantly more negative than for low-tech firms.

The results show limited support for hypothesis H3 because while the estimated accruals for both hi-tech and low-tech firms in the Post Crash Normalization Phase are significantly different from zero, the difference between hi-tech and low-tech firms are insignificantly different from zero.

Finally, the usage of the GICS classification helps to

discriminate the behaviors of hi-tech and low-tech firms so that they support H4 in contrast to the results reported by Kwon et al (2006).

References

Kwon S., Yin, Q. and Han, J. 2006. "The effect of differential accounting conservatism on the "over-valuation" of high-tech firms relative to low-tech firms", *Review of Quantitative Finance and Accounting* 27.

Xu, W. and Yan, Z. 2011. "Earnings management confronting market fall – evidence from Chinese and the U.S. information technology industry", Working Paper.

TABLE 1. DESCRIPTIVE STATISTICS

		HIGH TECH	LOW TECH	
	N	3838	8976	
				Mean Diff.
PRE (1995-1999)	AVGTA	1760.698 ***	2528.907 ***	-768.209 ##
	NI	-0.138 ***	-0.021 ***	-0.117 ##
	ΔNI	-0.012 *	0.012 ***	-0.024 ##
	CFO	-0.043 ***	0.042 ***	-0.085 ##
	ΔCFO	0.002	0.010 ***	-0.008 #
	REV	1.150 ***	1.333 ***	-0.184 ##
	ΔREV	0.189 ***	0.143 ***	0.046 ##
	N	3392	6907	
				Mean Diff.
CRASH (2000-2002)	AVGTA	2280.882 ***	3075.197 ***	-794.314 ##
	NI	-0.418 ***	-0.174 ***	-0.244 ##
	ΔNI	0.028 *	0.001	0.026
	CFO	-0.117 ***	-0.006	-0.111 ##
	ΔCFO	0.022 ***	0.011 ***	0.011
	REV	0.921 ***	1.226 ***	-0.306 ##
	ΔREV	0.021 **	0.055 ***	-0.034 ##
	N	6260	12908	
				Mean Diff.
POST (2003-2007)	AVGTA	2663.039 ***	3847.980 ***	-1184.940 ##
	NI	-0.373 ***	-0.188 ***	-0.185 ##
	ΔNI	0.023 **	-0.006	0.030 ##
	CFO	-0.101 ***	-0.019 ***	-0.082 ##
	ΔCFO	0.014 ***	-0.005 **	0.018 ##
	REV	1.049 ***	1.212 ***	-0.163 ##
	ΔREV	0.115 ***	0.120 ***	-0.006

***, **, and * indicates the value is significantly different from zero at the < 1% level, <5% level, and < 10% level, respectively (two-tailed)
###, ##, and # indicates the mean values are significantly different between high-tech and low-tech groups at the < 1% level, <5% level, and < 10% level, respectively (two-tailed)

AVGTA is average total assets; NI is net income; ΔNI is change in net income; CFO is operating cash flows; ΔCFO is change in operating cash flows; REV is total sales revenue; ΔREV is change in total sales revenue. All variables are deflated by average total assets and are winsorized at 1% (top 0.5%, bottom 0.5%)

FIGURE 2. DISCRETIONARY ACCRUALS

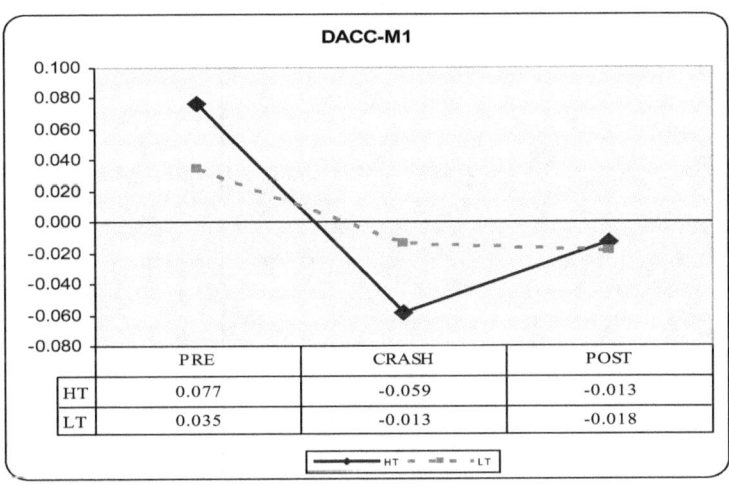

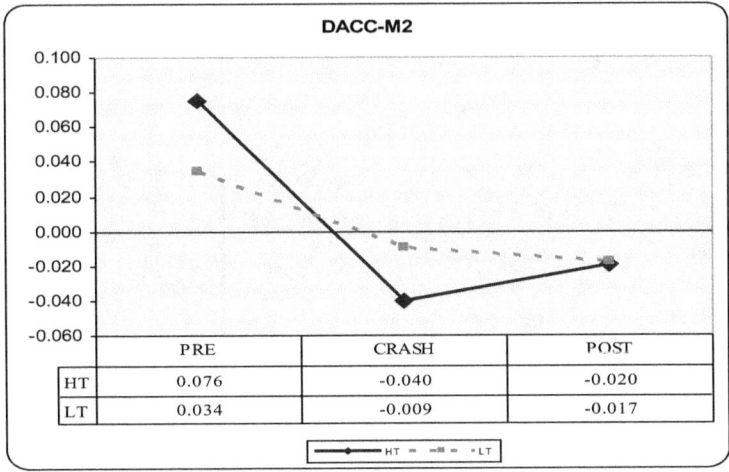

DACC-M1 and DACC-M2 are discretionary accruals estimated by regression models (1) and (2), respectively.

TABLE 2.
RESULTS FROM REGRESSION MODELS

Variables	G15 M(1)	G15 M(2)	G20 M(1)	G20 M(2)	G25 M(1)	G25 M(2)	G30 M(1)	G30 M(2)	G45 M(1)	G45 M(2)	G50 M(1)	G50 M(2)	G55 M(1)	G55 M(2)
ONE	-.381 ***	-.257 ***	-.471 ***	-.302 ***	-.518 ***	-.405 ***	-.514 ***	-.410 ***	-.590 ***	-.458 ***	-.710 ***	-.522 ***	-.573 ***	-.488 ***
$\Delta REV_{it} - \Delta REC_{it}$	.007	.000	.072 ***	.083 ***	.029 **	.037 ***	.109 ***	.148 ***	.048 ***	.061 ***	.032	.045	.088 ***	.094 ***
PPE_{it}	.097 ***	.018	-.036 *	-.108 ***	.049 **	-.095 ***	.007	-.069 *	-.166 ***	-.174 ***	.079	-.088	-.029 **	-.061 **
ΔCFO_{it}		-.855 ***		-.872 ***		-.642 ***		-.604 ***		-.636 ***		-.921 ***		-.815 ***
D_{LOSS}		.035 **		.070 ***		.039 ***		.088 ***		.045 ***		.001		.006
$D_{LOSS} * \Delta CFO_{it}$		1.669 ***		1.964 ***		1.222 ***		1.424 ***		1.328 ***		1.898 ***		1.009 ***
N	4153	4153	8948	8948	10215	10215	2948	2948	12039	12039	1451	1451	2527	2527
Adj. R^2	.360	.416	.368	.384	.352	.384	.384	.433	.398	.441	.405	.460	.786	.808

***, **, and * indicates the coefficient is significantly different from zero at the < 1% level, <5% level, and < 10% level, respectively (two-tailed)

Model (1)

$$TACC_{it} /TA_{it} = \alpha_1(1/TA_{it}) + \alpha_2(\Delta REV_{it} - \Delta REC_{it}) /TA_{it} + \alpha_3 PPE_{it} /TA_{it} + \varepsilon\text{-}DA_{it}$$

Where:

TAC_t = total accruals in year t, equals to net income less operating cash flows

TA_t = average total assets in year t

ΔREV_{it} = change in sales revenues;

ΔREC_{it} = change in total accounts receivables;

PPE_{it} = total property plant equipments;

DA_{it} = residual term of this regression, representing the estimated discretionary accruals.

Model (2)

$$TACC_{it} /TA_{it} = \alpha_1(1/TA_{it}) + \alpha_2(\Delta REV_{it} - \Delta REC_{it}) /TA_{it} + \alpha_3 PPE_{it} /TA_{it} + \alpha_4 \Delta CFO_{it}/TA_{it} + \alpha_5 D_{LOSS} + \alpha_6 D_{LOSS}*\Delta CFO_{it}/TA_{it} + \varepsilon\text{-}DA_{it}$$

Where:

ΔCFO_{it} = change in operating cash flows;

LOSS = dummy variable that equals to 1 if change in operating cash flows is negative, 0 otherwise; and

All numerical variables are deflated by average total assets and are winsorized at 1% (top 0.5%, bottom 0.5%)

TABLE 3. DISCRETIONARY ACCRUALS

		HIGH TECH	LOW TECH	
PRE (1995-1999)	N	3838	8976	
				Mean Diff.
	$DACC_{M(1)}$	0.077 ***	0.035 ***	0.042 ##
	$DACC_{M(2)}$	0.076 ***	0.034 ***	0.041 ##
CRASH (2000-2002)	N	3392	6907	
				Mean Diff.
	$DACC_{M(1)}$	-0.059 ***	-0.013 ***	-0.045 ##
	$DACC_{M(2)}$	-0.040 ***	-0.009 **	-0.031 ##
POST (2003-2007)	N	6260	12908	
				Mean Diff.
	$DACC_{M(1)}$	-0.013 **	-0.018 ***	0.006
	$DACC_{M(2)}$	-0.020 ***	-0.017 ***	-0.002

***, **, and * indicates the value is significantly different from zero at the < 1% level, <5% level, and < 10% level, respectively (two-tailed)
###, ##, and # indicates the mean values are significantly different between high-tech and low-tech groups at the < 1% level, <5% level, and < 10% level, respectively (two-tailed)

$DACC_{M(1)}$ and $DACC_{M(2)}$ are discretionary accruals estimated by regression models (1) and (2), respectively.

FIGURE 1. NET INCOME AND SALES

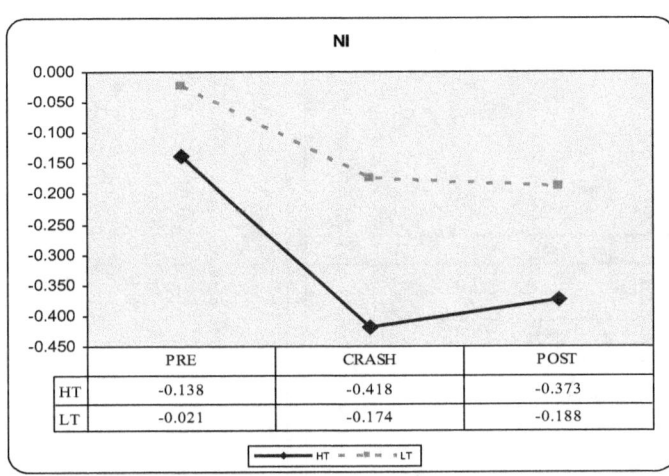

	PRE	CRASH	POST
HT	-0.138	-0.418	-0.373
LT	-0.021	-0.174	-0.188

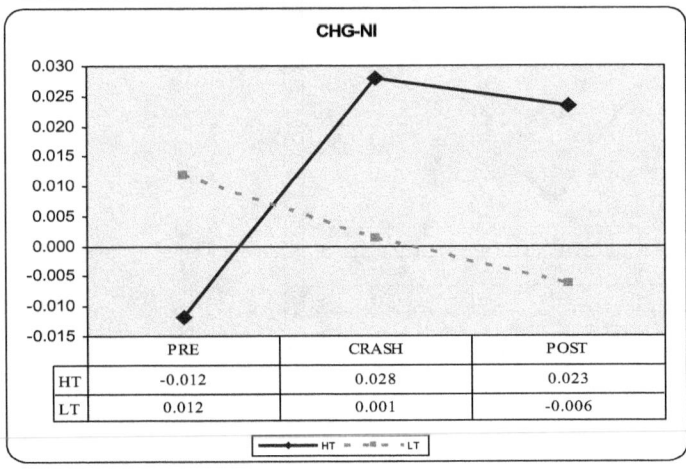

	PRE	CRASH	POST
HT	-0.012	0.028	0.023
LT	0.012	0.001	-0.006

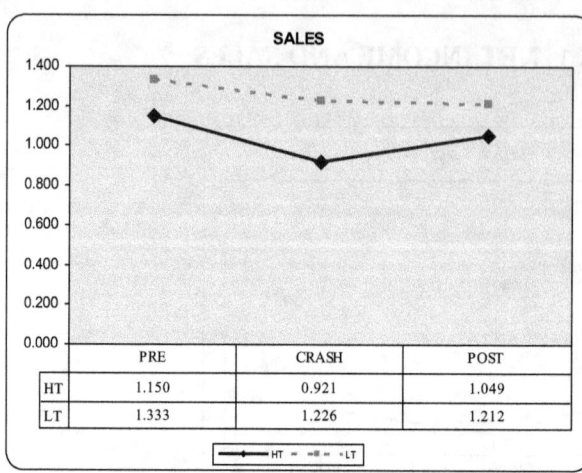

	PRE	CRASH	POST
HT	1.150	0.921	1.049
LT	1.333	1.226	1.212

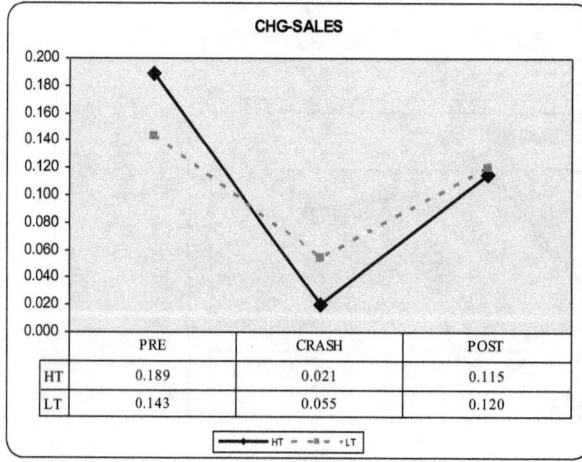

	PRE	CRASH	POST
HT	0.189	0.021	0.115
LT	0.143	0.055	0.120

CHAPTER SEVEN
STRUCTURED INVESTMENT VEHICLES
INNOVATION, REGULATION AND FINANCIAL
BUBBLES
EVOLUTION OF STRUCTURED INVESTMENT
VEHICLES

What's done cannot be undone.

M. Ehrlich   W. Rapp

Introduction

Financial bubbles, where asset prices have increased rapidly only to be followed by a subsequent crash, are as old as history. Kindleberger dates the first of "The Big 10 Financial Bubbles" as The Dutch Tulip Bubble of 1636 [Kindleberger & Aliber 2011]. Reinhart and Rogoff subtitled their book as "Eight Centuries of Folly" and refer to 12th Century China and the European Middle Ages [Reinhart & Rogoff 2009]. In this chapter, some common elements and paths that financial bubbles take are again reviewed but with the focus on the interplay of leverage, innovation and regulation as bubble enablers. It then uses the recent experience of Structured Investment Vehicles (SIVs) as a study to illustrate these points.

A Brief Tour of Some Historic Financial Bubbles

Tulips were a new import from Turkey and the Ottoman Empire around 1600 and were a luxury item popularized in still-life paintings of the time. By the 1630's several unique varietals, with distinctive coloration patterns due to infection by a tulip virus, were recognized but could only be propagated by buds formed on existing tulip bulbs. Bulbs planted in September would flower in May and then could be harvested for new buds during the summer months.

During the fall of 1636, Dutch tulip speculators began to purchase bulbs at community markets for delivery the following summer and made contracts to purchase at increasingly high prices. These were no-money-down futures contracts with neither initial or variation margin paid. Thus buyers of bulbs were using very extensive leverage in these purchases and prices skyrocketed. However by February of 1637, prices began to plummet and in late February the Dutch Parliament passed a law ruling that all futures contracts were to be considered options contracts and only required payment of 1/30th of the purchase price [Mackay 1841].

So here we have one of the earliest examples of an innovative new technology, propagating rare and unique tulip bulbs, combined with market activity and leverage to create a speculative financial bubble that burst and was followed by a government bailout with new regulations applying to existing contracts. [See Chapter 2 on Bubbles in Law.]

Another round of leverage, financial innovation and governmental policy changes sparked the famous bubble in shares of the South Sea Company. In 1711, Britain's Lord Treasurer Robert Harley needed to finance Britain's war debt with Spain and established a joint stock trading company known as the South Sea Company that would take on British debt and convert it to long-term low interest perpetuities in return for exclusive trading rights in South and Central America. The government planned to fund their perpetuity payments by charging tariffs on the goods arriving from South America even though such trade was likely to be minimal given Spain's control of their colonies' trade. Still this transaction created one of the earliest known examples of "off balance sheet" financing vehicles.

In 1719, a new round of debt to equity conversion was proposed. The British government would convert illiquid short-term debt into long-term low interest debt plus shares of the South Sea Company. With a fixed conversion price, investors were induced to participate if the share price was high. Shares were sold to politically prominent and influential investors for about £100 per share in late 1719, but they were not required to put any money down at the time. They would be able to profit when share prices rose and rise they did.

South Sea Company shares rose when Parliament passed a law to limit new joint stock companies to ones created either by an Act of Parliament or Royal Charter. With a pool of prominent investors talking the stock up and a series of rumors floated about the future value of the South American trade, South Sea Company shares traded near £1000 per share in August 1720. Unfortunately, in August the first of the installment payments became due and many investors could only afford to pay if they sold shares. Liquidity was further constrained by the collapse of the French Mississippi Company organized by John Law and shares of the South Sea Company tumbled back to the £100 level. Bankruptcy and scandal followed and many British Royals were ruined.

Financial innovation where the British government converted illiquid debt into highly leveraged tradable equity combined with the creation of new regulations regarding publicly traded stock companies and high expectations for new trading profits had created a speculative bubble in South Sea shares. In the aftermath, the estates of the directors were confiscated and bankers were vilified (Mackay 1841).

Later bubbles in the United States, including the US Railroad Speculations of the 1880's and the US Stock Market Bubble of 1927-29 exhibited many similar characteristics. Real estate booms in Japan, 1985-89, and the US, 2002-2007, were also fueled by leverage combined with waves of regulatory changes and financial innovation. In the current popular press, bubbles are frequently cited. Indeed recent references have been made to a "Golf Bubble" (Belson 2010) and an "Education Bubble" [See Chapter 1], though as explained in Chapter 1 the latter does not meet the bubble definition of a tradable asset.

Minsky Paradigm

Hyman Minsky was an American Economist who recognized financial markets were fragile and there was a natural life cycle for an economy. Minsky was a student of Joseph

Schumpeter when he got his Ph.D. in Economics at Harvard in the 1940's and Schumpeter was an expert in economic disequilibrium who understood that economic growth was based on "creative destruction" where new innovations overtook old market realities. These were frequently associated with disruptive technologies such as the railroads, electrification and the Internet. Market participants typically fail to identify bubbles as they develop because they believe "This time is different". Minsky recognized, though, there seemed to be a common critical path as markets moved from financial stability to crisis.

Minsky identified four phases of a financial bubble: Displacement, Euphoria, Overtrading, and Revulsion. Innovation is often at the heart of financial bubbles because new innovations lead to the new investments that are the initial displacements that move markets out of their steady equilibrium states. Examples include the New Tulip Varietals cited above or Emerging Markets and Frontiers like South America in the early 1700's. More recently new disruptive technologies have been catalysts that displace markets. Further new financial developments like Sub-Prime Mortgages, Credit Default Swaps, or Structured Investment Vehicles can also be market destabilizing.

These new innovations are not bad and often lead to economic growth and long-term economic productivity improvements. Furthermore many financial innovations like credit/debit cards, electronic funds transfers, and ATM machines have simplified financial dealing for many. Indeed even when bubbles induce overinvestment in promising new technologies, there may be long-term economic benefits. Today, centuries after the Tulip Mania, Holland is the world center for cut flowers, possibly due to the horticultural investments made during the 1600's.

The chaotic system of overbuilt railroads from the turn of the century are still today the lowest cost form of freight transport and the English Channel Car/Rail Tunnel, the Chunnel, is a terrific success despite having the initial company declare bankruptcy. Biotechnology overinvestment from the 1980's may have allowed the US to become the world's dominant pharmaceutical center. Overinvestment in fiber optic cable capacity during the 1990's has created the opportunity and capacity for new broadband products and Internet services.

A common element to nearly all bubbles seems to be leverage. This is where one can participate in a market without being required to pay the full investment price upfront and is seen in the examples cited above. Bubbles are built on leverage and financial innovations like derivatives are often used to create such leverage. But it is also part of the normal life cycle for people.

It would be a shame if every new young family had to wait until they had saved the full purchase price before being able to buy their first home. Leverage allows them to borrow money based on future income and use it to purchase their first house while their baby is still young. Similarly students can borrow money, using leverage to acquire an education that will allow them to earn more money in the future. It would be an unfair and less productive world if only the already rich could afford education. So we cannot say all leverage is bad, only that too much or misused and abused leverage is bad. In Minsky's terms the latter leads to Euphoria.

The forward trading in tulip bulbs, no-money-down purchases of shares in the South Sea Company and more recently the small down payment to get a subprime mortgage with low teaser rates were extreme forms of leverage. [See Chapters 4 and 5.] These transactions allowed market participants to bid up prices without requiring any resources upfront and exposing leveraged lenders to all the downside price risk.

Typically market participants develop future expectations based on recent observations, so with new innovations leading to new investments and increasing prices, they predict future price increases. With strong expectations of future price increases, it only makes sense to buy now and the incremental purchases become self-fulfilling with the new purchases driving prices still higher. Extreme leverage eliminates the constraint of current resources and euphoric price increases result.

Stock speculation leading to euphoric stock markets has often been based on extreme leverage. The 1907 Bank Panic in NYC was in part based on "bucket shop trading" where investors traded with brokers who operated like gambling bookies that took the bets on changes in share price and laid off none of the risk. They assumed that markets would go up and down normally so their trades over time would balance out. But when the markets all fell precipitously, the brokers went bankrupt and could not pay off investors or speculators as expected.

The 1929 Stock Market Crash was in part based on "margin trading" where investors could buy stocks with little or no money down. In both cases there was a severe economic contraction or recession following the bursting bubble. Then as is often the case the government responded after the fact to create new regulations to make sure that "that couldn't happen again". But new innovations will create new situations and market participants continue to believe "This time is different".

However regulations and laws passed in response to past bubbles can on occasion moderate or help manage future bubbles. The Dot.com boom and then 2001 bust is an example of this. While there was unquestionably a bubble in Internet technology companies' stocks and investors in many new Internet companies lost money, the overall economy was relatively stable and there was no immediate recession as a result of the bubble bursting due to high margin requirements and the securities laws passed in the 1930s and 40s.

It is apparent that the rapid pace of new Initial Public Offerings (IPO's) and the rapid growth of Venture Capital Funds during the late 1990's represented the Overtrading phase identified by Minsky. So why was the Revulsion and market price drop not followed by another economic contraction? One reasonable hypothesis is that the stringent stock market regulations that followed the Great Depression limited leverage so unlike 1929 the banks did not lose huge amounts of money from brokers' loans. Under Regulation T, stock investors must put up at least 50% of the stock price upfront if they want to invest and they must post additional variation margin if prices fall.

Investors in Internet technology companies thus knew that they were taking a personal investment risk and should have known not to invest more than they could afford to lose and repay. However keeping their optimism in check was the regulations that limited their debt repayment risk to no more than double their available cash. Further as prices declined brokers would be selling less stock to cover margin calls.

Hence, with extra liquidity provided by the Fed, the broader economy avoided a contraction. Unfortunately less than a decade later, the lessons of leverage were ignored and financial markets would fail again and the Great Recession of 2007-2009 would result where extreme leverage did play the major role, one form of which was SIVs.[57]

Structured Investment Vehicle (SIV) Case Study 2007-09

What caused the financial system meltdown of 2007-2009? While there are many contributors, the remainder of this chapter will focus on the interplay of leverage, financial innovation, and government regulation, all of which have been

---

[57] Interestingly the Dodd-Frank legislation that represented the usual closing of the barn door after the horse is stolen government approach to the aftermath requires that both banks and borrowers decrease their leverage and put more skin [own capital] in the game.

important factors in previous bubbles and their subsequent collapse. There were many new financial innovations that played a role, including Sub-Prime Mortgages, Credit Default Swaps, Collateralized Debt Obligations, and Structured Investment Vehicles (SIV's). This analysis will focus on SIV's.

In this regard Government regulation played a critical role too, though in the run up to the crisis, it was mostly in terms of deregulation. The Gramm-Leach-Bliley Act of 1999 ended the Depression era Glass-Steagall Act, capping nearly two decades of financial market deregulation. While most 1950-1970 era mortgages were made and funded by regulated Savings and Loan Institutions, by 2005, independent and unregulated mortgage brokers were arranging most mortgages [Chapter 5]. Bankers and financial market participants were thus seeking greater freedoms to allow them to make more profits. So they convinced US political leaders that the Depression era failures could never happen again because they had learned their lessons and thus the Times were different. The results speak for themselves.

Within a short period (1985-2000) after the law was changed a blizzard of new financial innovations were created just as with the South Sea Legislation described above and in Chapter 2. While these developments included many excellent improvements that enhanced economic growth and productivity, many new financial innovations were not only unfettered by regulation but more importantly were untested by difficult market conditions. Unfortunately it is now clear that some unregulated innovations had unforeseen consequences that were disastrous for our financial system. In a process Minsky might have recognized and Aliber did, seemingly reasonable financial innovations combined and evolved into critical weaknesses for the US and global financial systems.

SIV's did not exist before 1988. Yet over the next two decades SIV assets grew to over $400 billion and at one point represented nearly 5% of the US corporate debt market. However by the end of 2009, SIV's had become virtually extinct. So what is a SIV and what happened? SIV's are offshore investment companies that are not displayed on a bank's balance sheet (off-balance-sheet- entities). Typically they are sponsored by a bank or hedge fund that manages them and take fees as profits.

They invest in complex asset-backed credit market instruments that were traditionally funded on a bank's balance sheet. This includes credit card receivables, car loans, boat loans, accounts receivable loans, inventory loans, home equity loans, and mortgages. In theory, these are high quality assets, but in practice they are illiquid and hard to value. While a bank would normally fund these assets by taking deposits, unregulated SIV's could not take deposits. Therefore they issued AAA rated asset-backed commercial paper and medium term notes. SIV sponsors earned management fees based on the difference between the interest income the assets earned and the cost of financing or interest paid on the asset-backed commercial paper they issued.

In essence, SIV's were unregulated finance companies

engaged in banking. Without regulatory oversight, though, the market could not make sure they were carefully managed and ultimately they failed. In addition because they could not take deposits and were unregulated, FDIC insurance did not cover the commercial paper investors. Therefore as soon as there was a problem, or even the rumor of a problem, the commercial paper investors withdrew their funding. This rapid funding loss is analogous to the "bank runs" that existed before deposit insurance. Prior to deposit insurance created in the 1930s as one of the legislative responses to the Great Depression, the financial system endured periodic bank panics that caused many banks to fail and for depositors to lose their money. [See the description of the Panic of 1907 in Chapter 1.]

When depositors heard that a bank might be in trouble, they lined up to withdraw their deposits to make sure they were safe. Even a mere rumor of a bank being in trouble could lead to the self-fulfilling prophesy of a bank failing. After the Great Depression and the advent of the Federal Deposit Insurance Corporation, depositors no longer feared for the safety of their funds since they knew that the U.S. Government guaranteed their deposits, so bank runs became rare. So why then were SIVs created and allowed to recreate the potential for bank runs?

The First SIV

The post WWII growth of international trade and investment created a corresponding need for international banks that could move money globally. In order to harmonize international banking regulations across countries, the Bank for International Settlements brought together governmental finance leaders to discuss the problem and to facilitate international banking standards.

During the 1980's leaders from the economically largest countries met in Basel Switzerland to establish standards that each country would adopt and their agreement became known as the Basel Accords. A core requirement of these standards was a requirement that banks maintain an equity capital ratio of at least 8 percent of their risk-weighted assets. While some assets like cash and government bonds were exempted, the requirement's goal was to maintain an equity buffer that would cushion a bank against unexpected losses so depositors and counterparties with whom they traded securities or foreign exchange would bear less risk.

By 1988, when the regulations were required to be implemented in the U.S., most US banks already met the 8 percent capital ratio standard. However one bank was different. While most US banks at the time predominantly did business in only one state, Citibank had established an international franchise and was taking deposits and making loans in many different countries. As a result, its portfolio was much more diverse than most other US banks and so regulators had allowed them to operate with a much lower capital ratio.

In 1983, Citibank only maintained 4.8 percent of total assets as equity capital. Therefore to meet the new Basel standards, they were seemingly faced with two stark choices. Either they had to raise more capital and thereby dilute the return on equity for their existing shareholders, or they had to reduce their total assets and forego profitable new loan opportunities as well as tell existing clients they could not get any new loans. Yet in 1988 Citibank found a third option. Two astute Citibank bankers, Nick Sossidis in New York and Stephen Partridge-Hicks in London, noticed a loophole in the Basel capital requirements and they created a new type of investment that they called a Structured Investment Vehicle (Ehrlich, Anadarajan & Chou 2009).

SIV Structure

To create a SIV, the bankers needed to establish a new type of special purpose corporation and they selected the lightly regulated and tax advantaged location of the Cayman Islands to create an off-balance sheet bankruptcy remote corporation. It was bankruptcy remote because Citibank owned only a small part of its equity. A Cayman based attorney controlled the majority. However Citibank retained management and operating control. Since the legal ownership was not Citibank, it could be left unconsolidated on Citi's balance sheet. That is it would be off-balance sheet and therefore invisible for Basel capital requirements.

The bankers could then transfer a wide variety of high quality assets from Citibank's balance sheet into the new entity. By working closely with the rating agencies, they developed parameters of diversification and overcollateralization that satisfied requirements for an AAA rating. A crucial rating agency stipulation, though, required Citibank to maintain a 100 percent liquidity support guarantee for up to 360 days for the new entity. This meant if the entity ever needed cash, they could rely on Citibank for almost a full year. In this way Citibank was acting as the backup for the SIV just as the Federal Reserve provides funding support to Citibank.

With an AAA rating in place, the SIV liabilities were considered to be of comparable risk to US Treasury Bills and could be purchased by money market funds and other conservative investors. Indeed the new SIV could issue top rated commercial paper (CP) and medium term notes (MTNs) and use the proceeds to pay Citibank for the assets that were transferred.

From an investor's perspective, the CP and MTNs with maturities of less than 360 days were secured by both the assets in the SIV and also by Citibank. So there was no need to worry about a rapid funding loss or "run on the bank" because Citibank stood behind the SIV with available cash. Further from a Basle regulatory perspective, Citibank had transformed their balance sheet exposure from secured loans (with a 100 percent risk capital weight) to a variety of corporations to a secured line of credit to their new SIV.

The value of this transaction came from the Basel loophole that exempted secured lines of credit of up to one year from any capital requirements. So in the end Citibank kept control of the assets and was able to fund them, thus keeping the earnings as management fees all without any increase in capital requirements for new assets acquired or existing assets transferred. Over time, Citibank could thus replace maturing assets, add new assets and maintain the AAA rating as long as they followed the guidelines established with the rating agencies.

The regulatory agencies were aware of the new SIVs and must have given tacit approval. In essence, the SIV transaction was a regulatory arbitrage that allowed Citibank to maintain the economics of their business in the face of new regulatory requirements. The regulators had been comfortable with the lower capital ratios for Citibank earlier and presumably still were. Citibank could manage its business in the same way it had. Since it had control in a management contract rather than direct ownership and responsibility in its agreements with the rating agencies and its liquidity backup for the SIV assets, Citi bankers managed the SIV assets using the bank's traditional lending standards to control risk.

SIV Growth

By the mid 1990's other banks like Industrial Bank of Japan and Dresdner Bank began to recognize the benefit of creating an inexpensive funding vehicle for complex asset backed loans and created their own SIV's. At this time, SIV assets were a diverse group and included car and boat loans, credit card receivables, business loans backed by accounts receivables and inventory, home equity loans and other similar type assets. While these assets were too complex to sell into traditional capital markets, when bundled and rated AAA nearly any investor could buy them. The team that created the first SIV thus left Citibank and established a non-bank entity, Gordian Knot, to manage a new SIV. This was because a non-bank manager could purchase backup lines of credit from a regulated bank and meet the requirement for a liquidity support guarantee.

By 2001, there were 10 SIV's managed by five institutions. With a growing number of participants SIV liabilities became known as asset backed commercial paper (ABCP) and a new market was established. This new market was a public good and benefited both issuers and investors. As the availability of funds grew, the demand for secured loans grew and spreads began to shrink, reducing the funding costs for corporations. At the same time, money market investors could earn returns on their AAA rated ABCP that were higher than returns from comparable Treasury Bills, improving investment returns. The only two constraints on SIV growth were the challenge of finding enough high yielding high quality assets and the increased demand for liquidity support.

The 1998 failure of the hedge fund, Long Term Capital Management (LTCM) exposed the systemic risk of the leveraged hedge fund model that was also employed by Gordian Knot and their SIV, Sigma. The SIV structure was funded by CP and MTN's that typically were 30 to 180 days to maturity, but SIV assets were 3 to 4 year average life loans. As with LTCM, there was a potential for "mark-to-market" unrealized losses that could unsettle the market and scare some CP and MTN buyers away. Under the rating agency rules, the SIV would be required to sell assets and realize losses to maintain their rating, but this could cause a liquidity spiral with "fire sale" liquidations causing more mark-to-market losses. Regulated banks would not be subject to these "bank run" style funding losses, but a non-bank SIV manager like Gordian Knot could be forced out of business.

The Gordian Knot managers, the original inventors of the SIV, again worked with the rating agencies to mitigate this risk. With a decade of operating experience that demonstrated that SIV's were profitable and very low risk, they convinced the large rating agency, Moody's, in late 1999, to allow the SIV to issue 10 year capital notes that would be junior to the commercial paper and medium term notes. They would cover about 8 percent of the SIV's value, giving them a similar capital buffer as compared to the Basel standards.

The CP and MTN's retained their top AAA ratings and the capital notes were awarded an investment grade rating of BBB. The capital notes would earn the low interbank rate of LIBOR, but would also share in the management fees earned by the SIV's, which could add another 2-3 percent. Since comparable BBB corporate bonds were only yielding LIBOR plus 1 percent, the new notes were popular with investors looking for investment grade securities with higher yields.

Innovation Shifts Incentives

The incremental addition of the innovation of SIV capital notes had some unexpected results. The benign regulatory arbitrage that supported Citibank at the outset was replaced by a ratings arbitrage that put third party investors at risk and ultimately led to the meltdown of 2007. Under the original Citibank structure, the objective was to maintain their banking practices but to avoid the new regulatory capital charges. Citibank was left in the "first loss" position of bearing the cost of initial SIV losses, so they managed the SIV assets prudentially. The adoption of the SIV model by other firms created a vibrant market for asset backed commercial paper that funded a wide range of hard to finance assets.

But with the shift to capital note it was investors that took over the "first loss" position of the SIV's and thus the SIV capital base was supplied by rating and yield focused investors that had little understanding of the SIV assets. Without the risk of losses, though, and without any "skin in the game", incentives for prudential management by a SIV manager like Citibank was eroded.

Where the original SIV model had the bank sponsor bear both the losses and the gains from the SIV assets, the banks sought SIV assets that were of high quality and low risk. The constraints the rating agencies imposed for hedging and diversification therefore did not constrain asset selection since the SIV managers were already investing very carefully. With the advent of capital notes, the SIV sponsor was now sharing some of their fees with the capital note holders and in return the capital note holders took over the "first loss" position.

Thus for SIV managers to maximize their bonus, they needed to maximize the fee income received by the bank or hedge fund. Since some fees were now going to pay the capital note holders, the incentive for such SIV managers became to increase the size of the SIV and the yield on the assets. As they looked for high yielding, highly rated assets that would fit into the SIV within the rating agency model, they quickly found sub-prime mortgage-backed securities. Even if a SIV manager believed that sub-prime mortgages were risky, they were induced to add them to their portfolios because they increased the fee income and if there were a loss, the capital note holders would bear it. Under the rating agency's new capitalization rules, many new SIV sponsors entered the market to take advantage of it and a pattern of unhealthy SIV growth emerged.

The limits to SIV growth were now no longer based on the SIV sponsor's ability to find a bank to provide liquidity support or by the manager's ability to acquire good quality high yielding assets. Rather it was now based on the ability to find investors in capital notes. Without any "skin in the game" the SIV manager was no longer a banker with a fiduciary responsibility to the bank and its depositors but was a hedge fund manager who was only interested in maximizing fee income.

They did not care about the long run view of expected return of the assets in the portfolio, only whether they fit into the rating agency model that allowed the SIV an AAA rating. While not every SIV reduced their lending standards and some traditional bank sponsored SIV's behaved prudentially, the new entrants who were predominantly hedge fund managers were prepared to "game the system" and take advantage of the rating agency rules.

In 2002 there were 16 SIV's managed by 10 institutions with less than $100 billion in total assets. By mid 2007, there were 36 SIV's and SIV hybrids that were managing nearly $400 billion in total assets. The sole focus on high yielding assets drove portfolio selection toward sub-prime mortgage backed assets. Indeed there were special SIV hybrids known as SIV-lites that exclusively invested in bundled sub-prime mortgage backed securities. The non-bank hedge fund sponsors showed little compunction to game the system and SIV growth was heading for a crash.

The rating agencies that created the rules that allowed for unhealthy SIV growth had no incentive to change their policies. By the middle of 2007 over half of their earnings came from ratings on structured products like SIV's and they were especially profitable since they earned fees every month, not just at the inception as with a typical bond issue. The rating agencies justified the ratings by their risk estimates, but their data was all backward looking and for many new products such as the new type of SIVs, the time series was relatively short.

Therefore the investors who relied on the AAA ratings had

little interest in or understanding of the underlying assets. The SIV model, which was static, might have been altered as the market shifted, but rating agency managers felt it would be unfair to change the model in midstream. The revealing part of this is that the "customers" who would be unfairly hurt by a model change were the SIV managers, not the ultimate investors and risk bearers. Errors in assessing the risk of new securities like sub-prime mortgages compounded the SIV risks, but even if sub-prime mortgages were priced correctly, there was always going to be some asset class that was mispriced and whatever was mispriced was going to be what SIV managers sought for their portfolios.

Sub-Prime Crash of 2007

In early 2007, prices in the U.S. housing market began to decline and the key assumption underlying sub-prime mortgage valuation disappeared. Sub-prime defaults began to rise rapidly as housing prices dropped. The first victims were the Bear Stearns' hedge funds that held a leveraged portfolio of sub-prime collateralized debt obligations (CDO's). These funds lost their funding in June 2007 and within a month had failed.

Sophisticated investors began to question the SIV net asset valuations. Then as the market began establishing new lower valuations for sub-prime assets, the value of SIV holdings began to fall too. A SIV's net asset value (NAV) is the amount the market value of the portfolio exceeds the senior AAA rated debt level divided by its capital, which is mostly its capital notes. Since the rating agency rules were inflexible, as NAV's fell, SIV's were forced to sell assets or raise new capital to maintain their ratings. As the SIVs' NAVs fell the rating agencies forced them to liquidate portfolio assets as new capital investments dried up. With asset sales, prices fell further and the NAV's declined again. When the CP investors saw the NAV's declining, they began to question the assets behind their ABCP and they began to withdraw from the market.

By August of 2007, there were 30 SIV's and 6 SIV-lites with $412 billion of assets. Over half of the SIV managers were hedge fund sponsors and the losses from ABCP were disproportionately related to hedge fund sponsored SIV's. Many large bank sponsors of SIV's supported their SIV's and eventually took the SIV assets back onto their own balance sheets in order to protect their reputations. For the hedge fund sponsors, taking the assets back was not an option and in any case they were less concerned about their reputations. Nevertheless it was a classic boom and crash. A financial innovation had been developed for a logical purpose and had worked well. It then attracted speculators that forced out value investors and ultimately led to a collapse.

Implications and Lessons Learned

SIV's were a newly created financial market innovation that combined leverage and regulatory relief. This innovation was facilitated by the "for-profit" rating agencies that earned substantial fees based on the assets in the SIVs. SIV investors got a false sense of security from the rating agencies. Both the liquidity and credit risk were misunderstood and mispriced. Further relying on the AAA ratings was a major mistake.

Incentives matter and the banks, hedge funds and rating agencies had their own agendas. In this case, a seemingly reasonable series of innovations combined and became toxic when they shifted the incentives for SIV managers over time. The rating agencies gave no consideration to these management incentives when issuing their ratings and their risk estimation was entirely backward looking. It was therefore primarily based on the experience of the more prudently managed bank sponsored SIVs. The hedge fund managers entered the SIV market late to take advantage of the game where they could earn fees if all went well, but would leave the capital note and CP holders with the losses if anything went wrong. Thus their experience had relatively little input into the rating agencies' models.

The public good created by the advent of SIVs and the ABCP market could not be maintained in an unregulated free market. When investors could not understand the assets behind their securities and could not differentiate between "good" ABCP and "bad" ABCP, the whole market froze and failed to work. As part of the collateral damage, banks are now less willing to lend against complex assets since they must now be maintained on their own balance sheets. Further investors are now stuck with low yielding Treasury Bills in their money market accounts that provide a very poor return on their available cash balances.

Some of the various lessons learned from this episode include:

- Beware of new products without much history.
- Look carefully at the incentives motivating the people behind the products.
- Watch out for changes in rules and regulations that can change incentives.
- Buyers must understand the regulatory environment to reduce asymmetric information.
- Regulators, including rating agencies, need to be more proactive in developing and modifying rules for new investments to maintain healthy markets and not rely on historical data when the markets generating those numbers materially change.

Litigation

While learning something from a financial crisis is certainly useful and can inform the legislation aimed at preventing another similar event in the future, it does not get one's money back and tens even hundreds of billions of dollars were lost in the recent crisis, many through investment in SIV related assets. Therefore access to the courts and the assets of anyone still standing is a logical outcome. In fact it is a common aspect after crashes and is prominently noted by Kindleberger, Aliber, and Minsky.

However since generally it was sophisticated investors and financial participants that were involved in both sides of the SIV transactions, these cases have not been easy to win unless there was a clear breach of a statute such as ERISA or a fiduciary duty of prudence and care. A brief review of some of the more prominent cases indicates what is involved and the types of parties to these disputes.

These cases cover the Bear Stearns SIVs mentioned above, Cheyne Finance, Sigma Finance, Rhinebridge, STEP and Core USA while the defendants include the major rating agencies plus major financial institutions such as JPMorgan Chase, Citibank, Bank of NY Mellon, Morgan Stanley, Northern Trust and IKB Deutsche Industriebank. The plaintiffs are also generally large financial players such as Calpers or the Abu Dhabi Commercial Bank Co.

Specific Cases

In August 2011 Fitch Ratings Ltd. settled negligence claims brought by the California Public Employees' Retirement System over ratings it gave structured investment vehicles that later collapsed. It agreed to provide Calpers with documents from a similar lawsuit pending in New York. However, under the settlement Fitch made no payment to Calpers, the biggest U.S. pension fund.

Calpers sued Fitch, Moody's Investors Service Inc. and Standard & Poors over ratings for three SIVs -- Cheyne Finance LLC, Stanfield Victoria Funding LLC and Sigma Finance Inc. in which Calpers had invested $1.3 billion. Fitch will provide Calpers with a copy of its deposition taken in February and other documents it produced in a pending investor lawsuit against Moody's and Standard & Poor's the Abu Dhabi Commercial Bank filed over the Cheyne Finance SIV.

AFTRA, Sigma and JPMorgan

According to the New York Times, a group of JPMorgan's clients, the AFTRA retirement fund, invested $500 million in one of these SIVs, Sigma. The group's lawsuit against JPMorgan alleges even though Sigma was so deeply in debt it could not afford to issue any more commercial paper, JPMorgan fed it money so it would stay afloat and keep generating fees for JPMorgan through repo transactions. The repo transactions would earn JPMorgan $2 on every $1 it invested if Sigma defaulted.

The plaintiffs argue that in the summer of 2007, as the first tremors of the coming financial crisis were being felt, top executives at JPMorgan Chase were raising red flags about a troubled investment vehicle based in London called Sigma. But the bank chose not to move out $500 million in client assets it had put in Sigma two months earlier. The lawsuit thus asserts JPMorgan profited from its collapse a year later.

According to the suit while the clients lost nearly all their money, JPMorgan collected nearly $1.9 billion from Sigma's demise because as Sigma's troubles worsened, JPMorgan lent the vehicle billions of dollars and received valuable assets as security deposits or collateral.

BNYM Securities Lending Litigation

On December 19, 2008, CompSource Oklahoma, The Children's Hospital of Philadelphia Foundation, and The Children's Hospital of Philadelphia, Individually and in its

Capacity as Fiduciary of The Children's Hospital of Philadelphia Defined Benefit Master Trust, and the Board of Trustees of the Electrical Workers Local No. 26 Pension Trust Fund, in its Capacity as Fiduciary of the Electrical Workers Local No. 26 Pension Trust Fund, on behalf of themselves and all others similarly situated filed a suit against BNY Mellon, N.A., and The Bank of New York Mellon in a United States District Court in Oklahoma.

Plaintiffs represent an alleged class of persons and entities who were participants in Defendants' securities lending program and, through one or more of the collective investments vehicles managed by Defendants or its affiliates, incurred losses relating to investments in medium-term notes of Sigma Finance, Inc. ("SFI"). The case against BNY Mellon Corp. has been voluntarily dismissed based on its representations that it was merely a holding company and not involved with the securities lending program but the one against its subsidiary remains.

Specifically, Plaintiffs seek to represent a proposed Class of persons and entities that participated in Defendants' Securities Lending Program through which Defendants invested cash collateral, either directly or through a collective investment vehicle, in one or more SFI medium-term notes ("MTNs") and continued holding those MTNs as of the close of business September 30, 2008

Plaintiffs argue that under these Securities Lending Agreements, Defendants loaned securities owned by the Class

Members to third-party borrowers and received cash collateral. But it then invested the cash collateral, at its discretion, in an effort to earn an investment return on the cash collateral in excess of the rebate paid to the third-party borrowers. As compensation, Defendants received a percentage of the revenues generated for each Class Member.

According to the Securities Lending section of BNY Mellon's website, the stated purpose for its Securities Lending Program is "...generating returns and managing risk." Given that the funds Defendants invested for Class Members consisted of collateral that was required to be returned to borrowers upon repayment of the underlying securities loans, Defendants were required to invest the cash collateral conservatively and prudently. As alleged in the Complaint, each Securities Lending Agreement (and the investment mandates for each of the collective investment funds) required Defendants, among other things, to (a) safeguard principal, (b) maintain adequate liquidity, and (c) discharge its duties with respect to the investment of the collateral with care, skill, prudence, and diligence.

Despite these clear objectives and duties, it is argued BNY Mellon invested and lost a substantial portion of the cash collateral provided to Class Members MTNs issued by SFI, a Delaware corporation organized for the sole purpose of issuing debt securities for its Cayman Islands parent company, Sigma Finance Corporation ("Sigma"). The debt securities - here MTNs - were secured only by a "floating lien" on the assets of Sigma that were subordinated to the lien interests of Sigma's other creditors.

Shortly after Defendants purchased a substantial amount of Sigma MTNs using the cash collateral held by Class Members, analysts following Sigma and other structured investment vehicles ("SIVs") like Sigma warned about the lack of liquidity in the credit market and sharp declines in the market value of assets backing many SIVs, threatening their viability.

IKB Deutsche Industriebank AG

A federal lawsuit is proceeding as the judge has rejected a German bank's request to dismiss US lawsuits accusing it of fraudulently creating a risky debt vehicle it knew was likely to default, resulting in several hundred million dollars of investor losses. The lawsuits contend that IKB sponsored the creation of a structured investment vehicle, Rhinebridge, in June 2007 to dump investment losses onto unsuspecting investors and save itself from possible bankruptcy.

The same judge has rejected requests by rating agencies Moody's Investors Service and Standard & Poor's to dismiss them as defendants. The lawsuits were filed by Washington State's King County, which includes Seattle and manages accounts for more than 100 public agencies, and the Iowa Student Loan Liquidity Corp. The German bank is also a main investor in ABACUS 2007-AC1, the synthetic collateralized debt obligation that was the subject of a US Securities and Exchange Commission fraud lawsuit against Goldman Sachs Group Inc.

In the Rhinebridge case, the plaintiffs accuse IKB of

misrepresenting Rhinebridge's risks and its "triple-A" credit ratings when it was holding risky, subprime mortgage-backed assets. They called Rhinebridge "the shortest-lived 'triple-A' investment fund in the history of corporate finance." It was wound down August 2008, costing investors 45 percent of a $1.1 billion investment. The earlier ruling is significant because it represents one of the first times a court has refused to uphold First Amendment protections for ratings assigned by a rating agency to an investment product, potentially holding the agencies responsible for losses investors suffered by relying on the rating when the rated investments quickly failed.

Abu Dhabi Commercial Bank

In 2004, Abu Dhabi Commercial Bank and King County, Washington State purchased SIVs packaged, sold and rated by the defendants Morgan Stanley and two rating agencies, Moody's and Standard & Poor's. The plaintiffs claim common law fraud, negligent misrepresentation, breach of fiduciary duty and contract, and unjust enrichment.

The plaintiffs primarily allege the defendants worked together to package and sell SIVs while knowing the ratings assigned were false and misleading. They argue SIVs especially are dependent upon high ratings because not only is the SIV itself assigned a credit rating which is supposed to convey to investors its creditworthiness, but the collateral assets underlying the SIV are also given ratings.

Because of this the plaintiffs argue they were deliberately

misled because Morgan Stanley and the rating agencies knew the SIV's underlying capital, partially comprised of residential mortgage backed securities, did not warrant a high rating.

Northern Trust

On January 29, 2010 the Chicago Teachers Pension Fund and the Atlanta City Firefighters Fund filed a class action lawsuit against Northern Trust [Kugler 2010]. The lawsuit charges Northern Trust, which had a reputation as a conservative bank, during the recent financial crisis, engaged in highly risky securities lending and lost millions of client dollars in the process. The lawsuit argues Northern Trust, instead of investing Pension Fund money in conservative investments, placed the funds at risk through investments in activities such as those that brought down the financial system in 2008. "The STEP portfolio included hundreds of millions of dollars in exotic, unregistered securities issued by "structured investment vehicles" or "SIVs" — entities that were recently identified in hearings before the congressional Financial Crisis Inquiry Commission as one of the "causes of the financial crisis" that "served no good or productive purpose in the financial system" — and millions more in securities backed by risky residential mortgages and other consumer loans.

Both STEP and Core USA held hundreds of millions of dollars of securities backed by mortgages and other consumer loans, and billions more in securities issued by banks with massive exposure to mortgages and consumer loans...." Losses to the pension funds are in the hundreds of millions of dollars. These direct losses are of course in addition to the economic costs of the accompanying stock market collapse and economic downturn now known as the Great Recession.

References

Belson, K. "Golf Bubble", *The NY Times*, 28 March 2010

Ehrlich, M.A.; Anandarajan, A.; Chou, B, "Structured Investment Vehicles : The Unintended Consequences of Financial Innovation", *Bank Accounting and Finance*, 22(6), Oct/Nov 2009

Kugler, J. 2010. "Pension Board sues Northern Trust over huge investment losses", Substance News, IL. at http://www.substancenews.net/articles.php? page=1122.

Kindleberger, C. & Aliber, R. 2011. *Manias, Panics, and Crashes*, op. cit.

Mackay, C. 2012. *Extraordinary Popular Delusions and The Madness of Crowds*, Maestro Reprints.

Ribe, Abu Dhabi Commercial Bank Co. v. Morgan Stanley & Co., Inc., No. 08 Civ. 7508, 2009 U.S. Dist. LEXIS 79607 (S.D.N.Y. Sept. 2, 2009)

Rapp, W. 2010. op. cit.

Reinhart, C. & Rogoff, 2009. *This Time is Different*, op. cit.

CHAPTER EIGHT

MODEL OF SPECULATIVE HOUSING BUBBLES

Cauldron Burn And Cauldron Bubble

P. B. Chou

Introduction

An asset bubble, such as the housing bubble, occurs when the price of the asset is higher than the level that can be sustained by the economic fundamentals. The problem of identifying a bubble in the early stage is that it may be difficult to differentiate a boom from a bubble. Prior to 2004, many researchers, such as Labonte [2003] and Himmelberg *et al.* [2005], argued that the increases in the housing prices in the US were a boom phenomenon instead of a bubble. Today, there is now a more general agreement that a housing bubble occurred in some US cities between 1997 and 2006, as discussed, for example, by Mikhed and Zemčík [2009] and Coleman *et al.* [2008]. Therefore, it is important to study the dynamic properties of housing prices when such a bubble occurs.

To address this issue, Chou [2011] has proposed a simple Cobweb model to characterize a housing bubble due to the entry of speculators with bounded rationality. He shows that the combination of the number of speculators and the expected price increase can reinforce each other and sustain a housing bubble at a new steady state as a self-fulfilling prophecy, at least for a short period of time. The model also shows that the entry of speculators can lower the fluctuations of the housing price, while the exit of the speculators will increase the volatility of the housing price.

However, the expected price increase in that simple model is *exogenous*, and has limited explanatory power about how the housing price may change during the bubble. Based on assumption that speculators have bounded or adaptive rationality, the primary goal of this chapter is to extend the original model Chou [2011] proposed by making the expected price increase *endogenous* based on past price changes. Also, because Chou in the 2011 paper focused on the theoretical implication of the model, a secondary goal of this chapter is to strengthen the linkages between the theoretical and empirical studies of housing price bubbles.

The concept of bounded or adaptive rationality is more than a convenient academic assumption about how people form expectations. Shiller [2009] argues that "people tend to confuse price levels with rates of price change." He also mentions that "Karl Case and I asked random home buyers in the U.S. cities undergoing bubbles how much they think the price of their homes will rise each year on average over the next ten years. The medium answer was sometimes 10% a year." In addition, as discussed by Capozza et al. [2004], houses are quite heterogeneous so that participants in the housing market may have difficulty in assessing the instantaneous equilibrium price for a given property. An optimal "appraisal", as discussed by Quan and Quigley [1991], may be a weighted price between the current and past transaction prices of properties with the same or similar characteristics. Therefore, some degree of adaptive expectation based on past prices is inevitable in the housing market, particularly for speculators.

The contribution of this chapter is thus twofold. First, by extending the simple model proposed by Chou [2011] using an endogenous expected price increase, this chapter characterizes the dynamic property of housing prices before the bubble, during the bubble, and after the bubble bursts. Second, the material presented in this chapter can serve as a bridge between the theoretical and empirical approaches to housing price bubbles.

Section 2 is a brief review of the original model using exogenous price changes, which is the extended in Section 3 using endogenous price changes. In Section 4, some empirical studies are presented to reinforce the linkages between the theoretical model and the econometric studies. Section 5 is a discussion of the factors that can influence the housing demand and supply functions. Section 6 concludes the chapter but indicates some possible extensions for future research.

The Original Model of Housing Prices

2.1 The Original Model using Exogenous Price Changes

From the model proposed by Chou (2011), assume there are m non-speculators and x speculators in the housing market. For the m non-speculators, the individual demand function is $q_t^d = a - b P_t$. For the x speculators, the individual demand function is

$q_t^d = a - b P_t + c$. The coefficient c is the proxy for the subjective expected price change from the speculators' perspective. When all variables are in the log form, c will represent the expected *percentage* change from period t to period $(t+1)$. For non-speculators, $c = 0$. From the horizontal aggregation, the market demand function $Q_t^d = ma - mb P_t + xa - xb P_t + xc$, with $x \geq 0$.

For the market supply curve, assume there are n sellers of houses. The quantity supplied from each seller at time t depends on the expected price, P_t^e formed in the previous period $(t - 1)$. This is because it takes time for a house to be ready for market, such as the construction time for new houses, renovation time for old houses, and the preparation time for the speculators to buy houses and put them back into the market for speculation purposes. For simplicity, assume that the expected price in period t is equal to the previous price, P_{t-1}, based on the assumption of naïve expectation, an extreme case of adaptive expectation. Therefore, the market supply function is $Q_t^s = n h P_t^e$ $= n h P_{t-1}$, where n is the total number of sellers of houses in the market, with $h > 0$. When h increases, the supply function is more elastic to the (expected) price.

2.2 The Market Equilibrium with Speculators

With x speculators in the market, $x \geq 0$, the market demand becomes $Q_t^d = ma - mb P_t + xa - xb P_t + xc$. The equilibrium price becomes $P_t = \dfrac{ma + xa + xc}{mb + xb} - \dfrac{nh}{mb + xb} P_{t-1}$. Hence, the price over time can be described by $P_t = P^* + (-\dfrac{nh}{mb + xb})^t (P_0 - P^*)$, where the equilibrium price $P^* = \dfrac{ma + xa + xc}{mb + xb + nh}$ and $P_0 = \dfrac{ma}{mb + nh}$. P_0 is the original equilibrium price level when $x = 0$, and is also assumed to be the equilibrium price that can be sustained by the economic fundamentals.

In addition, because $-\dfrac{nh}{mb + xb} < 0$, P_t will oscillate over time towards or away from P^*. If $-1 < -\dfrac{nh}{mb + xb}$, or equivalently, $\dfrac{nh}{mb + xb} < 1$, the market price will converge to P^* over time. If $\dfrac{nh}{mb + xb} = 1$, P_t will oscillate around P^* with equal distance. And P_t will diverge (explosively) if $\dfrac{nh}{mb + xb} > 1$. Therefore, the entry of speculators has two effects. First, it will increase P^* because $\dfrac{\partial P^*}{\partial x} > 0$. Second, because as x increases, $\dfrac{nh}{mb + xb}$ will become smaller. Therefore, the entry of the speculators will speed up the convergence of the market price towards a higher *new* steady state price P^*.

The Modified Model with Endogenous Price Changes

3.1 The Adaptive Expectation and Upward-Sloping Demand

Function

As c represents the speculators' expected price change from t to $t+1$, from the adaptive expectation, we assume that c depends on the reaction of speculators to the price change from period $(t$-$1)$ to period t. That is, $c = (P^e_{t+1} - P_t) = r(P_t - P_{t-1})$, where r is the reaction coefficient to the price change, with $r > 0$ for speculators, and $r = 0$ for non-speculators.

In this case, the demand curve for a speculator is $Q^d_t = a - b P_t + r(P_t - P_{t-1}) = a + (r - b) P_t - r P_{t-1}$. This implies that if P_{t-1} can be treated as a pre-determined variable or a coefficient, the demand curve for a speculator is downward sloping if $r < b$, but upward sloping if $r > b$. For reasons of simplicity, we will assume that $r > b$ in this paper.

From the theory of microeconomics, the substitution effect should cause the buyers to buy less when the price increases, which is true for both the speculators and non-speculators. However, for the income effect, it may work differently for the speculators and non-speculators.   For non-speculators, the income effect may cause consumers to buy less when housing prices increase, which is consistent with the substitution effect. This is why the demand curve for non-speculators is downward sloping.   However, for the speculators, the increase in housing prices will cause the speculators to buy more houses because the speculators perceive buying new houses as investments such that the price increase will increase the speculators' future *expected* wealth or income. When the income effect dominates the substitution effect for speculators, the demand curve is upward sloping for speculators, and this is the focus of the model.

3.2 The Three Stages When Speculators Enter The Market

From the horizontal aggregation, the market demand function is $Q_t^d = ma - mb\,P_t + xa - xb\,P_t + xr(P_t - P_{t-1}) = (ma + xa) + (xr - mb - xb)\,P_t - xr\,P_{t-1}$. It is downward sloping if $xr - mb - xb < 0$, and is upward sloping if $xr - mb - xb > 0$ or $x(r-b) > mb$. In particular, when $x(r-b) > mb$, both x and r must be sufficiently large, including the possibility that some non-speculators may either exit the market or become speculators such that m decreases as x increases.

There can be at least two stages when a housing bubble is formed. In the first stage when very few speculators enter the market such that $xr - xb < mb$, the market demand function is downward sloping. In the second stage when many over-reactive optimistic speculators enter the market such that $xr - xb > mb$, the market demand function will become upward sloping. In fact, the first stage can be further divided into two more stages. In the first stage, when there are very few speculators, $x(r - b)$, is a very small number such that $xr + x(r- b) + nh < mb$. Later, however, when more speculators enter the market, $xr + x(r- b) + nh \geq mb$, but $x(r - b) < mb$ still holds. Therefore, there are in total three stages when speculators enter the market.

Assume that the market is in equilibrium, i.e., $Q_t^d = Q_t^s$, we have $(mb+ xb--xr) P_t = - (xr+nh) P_{t-1}+ (ma+ xa)$, which can be

simplified to $P_t = -\dfrac{xr + nh}{mb + xb - xr} P_{t-1} + \dfrac{ma + xa}{mb + xb - xr}$. The solution to

the market price over time is $P_t = P^* + (-\dfrac{xr + nh}{mb + xb - xr})^t (P_0 - P^*)$,

where $P^* = \dfrac{ma + xa}{mb + xb + nh}$ and $P_0 = \dfrac{ma}{mb + nh}$. The price P_0 is the

initial equilibrium price when $x = 0$. P_0 is assumed to be the

price level that can be sustained by the economic fundamentals.

Also, as $\dfrac{\partial P^*}{\partial x} > 0$, the entry of speculators will drive up the

equilibrium price.

As for the converging or the diverging path of housing

prices, it is more complicated because there are three stages

when the bubble is formed. In the first two stages when $xr - xb <$

$mb, -\dfrac{xr + nh}{mb + xb - xr} < 0$, the implication is that P_t over time will

oscillate on the convergent or divergent path. If $\dfrac{xr + nh}{mb + xb - xr} < 1$,

the market price will converge to P^* over time. If $\dfrac{xr + nh}{mb + xb - xr} = 1$,

P_t will oscillate around P^* with equal distance. And P_t will

diverge (explosively) if $\dfrac{xr + nh}{mb + xb - xr} > 1$.

3.3 The First Stage – Very Few Speculators

When there are very few speculators, $\dfrac{xr + nh}{mb + xb - xr} < 1$ will hold, which implies that $xr + nh < mb + xb - xr$, or simply, $xr + x(r-b) + nh < mb$. This means that it is the non-speculators that maintain the convergence or stability of the market price over

time. Also, because $\dfrac{\partial(\dfrac{xr + nh}{mb + xb - xr})}{\partial x} > 0$, as x increases,

$\dfrac{xr + nh}{mb + xb - xr}$ will increase, which means that the entry of speculators will slow down speed of convergence. Hence, this is the stage of *convergent oscillation* of the housing price. However, as x continues to increase, the housing price in the market may not converge to the new equilibrium price and can even become explosive. This is the new insight that is different from the original Chou model (2011) when speculators enter the market.

3.4 The Second stage – More Speculators

Moreover, as x increases, eventually $xr + x(r- b) + nh = mb$ will occur. This is when the housing price does not converge to the steady state price any more. The housing price over time will become a *random walk*, or a *unit root* problem from an econometric perspective. Nevertheless, many econometric studies treat this as the beginning of a housing bubble, as discussed, for example, by Mikhed and Zemčík (2009). When x continues to increase such that $xr + x(r- b) + nh > mb$, then the housing price path will become explosive.

This is the stage of "divergent oscillation" of the housing price when the housing bubble becomes seriously inflated, which will attract even more frenzied speculators to enter the housing market, including the possibility that m may also decrease when x increases over time. The reaction coefficient r may also increase when speculators become over-reactive or very optimistic in responding to any price increase.

3.5 The Third Stage – Too Many Speculators

Eventually, when there are a lot of speculators, $(mb + xb - xr) < 0$ will occur, and the term $(-\dfrac{xr + nh}{mb + xb - xr})$, or equivalently $(\dfrac{xr + nh}{xr - xb - mb})$, will become positive, which makes the market demand curve upward sloping. In this case, there will be *no* oscillation on the path of the equilibrium price. In addition,

because $\dfrac{\partial(\dfrac{xr + nh}{mb + xb - xr})}{\partial x} > 0$ or equivalently, $\dfrac{\partial(\dfrac{xr + nh}{xr - mb - xb})}{\partial x} < 0$,

the implication is that when x increases, $\dfrac{xr + nh}{xr - xb - mb}$ will decrease, thus increasing the possibility or the speed for the market price to converge towards the new equilibrium price.

However, if the market price can converge to the new steady state price, it means $\dfrac{xr + nh}{xr - xb - mb} < 1$ must hold, which can be simplified as $xr + nh < xr - xb - mb$, which is impossible because $xr + nh > xr > xr - xb - mb$. In other words, the ratio $\dfrac{xr + nh}{xr - xb - mb} > 1$ will always hold in the third stage when $(mb + xb - xr) < 0$.

Therefore, even if the entry of a lot of frenzied speculators may reduce the volatility of the housing price, it can *never* stabilize the price enough to converge towards a steady state price because the market price in the third stage will only become less explosive, but explosive nonetheless. Therefore, this is the stage when housing prices become "divergent without oscillation".

In addition, because the inequality $\dfrac{xr + nh}{xr - xb - mb} > 1$ now holds, the diverging housing price will increase or decrease over time at an increasing rate. Most importantly, when $(mb+xb--xr) < 0, \dfrac{ma + xa}{mb + xb - xr}$, the last term of the difference equation $P_t = $

$\dfrac{xr + nh}{xr - mb - xb} P_{t-1} + \dfrac{ma + xa}{mb + xb - xr}$, will become negative. Hence, housing prices over time will decrease at an increasing rate. This is also the time when the housing bubble begins to burst. Therefore, by making c endogenous, we have shown that the housing price will eventually decrease rapidly when there are too many speculators in the housing market. This occurs in the third stage when the housing price becomes "divergent without oscillation".

3.6 The Aftermath

Exhibit 1

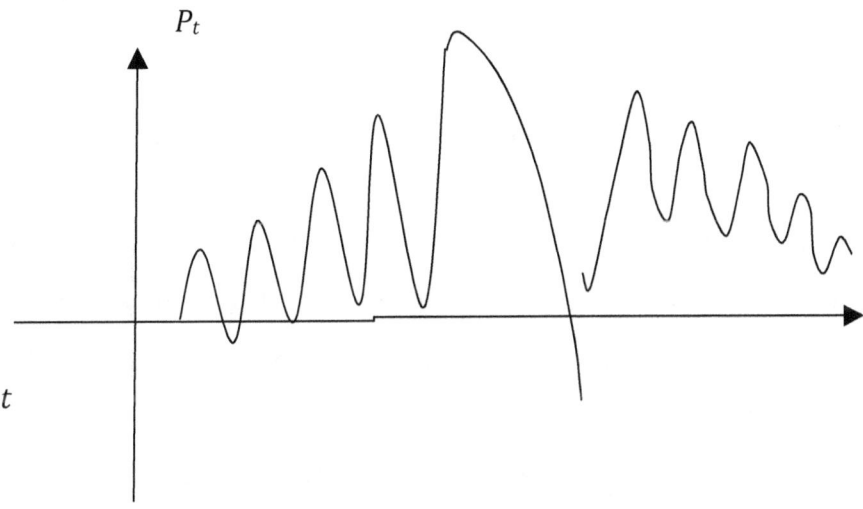

Finally, the price decreases, x will decrease, and eventually $(mb+xb--xr)$ will become positive again. The new equilibrium price will be lower as x decreases. The housing price will become a *diverging oscillation* first when $\dfrac{xr + nh}{xb + mb - xr} > 1$. Then as x continues to decrease, $\dfrac{xr + nh}{xb + mb - xr} < 1$ will eventually hold again, which makes the housing price to again become "convergent oscillation".

However, because the supply of houses may have increased, i.e., n or h may have increased, during the bubble and the speculators may also be stuck with houses that they cannot sell, the new equilibrium price, $P^* = \dfrac{ma + xa}{mb + xb + nh}$, will be lower than the original one before the housing bubble occurs. The re-entry of non-speculators will also help stabilize the housing price

toward a lower new equilibrium price. However, as $\dfrac{xr + nh}{xb + mb - xr}$

will be larger due to the increase in n or h, the speed of convergence to the new equilibrium price will be slower.

To some extent, this is consistent with the perspective that housing prices are sticky downwards, as discussed, for example, by Gao *et al.* (2009). "When a housing market is weak and starts to decline, the downward movement will not be as rapid as the upward movement when the housing market is strong, because sellers in weak markets are often unwilling to sell their homes at market-clearing prices." That is, the downward rigidity of housing prices will slow the convergence process towards the new equilibrium price that could be supported by the economic fundamentals. Therefore, the recovery time after the housing bubble bursts may be longer than the time for the bubble to form.

Selective Relevant Empirical Studies

4.1 The Bubble, Convergence, And Divergence Of Housing Prices

Mikhed and Zemčík [2009] use aggregate data and panel data to determine whether the recently very high and then rapidly decreasing US housing prices reflect economic fundamentals, such as personal income, population, house rent, stock market wealth, building costs, and mortgage rates. They believe that "a bubble in the price of housing may be identified if this price has a unit root, but housing demand and supply shifters are stationary or these shifters are not co-integrated with the price." Hence, they also conclude that the "house price does not align with the fundamentals in sub-samples prior to 1996 and from 1997 to 2006.

Exhibit 2

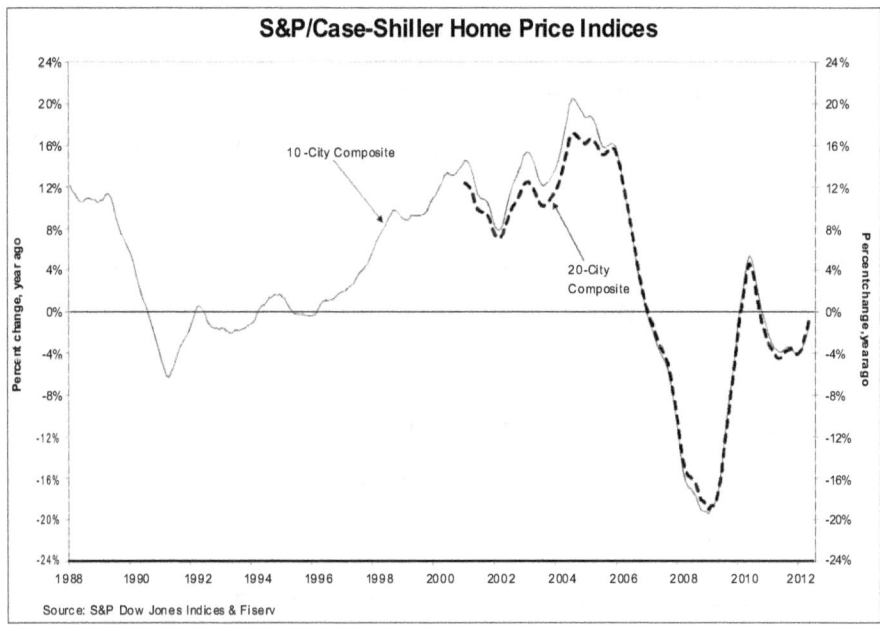

It appears that real estate prices take long swings from their fundamental value and it can take decades before they revert to it. As a result, "three peaks followed by a rapid decline can be identified in the house price series: 1979, 1989, and 2006. "The most recent correction (a collapsed bubble) occurred around 2006."

Ray and Ray [2009] explore the long-term movement in housing prices in selected American cities. By using the monthly

S&P/Case-Shiller price index, they undertake an Augmented Dickey Fuller (unit root) test in each city. One important result of their research is that they identify three distinct cycles of convergence-divergence in housing prices across the US. In particular, they find that the US housing prices broadly converged between January 1987 and January 2000.

Then there is a rapid divergence in prices, and this trend continues until the middle of 2006. After about June of 2006, housing prices started to correct themselves, which results in *convergence* once again. These results are consistent with the theoretical implications of Section 3. The entry of speculators can cause the housing price to diverge during the bubble, but the price will eventually converge again after the bubble bursts.

4.2 Adaptive or Backward-Looking Expectations

Riddle [1999] investigates the relative influence of speculative and economic demand on the median house price on the Santa Barbara South Coast by decomposing the house price into economic forces and speculative demands. Her results show that a speculative housing market bubble formed in the later part of 1987 and then collapsed in mid-1990. Therefore consistent with the theoretical model presented in Section 3 of this Chapter, she concludes that expectations are based on past values of appreciation, that is, backward-looking expectations as opposed to market fundamentals. Once prices begin to rise, feedback mechanisms accentuate the rise. Price declines are also exaggerated since feedback also impacts traders selling or trying to sell their houses as housing prices fall.

In addition, Capozza et al. [2004], Case and Shiller [1988, 1989] and Shiller [1990] posit that serial correlation in real estate markets is partially due to backward-looking expectations of the market participants. Case and Shiller [1988] have conducted surveys of buyers, showing that buyers in booming markets have greater expected price appreciation than buyers in a control market. In addition, "Buyers in the booming market indicate that they treat the purchase of a home more as an investment (as opposed to the consumption value of a house) than those in the control market." As a result, "strong markets should have more serial correlation than markets with slower growth." Their conclusion is consistent with the model discussed in Section 3 of this Chapter. That is when x or r increase, $\dfrac{xr + nh}{mb + xb - xr}$ will increase, which increases the serial correlation of housing prices over time.

4.3 The Convergence And Divergence With Oscillation – The 74%

From the perspective of the second-order difference equation, Capozza *et al.* (2004) analyze the dynamic properties of housing prices of the illiquid US single-family housing markets with the focus on serial correlation, that is, the autocorrelation, and mean reversion, or reversion to the long-run equilibrium price. They identify the serial correlation and mean reversion parameters for which prices will overshoot equilibrium (cycles), and/or diverge permanently from equilibrium, although results vary with the location of the metropolitan statistical area (MSA).

The overshooting of the housing price occurs when the correlation and reversion coefficients pairs assume values in the "oscillatory" region where the roots of the "characteristic" or "complementary" function of the difference equation are complex. Most importantly, from a mathematical perspective, a coefficient pair that lies in the divergent or explosive region is one way to define a "bubble." This divergent behavior arises when the coefficient for serial correlation exceeds one.

In particular, the authors use the following equation to include the serial correlation and mean reversion: $\Delta P_t = \alpha \Delta P_{t-1} + \beta(P_{t-1}^* - P_{t-1}) + \gamma \Delta P_t^*$, where P_t is the log of real house values at time t, with Δ as the difference operator. Also, α is the short-term serial correlation coefficient, and β is the long-term mean reversion coefficient with $0 < \beta < 1$. The smaller the β, the faster the adjustment is to the long-term price level determined by the economic fundamentals. The coefficient γ is the contemporaneous partial adjustment of prices to current shocks with $0 \le \gamma \le 1$.

This equation can also be rewritten in a difference equation by substituting $(P_t - P_{t-1})$ for ΔP_t. Then the equation becomes a second-order difference equation $P_t - (1 + \alpha - \beta)P_{t-1} + \alpha P_{t-2} = \gamma P_t^* + (\beta - \gamma)P_{t-1}^*$. To simplify the discussion, the authors focus on the case when $P_t^* = P^*$ such that the right hand side becomes a constant K. That is,

$P_t - (1 + \alpha - \beta)P_{t-1} + \alpha P_{t-2} = K$, which is a second-order difference equation.

The authors also empirically estimate the serial correlation and mean reversion coefficients from a large panel data set of 62 MSAs from 1979 to 1995. They summarize the distribution of the fitted parameters into four regions.

Region I Convergent, No Oscillation - 26%

Region II   Divergent, No Oscillation - 0%

Region III   Convergent Oscillation - 67%

Region IV   Divergent Oscillation - 7%

The authors find that the mean reversion coefficient varies between 0.05 and 0.45, and the autocorrelation coefficient varies from about –0.2 to 1.7. The average fitted values for serial correlation (= 0.47) and mean version (= 0.23) lie in the convergent oscillatory region, but specific observations fall in both the damped and oscillatory regions and in both the convergent and divergent regions. They conclude that the dynamic properties of housing markets are specific to the given time and location. Location, Location, Location!!

Therefore, the simple model in Section 3 can explain 67% of the dynamic property of the housing price, the case of convergent oscillation. In addition, the model can also explain the 7% of divergent oscillation. Although the authors did not find the empirical evidence of divergent price without oscillation, or the special case when bubble bursts, this can be a direction for future research.

4.4 The Convergence without Oscillation –The 26%

Although convergence without oscillation is beyond the theoretical implication of our current model, empirically, researchers other than Capozza et al. (2004) have found evidence of such a dynamic property of a housing price that converges without oscillation. For example, Englund and Ioannides [1997] investigate the housing price dynamics in 15 OECD countries by using the autoregressive regressions of the yearly change in log real housing prices $P_t - P_{t-1}$ in 15 OECD countries, where P_{t-i} , $i = 0$, 1, 2, ... is the log real housing price. The results include a highly significant first-order autocorrelation for lags of around 0.45, and obtain evidence of negative autocorrelation for lags up to 5 years.

In particular, for the case of one lag, $P_t - P_{t-1} = 0.0041 + 0.412 \ (P_{t-1} - P_{t-2})$. For the case of two lags, $P_t - P_{t-1} = 0.0035 + 0.472 \ (P_{t-1} - P_{t-2}) - 0.208 \ (P_{t-2} - P_{t-3})$. For both cases, the constant is not statistically significant, but the other coefficients are. In addition, for the cases of more than two lags, the intercepts are all positive. However, only the coefficient of $(P_{t-1} - P_{t-2})$ is positive, while the coefficients of all the other log price differences are negative. For the purpose of the current chapter, the focus was only on the case of $P_t - P_{t-1} = 0.0041 + 0.412 \ (P_{t-1} - P_{t-2})$. The coefficient of $(P_{t-1} - P_{t-2})$ here is 0.412, which implies that the housing price will converge to the steady state. At the same time, although the coefficient of mean reversion is unknown, if the methodology of solving the second-order difference equation is followed, it changes to $P_t - 1.412P_{t-1} + 0.412P_{t-2} =$ 0.0041. In this case, as $1.412^2 - (4)(0.412) = 0.3457 > 0$, this means that two roots are real numbers, and it can be an example of convergence without oscillation.

The Empirical Perspectives of Housing Demand and Supply

In this chapter, the focus is on the impact of the entry of speculators with adaptive or backward-looking expectations[58] to the housing price. While price determinants cause the movement of the demand and supply curves, the non-price determinants can shift the demand and supply curves and influence the real housing price over time. From an econometric perspective, demand and supply functions in the housing market can be estimated, for example, for each MSA because location matters to the housing price.[59]

5.1 The Demand Function

In general, in the demand function, the quantity of housing demanded Q_t^d should be a function of the following variables, adjusted by inflation, with the relationship with Q_t^d as follows:

(1) housing prices (inverse relationship)

(2) (after-tax) income (direct relationship)

---

[58] See Leung et al. (2007) for more discussions.
[59] See Chow and Niu (2009) for an example.

(3) mortgage rate or interest rate[60] (inverse relationship)

(4) other financial assets or wealth (direct relationship)

(5) demographics, such as baby boom, or population of the MSA (direct relationship)

(6) macroeconomic variables, such as unemployment rate, and financial controls (inverse relationship)

(7) other factors, such as the rate of return from other investments, the buyers' expectations, loan-type intensity[61] , the easiness to get (sub-prime) mortgages, or any other policy change that can influence the demand function.

The "(7) other factors" are just as important as the economic fundamentals. For example, it is possible that "the collapse of the tech-stock bubble in the year 2000 prompted many people, searching for other types of investments, to focus on real estate." [62] As a result, the housing bubble may have started about 2000. At the same time, the interest or mortgage rates were kept low under the Fed's easy money policy, which made property investments even more attractive. Later, house prices reached levels most ordinary people could not afford, but then Wall Street and mortgage banks responded by relaxing lending standards further with loans that kept payments very low in the initial years. It was also possible for people to lie about

---

[60] Alternatively, we can use the some combination of mortgage rate and income tax rate, such as the user cost of capital = (mortgage rate + property tax rate) * (1 – income tax rate) – inflation rate + 0.03. See Capozza et al. [2004] for more details.

[61] Coleman et al. [2008].

[62] http://politicalcalculations.blogspot.com/2010/02/better-method-for-detecting-housing.html

their incomes. [See Chapter 5.] That helped push home prices up much higher till the home price bubble started down in 2005 and 2006.

5.2 The Supply Function

In addition, in the supply function, the quantity supplied Q_t^s in general should be a function of the following variables, adjusted by inflation, with the relationship with Q_t^s as follows:

(1) housing prices (direct relationship)

(2) construction costs for new housing (negative relationship)

(3) housing market supply regulatory constraints or restrictions (negative relationship), for example, land supply index[63], a measure of the percentage of the land in the city that is available for development

(4) other factors, such as the expectations of sellers, and any other policy change that can influence the supply function such as the availability of construction loans.

5.3 Log Transformation

Although it is possible to test whether the market is in equilibrium, as discussed for example, by Chow and Niu [2009], it is convenient to assume that the housing market is in equilibrium such that the quantity demanded equals the quantity supplied. As a result, one can derive the housing prices as a function of these variables or new variables generated from these variables (based on a two-stage least square or indirect least square method) that

---

[63] See Capozza et al. [1997] for details.

reflect the fundamentals of housing prices. It is then possible to estimate the impact of these different fundamentals on housing prices across the different MSAs.

At the same time, it can be determined whether the log transformation of the variables can increase the explanatory power of the model. Many researchers, such as Coleman *et al* (2008), have assumed that both the demand and supply functions have log-linear forms. That is, the quantity demanded Q_t^d is a product of the variables mentioned above such that the natural log of the quantity demanded Q_t^d becomes a linear function of the log form of these variables in the demand function. Similarly, the log form of the quantity supplied Q_t^s will become a linear function of the log variables in the supply function.

5.4 Serial Correlation, Mean Reversion, And Fundamentals

Finally, although the model presented in this chapter cannot address both serial correlation and mean reversion. As discussed by Capozza *et al.* [2004], "higher real income and population growth and a high level of construction costs and regulation are expected to increase serial correlation. Higher real income growth, larger MSA size (population), and a faster growing city with lower level of real construction costs/regulation should increase mean reversion." Further, as discussed by Mikhed and Zemčík [2009], it is critical to use the factors that can influence housing demand and supply as the economic fundamentals to establish the price level and thus identify any upward deviation from this as a bubble.

Conclusion And Extensions

By making the price increase endogenous based on the past price difference, this research explores the impact of speculators with adaptive or backward-looking expectations to the dynamic property of housing prices. In particular, it shows that when very few speculators first enter the market, the housing price should be convergent with oscillation if there are enough non-speculators. It is the first stage. When a lot more speculators enter the market with strong reactions to any price increase, the bubble will start to form.

This is the second stage when the housing price becomes divergent with oscillation. Eventually, when there are too many speculators in the market, the bubble will burst, and the price will become divergent without oscillation. This is the third stage when the housing price decreases at an increasing rate. When the number of speculators decreases, the price dynamics will operate in reverse order. It will be the non-speculators that eventually re-stabilize the price to a new but lower equilibrium price. The price recovery speed is also slower because of the increased supply from the bubble and the downward rigidity in housing prices.

There are empirical studies consistent with the dynamic properties characterized by the theoretical model. The mathematical model provides three possible properties for the housing price that can explain up to 74% of the results estimated by Capozza et al [2004]. In addition, there are also other non-price determinants of the market demand and supply functions that can shift the demand and supply curves, changing housing prices. These determinants can also influence the serial correlation and mean reversion. As discussed by Capozza et al [2004], "serial correlation is higher in MSAs with higher real incomes, population growth, and real construction costs. Mean reversion is greater in larger MSAs and faster growing cities with lower construction costs."

There are several ways to extend the research presented in this chapter. First, instead of the first-order difference equation, the mathematical model can be extended to a second-order difference equation, which may provide more insights into the dynamic properties of housing prices. In addition, the current theoretical model can only explain about 74 % of the market's dynamic properties based on the discussion by Capozza et al [2004]. Hence, a second way to extend the model is to incorporate the possibility of a housing price convergent without oscillation to explain the remaining 26%.

A third way to extend the research is to examine the methodologies and findings for ways to identify housing bubbles, including the empirical evidence for divergent prices without oscillation when a bubble bursts. This would further strengthen linkages between the theory presented here and empirical approaches to the dynamic properties of housing prices. Finally it could incorporate policy variables with possible implications for regulators and central banks in determining the optimal way to smooth out housing bubbles in their early stages rather than having to clean up the mess in the aftermath of a major boom and bust such as the recent Great Recession.

References

Baddeley, M. 2005. "Housing Bubbles, Herds, and Frenzies: Evidence from British Housing Markets", working paper, *CEPP Policy Brief*, No. 02/05.

Capozza, D., Hendershott, P., & Mack, C. 2004. "An Anatomy of Price Dynamics in Illiquid Markets: Analysis and Evidence from Local Housing Markets", *Real Estate Economics*, V. 32, N. 1.

Capozza, D., Kazarian, D., & Thomson T. 1997. "Mortgage Default in Local Markets", *Real Estate Economics*, Vol. 26, no. 4.

Case, K. & Shiller, R. (1988), "The Behavior of Home Buyers in Boom and Post-Boom Markets", *New England Economic Review*, November/December.

Case, K. & Shiller, R. 1989. "The Efficiency of the Market for Single Family Homes", *The American Economic Review*, V. 79.

Case, K. & Shiller, R. 2003. "Is There a Bubble in the Housing Market?", *Brookings Papers on Economic Activity*, No. 2.

Chou, P. 2011. "A Simple Model for Speculative Housing Bubbles", Leir Center For Financial Bubble Research Working Paper #6, available at http://www.Leirbubble center.org/2011/07/simple-cobweb-model-of-speculative.html.

Chow, G. & Niu, L. 2009. "Demand and Supply for Residential Housing in Urban China", working paper.

Coleman, M., LaCour-Little M., & Vandell K. 2008. "Subprime Lending and the Housing Bubble: Tail Wags Dog?", *Journal of Housing Economics*, 17.

Dickey, D. &Fuller, W. 1979. "Distribution of the Estimators for Autoregressive Time Series with a Unit Root", *Journal of the American Statistical Association*, No. 74.

Englund, P. & Ioannides Y. 1997. "House Price Dynamics: An International Empirical Perspective", *Journal of Housing Economics*, 6.

Ferguson, C. 1960. "Learning, Expectations, and the Cobweb Model", *Journal of Economics*, Numbers 3-4.

Foley, P. 2001. "Are Irish Housing Prices Determined by Fundamentals?", Working paper, 04-01, University College Cork, Ireland.

Gao, A., Lin, Z., & Na, C. 2009. "Housing Market Dynamics: Evidence of Mean Reversion and Downward Rigidity", *Journal of Housing Economics*, V. 18.

Glaeser, E., Gyourko J. & Saiz, A. 2008. "Housing Supply and Housing Bubbles", *Journal of Urban Economics*, Vol. 64, No. 2.

Goodman, A. & Thibodeau, T. 2008. "Where are the Speculative Bubbles in US Housing Markets?", *Journal of Housing Economics*, 17.

Green R., Malpezzi, S., & Mayo S. 2005. "Metropolitan-Specific Estimates of the Price Elasticity of Supply of Housing, and their Sources", Regulation and the High Cost of Housing, *AEA Papers and Proceedings*, 95(2).

Himmelberg, C., Mayer, C., & Sinai, T. 2005. "Assessing High House Prices: Bubbles, Fundamentals, and Misperceptions", *Journal of Economic Perspectives*, 19(4).

Kaizoji, T. 2009. "Root Causes of the Housing Bubble", MPRA working paper, http://mpra.ub.uni-muenchen.de/16808/.

Kranendonk H. & Verbruggen J. 2008. "Are Houses Overvalued in the Netherlands?", working paper.

Labonte M. 2003. "U.S. Housing Prices: Is There a Bubble?", *Report for Congress*.

Lai R. & Van O. 2008. "A Regime Shift of the Recent Housing bubble in The United States", working paper.

Lai Y., Xu, H., & Jia J. 2009. "Study on Measuring Methods of Real Estate Speculative Bubble", *Journal of Service and Science Management*, 2.

Leung A., Xu, J., &Tsui, W. 2007. "Nonlinear Delay Difference Equations for Housing Dynamics Assuming Heterogeneous Backward-looking Expectations", *Applied Mathematics and Mechanics*, 28(6).

Malpezzi S. & Wachter S. 2005. "The Role of Speculation in Real Estate Cycles", *Journal of Real Estate Literature*, V. 13, N. 2.

Mikhed, V. & Zemčík P. 2009. "Do House Prices Reflect Fundamentals? Aggregate and Panel data Evidence", *Journal of Housing Economics*, 18.

Quan, D. & Quigley, J. 1991. "Price Formation and the Appraisal Function in Real Estate Markets", *Journal of Real Estate Finance and Economics*, V. 4.

Ray, A. & Ray I. 2008. "Stability of Housing Prices in Major US Cities: A Time Series Analysis of S&P/Case-Shiller Housing Price Indices", *Journal of Money, Investment and Banking*, No. 7.

Riddel, M. 1999. "Fundamentals, Feedback Trading, and Housing Market Speculation: Evidence from California", *Journal of Housing Economics*, 8.

Shiller, R. 1990. "Market Volatility and Investor Behavior", *The American Economic review*, V. 80.

Shiller, R. 2009. "Unlearned Lessons from the Housing Bubble", *The Economists' Voice*, www.bepress.com/ev.

CHAPTER NINE

SURVEY OF SOME ECONOMETRIC MODELS THAT QUANTITATIVELY IDENTIFY BUBBLES

In thunder, lightning, or in rain?

P. B. Chou

Introduction

The economic and financial damage wrecked by the bursting of asset bubbles can have devastating impacts on investors' fortunes and the welfare of a society. Krueger (2005) points out that the rise and fall of Internet stock prices during the Internet bubble destroyed about $8 trillion of shareholders' wealth. More recently, the bursting of the US and other housing bubbles such as Ireland and Spain and the evaporation of toxic financial assets created worldwide financial crises. This impacted many nations, their economies and their financial systems. [See prior Chapters in this Book.] Therefore understanding recent developments in econometric techniques for identifying asset bubbles is an important step for researchers to help policy makers develop preemptive measures to ameliorate the negative impacts of speculative bubbles before they get too big and collapse, especially those involving banks and the heavy use of leverage.

An asset bubble occurs when the price of the asset is higher than the level that can be sustained by the economic fundamentals. However, as Alan Greenspan, Fed chairman at the time of emerging Internet Bubble, stated so poignantly: "How do we know when irrational exuberance has unduly escalated asset values?"[64], the problem of identifying a bubble in its early stage is that it can be difficult to differentiate a boom based on a fundamental economic expansion from a bubble. In addition, as argued by Guenster et al [2009] and Abreu and Brunnermeier [2003], when an asset bubble occurs, the price of the asset grows faster than fundamental values, in combination with a sudden acceleration of real price growth. Hence, it is also about how fast the asset price will increase compared to the asset's fundamental value, which in turn is related to the statistical time series of both the asset price and its fundamental value over time. A related issue is how fast is too fast? But as noted elsewhere in this book it seems to be when price increases draw speculators into the market and stimulate further price increases.

An economist's perspective would be, "If you cannot quantify it, you don't understand it." There is also a similar saying in management that "If you cannot measure it, you cannot manage it." Therefore if an asset bubble can be identified and its likely evolution measured in its early stages, this can benefit those that might want to understand and/or manage it ranging from the academic and investment communities to company executives, central bankers, and public policy makers. For this reason this chapter will review and evaluate some recently developed methodologies that quantitatively identify bubbles, and their level

---

[64] See Greenspan [1996] for details.

of "irrational exuberance". They do this through examining and analyzing the time series properties of some important asset price bubbles.

There have of course been many efforts to identify asset bubbles. Some of them are less rigorous than others because they are based on intuition and observations or graphical analysis of asset prices over time. On the website, Political calculation[65], the author(s) compare medium new house prices and the median household income for the years from 1967 to 2010. The authors find that there is a shift of the trend after 1986, but, more importantly, they identify a U.S. housing bubble from 2000 to 2007 when the housing price deviates from the trajectory of the medium income over time, as shown in following graph Exhibit.

However, from a researcher's perspective, while such a graphical analysis to determine there was a housing bubble is a convenient visual confirmation after the fact, it has some potential problems. First, the medium house price can only serve as a proxy for the economic fundamentals underlying the housing price. This is because there are other factors that can influence the benchmark or long-run equilibrium housing prices, such as population growth (rate), house rent, stock market wealth, building or construction costs, mortgage rate, and the location of a city or metropolitan significant area (MSA), as discussed, for example, by Mikhed and Zemčík [2009] as well as in Chapter 8.

---

[65]See: http://politicalcalculations.blogspot.com/2010/02/better-method-for-detecting-housing.htmlandhttp://politicalcalculations.blogspot.com/2011/12/revisiting-us-housing-bubble.html for details.

Exhibit 1

Median New House Prices vs Median Household Income
in the United States, 1967-2010

Source: U.S. Census Bureau

© Political Calculations 2011

Second, the comparison between medium new house prices and the median household income is based on yearly data, which is subject to data availability. In particular, the median household income is usually available only on a yearly basis, although it can be estimated between years. In this case, there is no good way to estimate the starting and ending time of a bubble if it occurs during the data gaps. Hence, such an approach may have limited ex ante or real time pro-active policy implications in the bubble formation process.

Third, and most importantly, such a technique is not rigorous since there is no quantitative characterization of the bubble. In particular, there is no test statistic such that statistical methods or econometrics can be applied to determine a statistically significant starting date and ending date for a bubble.[66] This chapter's goal is to survey the current studies that have tried to quantitatively identify bubbles and to evaluate their actual results.

Section 2 introduces some basic terminologies and concepts that are widely used in econometrics and statistics. Section 3 discusses the standard left-tailed Augmented Dickey-Fully (ADF) test as a way to determine the formation of a bubble. In addition, instead of a left-tailed ADF test, Section 4 introduces a recently developed right-tailed ADF test, the SADF test, to directly examine the evidence of asset bubbles. Section 5 discusses the development of alternative tests to the SADF test and a generalized version of the PWY test, the GSADF test, which has higher power in detecting bubbles than other tests particularly when there are multiple bubbles occurring during the same long time period. In Section 6, three additional quantitative methods for determining asset bubbles are reviewed. Section 7 presents the conclusions.

Basic Terminologies and Concepts[67]

2.1 Random Walk and Unit Root

Suppose y_t is generated by the following model:

$y_t - y_{t-1} = \beta + u_t$, where u_t is a stationary series with mean zero and variance σ^2. In this case, the first difference of y_t, i.e.,

---

[66] There are several ways to statistically test the relationship between the housing price and medium income, which will be discussed in Sections 3 & 4.
[67] Sections 2.1-2.3 are partially based on Maddala [1992].

$\Delta y_t = y_t - y_{t-1}$, is stationary with a mean β. This model is also known as the random-walk model with drift if $\beta \neq 0$, or a random walk without drift if $\beta = 0$.

2.2 Unit Root Tests – ADF Test

Empirically, whether y_t has a unit root or not needs to be tested. Suppose $y_t = \rho y_{t-1} + u_t$. A unit root is present if $\rho = 1$. Then the regression can be re-written as follows: $\Delta y_t = (\rho - 1)y_{t-1} + u_t = \delta y_{t-1} + u_t$, where $\delta = \rho - 1$. This model can be tested for a unit root if $\delta = 0$, which is called the Dickey Fuller Test. There are also two additional versions of this test, $\Delta y_t = \beta + \delta y_{t-1} + u_t$ and $\Delta y_t = \beta + \gamma t + \delta y_{t-1} + u_t$.[68] In addition, a more general test is called the augmented Dickey-Fuller (ADF) test, which includes the possibility of lagged variables Δy_t. For example, the model can be modified as follows:

$$\Delta y_t = \beta + \delta y_{t-1} + \sum_{j=1}^{k} \theta_i \Delta y_{t-j} + u_t,$$ where $\delta = (\rho - 1)$. In the standard left-tailed ADF test, the null hypothesis is $H_0: \delta = 0$ (unit root behavior) against the alternative hypothesis $H_1: \delta < 0$ (stationary behavior).

2.3 Co-integration

A time series y_t is said to be integrated of order 1 or I(1) if Δy_t is a stationary time series. A stationary time series is thus I(0). A random walk is a special case of an I(1) series or process.

---

[68] See Dickey and Fuller [1979] for details.

This is because if y_t is a random walk, Δy_t is white noise, a special case of a stationary series. In addition, a times series y_t is integrated of order 2 or is I(2) if Δy_t is I(1). In addition, if y_t is I(1) and u_t is I(0), then their sum $S_t = y_t + u_t$ is I(1).

Suppose that y_t is I(1) and x_t is also I(1), then y_t and x_t are co-integrated if there exists a β such that $y_t - \beta x_t$ is I(0), which can be denoted as CI(1, 1). In other words, the regression equation $y_t = \beta x_t + u_t$ is meaningful because y_t and x_t do not drift away from each other over time. This implies there is a long-run equilibrium relationship between y_t and x_t.

In addition, if x_t and y_t are co-integrated such that $u_t = y_t - \beta x_t$ is I(0), then the unit root test can be applied to u_t. The null hypothesis is H_0: u_t has a unit root or x_t and y_t are not co-integrated, against the alternative hypothesis, H_1: x_t and y_t are co-integrated.

For the purpose of identifying bubbles, prices in the long run equilibrium are usually assumed as determined by the economic fundamentals. As a result, a bubble occurs only if the price level is not co-integrated with all the fundamentals since this implies there is no long run equilibrium relationship between the price and the fundamentals.

2.4 Unit Root Test and Co-integration Test

As discussed by Yiu and Jin [2012], "there are four possible scenarios of the unit root test on the asset price and fundamental value series: (A) asset price and fundamental values are both stationary in level; (B) asset price is stationary but fundamental value is non-stationary in level; (C) asset price is non-stationary and fundamental value is stationary in level; (D) asset price and fundamental value are both non-stationary in level. Scenario A indicates no bubble; Scenario B indicates an incorrect model; Scenario C suggests the presence of bubbles in the asset price; and Scenario D needs a co-integration test between asset price and its fundamental, assuming their first differences are stationary."

Unit Root Test – The ADF Test

As the asset price can deviate from the fundamental values, Campbell and Shiller [1987] propose a method to use a unit root test as a first step to detect bubbles. If there is a bubble, the asset price and the fundamental value can be characterized by two possible cases. The first case is Scenario C discussed above in which the asset price is non-stationary (not mean reverting) in level, but the fundamental value is stationary. The second case is Scenario D, where both the asset price and fundamental value are non-stationary. Because of this, the second case calls for a co-integration test as a second step. If a bubble is present, the asset price and its associated fundamental value will not be co-integrated (not have co-movement in the long run), assuming they are both non-stationary in levels but stationary in the first differences.

Similarly, based on the unit root and co-integration tests,

Diba and Grossman [1988] point out that the bubble detection is equivalent to the identification of the explosive behavior in the gap between the asset price and its associated fundamentals. Since then, the standard unit root test (left-tailed ADF Test) and co-integration test on the price series and fundamental value series have been widely used for detecting asset bubbles because of its easy implementation.

Nevertheless, when Diba and Grossman [1988] apply the unit root test to the real US Standard and Poor's Composite stock price index data from 1871 to 1986, they find that stock prices are non-stationary in levels but stationary in differences. The authors also confirm the co-integration relationship between stock prices and dividends over the same period. This supports the argument prices did not diverge from the long-run fundamentals, giving evidence against the formation of stock market bubbles.

More recently Ray and Ray [2009] explored the long-term movement in housing prices in selected American cities. By using the monthly S&P/Case-Shiller price index, they undertook an ADF test in each city. One important finding is that there are three distinct cycles of convergence-divergence in housing prices across the US. In particular, Ray and Ray found that US housing prices broadly *converged* between January 1987 and January 2000. Then there was a rapid *divergence* in prices that continued until the middle of 2006. After about June 2006, housing prices began correcting, resulting again in a *convergence*. Therefore, housing prices can diverge during a bubble, but will eventually converge again after the bubble bursts.[69]

Mikhed and Zemčík [2009] use aggregated data and panel data to determine whether recently high and subsequent rapidly decreasing US house prices reflect their economic fundamentals, such as personal income, population, house rent, stock market wealth, building costs, and mortgage rates. They believe that "a bubble in the price of housing may be identified if this price has a unit root, but housing demand and supply shifts are stationary or these shifts are not co-integrated with the price." Hence, they also conclude that the "house price does not align with the fundamentals in sub-samples prior to 1996 and from 1997 to 2006, and "three peaks followed by a rapid decline can be identified in the house price series: 1979, 1989, and 2006, and "the most recent correction (a collapsed bubble) occurred around 2006."

In addition, Clark and Coggin [2011] examine the existence of a US housing price bubble using quarterly data from the first quarter of 1975 through the second quarter of 2005. The authors find that US house prices and the fundamental economic variables are non-stationary unit root variables that are *not* co-integrated, even after allowing for structural breaks. These results confirm the existence of a US housing price bubble for this period.

The PWY Test

---

[69] This result is consistent with the theoretical model discussed in Chapter 8 in which the housing price will converge with oscillation before the bubble, diverge with oscillation during the bubble, and then diverge without oscillation after the price starts to decrease.

4.1 The Limitations Of The Unit Root Test

Despite the popularity of the ADF test, the results from the unit root test need to be interpreted with caution. As discussed by Yiu and Jin [2012], "when the asset price and its fundamental value are found to be co-integrated, the null hypothesis of no bubble is confirmed. However, the reverse may not be necessarily true, because the presence of a rational bubble may be one of the many possible reasons. Other possible factors include, for example, the non-stationary nature of unobservable variables."

Moreover, because the standard ADF test "utilizes a linear model to detect any non-linear growth of the bubble component, the power of detecting explosive bubble behavior and identifying the origination and collapse of a bubble, particularly the collapse" is limited. Similarly, as argued by Evan [1991], as well as Phillips, Wu, and Yu [2011], "standard unit root test and co-integration tests are inappropriate tools for detecting bubble behavior because they cannot effectively distinguish between a stationary process and a periodically collapsing bubble model." This is because patterns of periodically collapsing bubbles in the data look more like data generated from an I(1) process, such as a unit root, or even a stationary auto-regression process than a potentially explosive process.[70] In addition, even if the process is explosive, within a limited time period when a bubble is first

---

[70] See http://knowledge.smu.edu.sg/article.cfm?articleid=1385 and Mokhtar et al. (2006) for similar discussions.

developing, the magnitude of the bubble may be small relative to the fundamentals. This may result in underestimating the bubble's true growth rate.

4.2 The PWY Test-SADF Test

To overcome these problems, Phillips, Wu, and Yu [2011][71] propose a newly developed method, the PWY test, to determine the existence of an asset bubble. Instead of the standard left-tailed ADF test, the PWY method arranges the right-tailed ADF test to both the price and dividend. By using the same symbols as in Section 2 such that $\delta = \rho - 1$, the null hypothesis is $H_0: \delta = 0$ (unit root behavior) versus the alternative hypothesis of $H_1: \delta > 0$ (*mildly* explosive). The PWY test therefore looks directly for evidence of non-linear explosive behavior in the asset price.

Also, in terms of forward recursive regressions, the super ADF test (SADF test) is repeated using subsets of the sample data increased one observation at a time. A bubble's origination is dated as the first recursion for which the value of the t-statistic of the estimated ρ or $\delta = \rho - 1$ is equal to or above the right side critical value of a particular significance level.

The collapse date is identified as the first subsequent recursion for which the t-statistic decreases to the level that is equal to or below the critical value. In other words, the SADF test not only can determine the origination of a bubble by estimating the date of a regime switch from a random walk to an explosive

---

[71] The same authors first proposed the PWY test in a Yale University Working paper in 2009.

process, but also can determine the collapse of a bubble by estimating the date when the there is a regime switch from an explosive process to a random walk. Therefore, the forward recursive procedure is stronger than the standard ADF test or co-integration test in identifying the beginning and collapse of an asset bubble.

In addition, as the authors seek to quantify the "exuberance", coined by Greenspan [1996], in terms of a mildly explosive auto-regressive behavior, they examine the Internet bubble for the Nasdaq price index, adjusted by inflation. By using a 5% significance level as the critical value, their results show that the Nasdaq's price level was explosive, while the dividend level was not. This result supports the existence of a bubble. They also determined that the Internet bubble emerged from July 1995 until February 2001, and then started again from April 2001 but burst in July 2001 when prices finally collapsed.

4.3 More Applications of the PWY Test

4.3.1 Recent U.S. Bubbles

In a recent study, Caballero et al [2008] argue that "the internet bubble in the 1990s, the asset bubbles over 2005 to 2006, the subprime crisis in 2007, and the commodity bubbles in 2008 are closely related." To econometrically test such a statement, Phillips and Yu [2011] apply the PWY test with some modification and improvement to determine the origination and ending times of three financial time series during the subprime crisis, including "a financial asset price (the house price index), a commodity price (the crude oil price), and one bond price (the spread between Baa and Aaa)." The authors not only identify different bubble behavior statistically, but also provide consistent dating of the origination and collapse of the bubbles.

The empirical estimates of the origination and collapse of these financial variables show that there is some migration or transmission mechanism among them. In particular, as noted above, Phillips, Wu, and Yu [2011] estimate that the origination date of the Internet bubble was July 1995, and the termination date was July 2001. Then a real estate bubble emerged in February 2002 and collapsed in December 2007, soon after the subprime mortgage crisis erupted. Then the bubble phenomenon migrated to certain bond and the commodity markets. The bubble in crude oil started in March 2008 and ended in July 2008. Then the bubble in bonds appeared on September 22, 2008 and collapsed April 20, 2009.

Their "estimates suggest that the bubbles emerged in the housing market before the subprime crisis, and collapsed with the subprime crisis. The bubble then migrated from the housing market to the selective commodity markets and the bond market after the crisis erupted into the public arena. All these bubbles collapsed as the financial crisis impacted the real economic activity." Therefore, "the estimated sequence is broadly consistent with the statement made by Caballero et al [2008]."

Most importantly, the PWY test "can be used to provide early warning diagnostics for market exuberance as they provide consistent tests for mildly explosive behavior. Such diagnostics may assist policy makers in framing early preventive monetary policy responses or other regulatory actions or interventions" to alleviate the possible negative impacts of speculative asset bubbles.

4.3.2 Hong Kong Housing Bubbles

Yiu and Jin [2012] also apply the PWY Test to identify housing bubbles in the Hong Kong residential property market. Unlike the Phillips, Wu, and Yu [2011] who test the price and fundamental series separately, Yiu and Jin [2012] examine the differential between the property price and the fundamental, rent, directly based on the price/rent ratio, which is calculated as the log difference between the real property price index and real rent index of the Hong Kong residential property market. The log difference is expected to have an explosive feature if an asset bubble occurs. One reason for doing so is that price and rent are non-stationary.

Accordingly, "the origination of the bubble is identified in February 1997 when the *t*-statistic for the first time exceeds both the 5% and 10% critical values. However, the collapse date of the bubble depends on which significance level is used. If the 5% significance level of the *t*-statistic is used, the end date was July 1997 when the real price dropped 4.1% from the peak in May 1997. On the other hand, if the 10% significance level is used, the end date was November 1997 when the real price fell 9.2% from the peak."

In addition, the method detects explosive growth of the price-rent differential in Hong Kong since July 2009, indicating strong upward price pressure. "During the first quarter of 2011, the result also shows clear explosive behavior of the differential which signals an asset-bubble formation. Most importantly, their results show the potential of the PWY Test to be used of timely monitoring of bubble formation in asset markets since the method will provide updated indications of bubble formation, once new data become available, i.e., with time lag of about six weeks." Although the identification of the starting date of a bubble cannot lead to the prediction of the collapse time of the bubble, it can give policy makers some early warning so that pro-active policy actions can be taken in a timely manner.

PWY Test and Other Associated Tests

5.1 The PWY Test vs. Alternative Tests

By using the PWY test as the benchmark, Homm and Breitung [2012] compare several alternative modified tests, originally proposed by Bhargava [1986], Busetti and Taylor [2004], and Kim [2000], for rational bubbles and investigate the power properties of these tests. The focus is on the case where bubble detection is reduced to testing for a regime change from a random walk to an explosive process. In addition, the authors apply the modified sequential Chow-Test for structural breaks. When there is only one regime change, the sequential Chow-Test and the modified Busetti and Taylor [2005] test procedures exhibit the highest power when the change from I(1) to explosive occurs late in the sample.

Moreover, with regard to the estimation of the date when a bubble emerges, a breakpoint estimator derived from the sequential Chow-Test turns out to be the most accurate when compared to the PWY test. However, this result does not hold if there are multiple bubbles and crashes, that is, multiple structural breaks. In that case, the PWY test is much more robust against multiple structural breaks than all other tests.

The authors also analyze the Nasdaq composite index and various other financial time series, such as the S&P 500, Nikkei 225, Hang Seng, and Shanghai Indices. As a result, the PWY test provides strong evidence for a bubble presence in the Nasdaq index and other stock markets. Similar results are derived using the sequential Chow-Test and Busetti and Taylor [2004] test, thus reinforcing the PWY test results.

Furthermore, the authors redesigned all tests as monitoring procedures, with the focus on FLUC (similar to the PWY test) and CUSUM procedures as a real time monitoring approach to detect the origination date of emerging bubbles. The estimation of the origination date for the Nasdaq bubble was June 1995. Based on the monthly data, the authors also estimate the bubble origination dates for different stock markets. They are 1990-10-31 for S&P 500, 1982-10-03 for Nikkei 225, 2003-03-31 for Hang Seng, and 2005-12-02 for Shanghai. Likewise, the estimated origination dates for housing bubbles are 1999-06-15 for the U.S., 1997Q4 for Spain, 1999-01-15 for the U.K., and 1985 for Japan.

5.2 The Test for Multiple Bubbles-The GSADF Test

Gilbert [2010] applies the PWY text to commodity futures' prices and discusses the method's power of detecting multiple bubbles. However the author finds the PWY test is not a very effective test for multiple bubbles, in particular when the explosive behavior is more pronounced in the first bubble. In addition, Phillips, Shi, and Yu [2012] admit that the "complexity of the non-linear structure inherent in multiple bubble phenomena within the same sample period makes econometric analysis particularly difficult."

They also "show how the testing procedure and dating algorithm of the PWY test are affected by multiple bubbles and may fail to be consistent." Therefore, the authors generalize the SADF test to GSADF test to overcome such difficulties. Their simulation results show that the GSADF test significantly improves discriminatory power in detecting multiple bubbles and collapses.

Phillips, Shi, and Yu]2012) also conduct empirical applications of the GSADF test to the price-dividend ratio of the S&P 500 stock market monthly data from January 1871 to December 2010. These results identify many key historical episodes of *both* exuberance and collapse during this period. These include the Great 1929 Crash (1929M01-M09), the immediate WW II and Korean War postwar boom 1954 (1954M12-1955M12), black Monday October 1987 (1987M02-

M09), the dot.com bubble (1995M12-2001M06), and the subprime mortgage crisis (2008M10-M09). These cover " the episodes with the durations greater than or equal to half of year". For the other episodes that are less than six months, the authors also identify the "explosive recovery phase from the panic of 1873 (1879M10-1880M02), the banking panic of 1907 (1907M10-M11), and the 1974 stock market crash (1974M09)." In contrast, the SADF test (PWY test) only identifies two explosive periods: the recovery phase of the panic of 1873 (1879M10-1880M04) and the Internet bubble (1997M07-2001M08).

The authors also apply the CUSUM procedure proposed by Homm and Beritung [2012] to the same data to detect for the emergence of bubbles. The results show that the CUSUM procedure identifies some bubble episodes for periods before 1990. However, "for the past-1990 sample, the procedure detects only the great crash and the dot.com bubble episodes." Hence, CUSUM does not provide early warning alert or acknowledgement of black Monday in October 1987 or the subprime mortgage crisis in 2008. As the new recursive procedures GSADF is more sensitive in identifying multiple bubbles and collapses than the SADF or the CUSUM, GSADF therefore is a better tool for central bankers and fiscal regulators looking for practical applications and surveillance strategies.

Other Tests For Detecting Bubbles

6.1 State-space Model With Markov-Switching

Similar to the PWY test, there are other studies that use

direct tests for speculative bubbles by explicitly formulating the existence of a bubble in the alternative hypothesis. Examples of such direct test procedures can be found in research such as West [1987] and Wu [1997]. By following such a research approach, Al-Anaswah and Wilfling [2011] adopted a state-space model with Markov-switching methodology to detect speculative price bubbles in the stock market. This approach was originally used by researchers such as Kim and Nelson (1999) to detect turning points in business cycles. Hence, Al-Anaswah and Wilfling (2011) utilize a two-regime Markov-switching specification for the unobservable bubble process. One regime is when the bubble survives, while the other is when it collapses. A bursting bubble is identified if the two regimes can be separated.

The authors test artificial data and real world bubbles, specifically, the famous bubbles discussed by Kindleberger and Aliber [2011] such as the Dutch Tulip Bulb Bubble in 1636, the South See Bubble in 1720, the Mississippi Bubble in 1720, and so on. The authors thus test several famous bubbles, and can identify most, if not all, such as the Black Monday, and the bursting of the Internet bubble.

In addition, the authors use the entire monthly data set of the US stock market from January 1871 to June 2004, but cannot find significant results until they separate the data into three sub-periods. Therefore, despite its ability to detect bubbles, this technique may not have the same power in detecting and particularly date-stamping bubbles as the GSADF procedure.

6.2 The Duration Dependence Test

As discussed by Mokhtar et al [2006], "the majority of published studies examining the existence of speculative bubbles are concentrated on the techniques used to detect rational speculative bubbles in the stock market." "These techniques can be grouped into four main categories: (1) tests for bubble premiums, (2) tests for excess volatility, and (3) tests for the co-integration of dividends and prices, and (4) the duration dependence test."

For the research in category (1), "a bubble premium is the excess returns the investor demand above the fundamental return in the presence of speculative bubble. This return has an explosive nature as it increases geometrically through time, and incorporates the actual excess return of the stock over the risk free rate." However, "the broad consensus of this literature is that tests for the presence of a bubble premium face serious problems and may not be able to prove or adequately disprove the existence of rational speculative bubble." [72]

For category (2), if a speculative bubble is present, the variance of the stock price will be higher than the variance of the fundamental price. Examples can be found in the studies such as Shiller [1981], West [1987], and Wu [1997]. For category (3), it is obvious that Mokhtar et al [2006] were not aware of the recently developed PWY test [2009] and other tests that would solve the underlying problems of the unit-root test and the co-integration

---

[72] See the discussion of Liu et al. (1995) for further interest.

test that detect bubbles indirectly. Therefore, the authors focus on category (4).

From a behavioral finance perspective, the authors "investigate the presence of rational speculative bubbles in Malaysian stock market by employing the duration dependence test based on the Weibull's hazard model and Log Logistic hazard model." From the abnormal monthly real returns and three time frames – before (1994-1996), during (1997-1998), and after (1999-2003) the Asian financial crisis in 1997, the authors confirm the existence of rational speculative bubbles in the Malaysian stock market before and after the crisis, although the post-crisis bubble is smaller than the pre-crisis one. The weakness of this approach, though, is its inability to date-stamp the bubble's origination and collapse, which also could be resolved by utilizing the recently developed SADF or GSADF tests.

6.3 Asset Price Volatility

In the field of mathematical finance, Jarrow et al [2011] recently proposed another new methodology to detect bubbles based on asset price volatility. They characterize asset price bubbles as frictionless, competitive, and continuous trading models using an arbitrage-free Martingale pricing technology. The asset pricing process is defined in terms of a standard stochastic differential equation driven by Brownian motion. The determination of a bubble depends on whether the price process under a risk neutral measure is a Martingale or a strict local Martingale. The difference between them hinges on the asymptotic behavior of the asset's price volatility. If the volatility of the asset price is high, then a bubble exists.

The authors also apply the same methodology to several stock prices during the Internet bubble: Lastminute.com, eToys, Infospace, and Geocities. In eToys' case, the result is inconclusive about whether a bubble occurred. For Lastminute.com and Infospace, the methodology supports the existence of a price bubble. However, for Geocities, the result does not indicate a price bubble. Therefore, this research should be viewed as an early effort to detect bubbles in real time. Probably more applications need to be done testing known famous historical bubbles instead of the stock prices of a few firms.

Conclusions

7.1 The Tests And The Identification of Bubbles

In this chapter, different methodologies to quantitatively detect bubbles are reviewed, including the ADF test, SADF (PWY) Test, GSADF Test, the sequential Chow-Test, Bhargava [1986] test, Busetti and Taylor [2004] test, and Kim [2000] test, the CUSUM test, Test based on state-space model with Markov Switching, duration dependence test, and mathematical finance's asset price volatility test.

The various applications of these tests have successfully identified most, if not all, famous historical stock price bubbles such as the Nasdaq (1995), the S&P 500 (1999), the Nikkei 225 (1982), the Hang Seng (2003), and the Shanghai (2005), as well as some in countries such as Malaysia and Indonesia. Similarly, housing bubbles were identified in the U.S. (1999), Spain (1997Q4), the U.K. (1999), and Japan (1985).

In addition, using the GSADF Test, both the origination and collapse dates were identified, including the Great Crash (1929M01-M09), the 1954 postwar boom (1954M12-1955M12), black Monday October 1987 (1987M02-M09), the dot.com Internet bubble (1995M12-2001M06), the subprime mortgage crisis (2008M10-M09), the recovery from the 1873 panic (1879M10-1880M02), the 1907 banking panic (1907M10-M11), and the 1974 stock market crash (1974M09). Sometimes, different tests gave slightly different results. For example, the SADF test only identifies two explosive periods – the 1873 panic recovery (1879M10-1880M04) and the Internet bubble (1997M07-2001M08).

7.2 More Comparisons And Policy Options

When there were no reliable statistical or econometric methods to detect bubbles or "exuberance", either rational or irrational, people could only *intuitively* or *graphically* "detect" a bubble when the asset price continues to increase unreasonably in comparison with the economic fundamentals. Although one may argue that "When you are in a bubble, you know it," such a statement is not very useful for policy makers or regulators.

By the time the asset price reaches its historical peak, an imminent bubble implosion and its destabilizing effects on wealth and the economy will be inevitable. By then there is little that policymakers can do to smoothly deflate the bubble and they are relegated to dealing with the aftermath. This is why historically central banks and politicians have focused on managing the mess after the bubble's collapse and passing legislation or imposing regulations to prevent or ameliorate the next one. Yet this has started to change with better research and policy makers seem more interested in early warnings and pro-active policy actions to recognize and manage bubbles without damaging the real economy.

Now these newly developed econometric and mathematical techniques to monitor asset prices make it possible to more rigorously detect a bubble before it collapses. However, just because a bubble has been identified, it does not mean that the bubble is due to pop soon or that when it does pop its impact on the economy will be material. Therefore, the next research and policy agenda is to further compare these tests in terms of their strengths and weaknesses such that the most efficient ways to combine these tests given data availability can be established. The goal would be to determine reliable early warnings for both the origination and *predicted* collapsing dates of a bubble combined with developing mechanisms to monitor bubbles in real time. The second major objective would be to develop policy options and measures that could be executed in a timely manner for maximum effect based on metrics using these new statistical and mathematical techniques.

7.3 Unit Root Test Vs. PWY Test Vs. Other Tests

As an asset price may change from a random walk to

explosive behavior when a bubble emerges or from explosive behavior to random walk after it collapses, the tests reviewed in this chapter are not necessarily contradictory. Rather they should be viewed as complements instead of substitutes. While it is true the presence of the random walk or unit root may not be clear evidence of an emerging bubble, it may serve as an early warning if the asset price continues to become divergent or explosive statistically based on the SADF or related tests. Similarly, if an explosive asset price starts to show patterns that are similar to the unit root, once again, it may serve as an early warning the bubble will collapse soon, which can be verified later with a rigorous test such as SADF.

Since the GSADF test is more sensitive than CUSUM and SADF in detecting asset bubbles, particularly when there are multiple bubbles, if the policy makers or regulators are less risk averse towards a bubble, they can adopt tests predictive of later bubble formation such as CUSUM and SADF instead of GSADF. Yet, in either case, policy makers will need experts to statistically determine and predict asset bubbles and to help establish the criterion and consensus concerning when action should be taken. Although every bubble is different, bubbles and their subsequent crashes can be correlated with each other. Therefore, it is important that policy makers have a bubble monitoring system of bubbles with strategies and regulatory tools to handle every stage in a bubble's development as identified from these tests.

7.4 Significance Levels

Similarly, as different confidence or significance levels are not necessarily contradictory, choosing a significance level may also depend on the risk aversion of policy makers towards a particular bubble. While a 1% significance level may be the best predictor, a 10% significance level may provide the earliest warning though with less certainty. Policy makers thus need to establish their own comfort levels with probably greater concern for bubbles that put the financial system at risk such as the subprime mortgage crisis as compared to the recent collapse in social media stocks the caused barely a ripple on the US economy.

7.5 Efficiency of the Markets

As discussed by Mokhtar et al [2006], one reason the Malaysian bubble in the post-Asian crisis period was smaller than the one in the pre-crisis period is that based on experience the market became more efficient in handling bubble risk. After the Asian crisis, specific actions were taken, including "ownership rules, liberalization of investment rules, improvement of banking sector prudential regulation, capital market reform, corporate governance reforms and corporate restructuring. These measures successfully brought confidence among local as well as foreign investors towards the Malaysian stock market." Hence, policy changes improved the economic fundamentals through capital and currency controls that improved market efficiency, and thus reduced the impact of the post-crisis bubble.

In the recent US case the policy focus of the Dodd-Frank Act discussed elsewhere in this book is that it seeks to strengthen the prudential regulation of financial institutions and prevent the next financial bubble. This should also help improve the global economic environment and increase employment through more lending to businesses and housing. Related actions have taken place internationally. Indeed the euro crisis is another example of how bubbles and crashes across countries have become correlated due to the globalization of trade, investment and finance. Therefore how to improve the economic efficiency of a country or countries and prevent or alleviate future bubbles that can negatively impact that goal should be an important research topic of interest to all policy makers.

References

Abreu, D. & Brunnermeier, M. 2003. "Bubbles and Crashes," *Econometrica*, V. 71, No. 1.

Al-Anaswah, N. & Wilfling B. 2011. "Identification of Speculative Bubbles Using State-Space Models with Markov-Switching," *Journal of Banking & Finance*, V. 35.

Bhargava, A. 1986. "On the Theory of Testing for Unit Roots in Observed Time Series," *Review of Economic Studies*, V. 53.

Busetti, F. & Taylor, A. 2004. "Tests of Stationarity against a Change in Persistence," *Journal of Econometrics*, V. 123.

Caballero, R., Farhi, E., & Gourincha, P. 2008. "Financial Crash, Commodity Prices, and Global Imbalances," *Brookings Papers on Economic Activity*, Fall.

Campbell, J. & Shiller R. 1987. "Co-integration and Tests of Present Value Models," *Journal of Political Economy*, V. 95.

Chou, P. 2012. "A Model for Housing Price and Bubbles", working paper.

Chow, G. & Niu, L. 2009. "Demand and Supply for Residential Housing in Urban China", op. cit.

Clark, S. & Coggin, T. 2011. "Was There a U.S. House Price Bubble? An Econometric Analysis Using National and Regional Panel Data," *The Quarterly Review of Economics and Finance*, V. 51.

Dickey, D. & Fuller, W. 1979. "Distribution of the Estimators for Autoregressive Time Series with a Unit Root," *Journal of the American Statistical Association*, No. 74.

Diba, B. & Grossman H. 1988. "Explosive Rational Bubbles in Stock Prices," *American Economic Review*, V.78.

Evans, G. 1991. "Pitfalls in Testing for Explosive Bubbles in Asset Prices," *American Economic Review*, V. 81.

Greenspan, A. 1996. "Minutes of the Federal Open Market Committee," available from www.federal.reserve.gov.

Guenster, N., Kole, E, & Jasobsen, B. 2009. "Riding Bubbles", working paper.

Homm, U. & Breitung, J. 2012. "Testing for Speculative Bubbles in Stock Markets – A Comparison of Alternative Methods," *Journal of Financial Econometrics*, V. 10, No. 1.

Jarrow, R., Kchia, Y., & Protter, P. 2011. "How to Detect an Asset Bubble," *SIAM Journal on Financial Mathematics*, V. 2.

Kim, C. & Nelson, C. 1999. *State Space Models with Regime Switching*, MIT Press, Cambridge, MA.

Kim, J. 2000. "Detection of Change in Persistence of a Linear Time Series," *Journal of Econometrics*, V. 95.

Kindleberger, C. &, R. 2011. *Maniacs, Panics, and Crashes*, John Wiley op. cit.

Krueger, A. 2005. "Bubbles Old and New: Economists Wrestle with a Theoretical Impossibility," *New York Times*, NY.

Liu, T., Santoni, G., & Stone, C. 1995. "In Search of Stock Market Bubbles: A Comment on Rapport and White," *Journal of Economic History*, V. 55.

Maddala, G. 1992. *Introduction to Econometrics*, 2nd edition, Macmillan, NY.

Mikhed, V. & Zemčík P. 2009. "Do House Prices Reflect Fundamentals? Aggregate and Panel data Evidence," *Journal of Housing Economics*, 18.

Mokhtar, S., Nassir A., & Hassan T. 2006. "Detecting Rational Speculative Bubbles in the Malaysian Stock Market," *International Research Journal of Finance and Economics*, No. 6.

Phillips, P., Wu, Y., & Yu, J. 2011. "Explosive Behavior in the 1990s Nasdaq: When Did Exuberance Escalate Asset Values?" *International Economics Review*, 52, No. 1.

Phillips, P. & Yu, J. 2011. "Dating the Timeline of Financial Bubbles during the Subprime Crisis," *Quantitative Economics*, V. 2.

Phillips, P., Shi, S., & Yu, J. 2012. "Testing for Multiple Bubbles," *Cowles Foundation Discussion Paper, No. 1843*, Yale University, New Haven, CT.

Ray, A. & Ray I., op. cit.

Shiller, R. 1981. "Do Stock Prices Move Too Much to be Justified by Subsequent Changes in Dividends?", *American Economic Review*, V. 71.

Shiller, R. 1990. "Market Volatility and Investor Behavior," *American Economic review*, V. 80.

West, K. 1987. "A Specification Test of Speculative Bubbles," *Quarterly Journal of Economics*, V. 102.

Wu, Y. 1997. "Rational Bubbles in the Stock Market: Accounting for the U.S. Stock Price Volatility," *Economic Inquiry*, V. 35.

Yiu, M. & Jin, L. 2012. Detecting Bubbles in the Hong Kong Residential Property Market: An Explosive-Pattern Approach, *Hong Kong Institute for Monetary Research Working Paper No. 1/2012*.

THE JOURNEY
SOME CONCLUSIONS AND FUTURE RESEARCH
REGARDING FINANCIAL BUBBLES

That will be ere the set of sun.

W. Rapp

Historically as explained in this volume, unfortunately most bubbles have been recognized and analyzed specifically after the fact, "When the Hurley Burley's done and the Battle Lost and Won." Further policy makers have generally only taken action in dealing with the aftermath. This is true of the recent housing and financial crisis as well as prior crises within current memory such as the S&L crisis of the 1980s or the Internet boom and bust in the 1990s.

The Leir Conferences and the Leir Center For Financial Bubble Research, however, have sought to move beyond retrospection or intuition to develop through research and its dissemination metrics and methods to recognize Bubbles while they are developing including identifying the different types of bubbles and their various stages. Through this effort the Center seeks to better inform policy makers, regulators, investors, financial institutions and the general public about Financial Bubbles and how they should be recognized and managed.

In this regard Bubbles are seen as rapid rises in real prices for an asset above its economic or intrinsic value and so not sustainable. Rapid price increases for an asset relative to the general price level are seen as attracting speculator interest that further drives up asset prices, something that can actually be identified and measured from both a qualitative and quantitative perspective. These signals include herding, more market volatility and high optimism. The initial paper by Dr. Chou for example argued a period of less volatility if the price shock was external but his revised paper published in this volume shows an immediate increase in the price action if this is endogenous as is true for most bubbles.

Speculators will then drive out value investors. However when some speculators start to leave price deceleration can signal a maturing and measurable loss of momentum. At the same time policy makers appear reluctant to act early, because they see benefits from the perceived economic prosperity while the public is optimistic due to its enjoying a false sense of prosperity, even though the eventual pain can be extreme when the bubble collapses. So there is a public policy need to manage bubbles and lean against the public's measurable excess optimism.

Some important Bubble types are financial bubbles in stocks, emerging markets, bonds, real estate, commodities and new technologies.

It is important to differentiate bubbles because disruptive technologies can attract risk capital as in the case of the boom in social media investments whereas real estate lending booms financed by bank loans are always bad due to the excess leverage and credit risk involved. The former can avoid a financial crisis such as the Internet or the collapse in social media stocks whereas the latter generally cannot as seen in the Great Recession. Government Regulations can initiate, manage and avoid some Bubbles since they all seem to require an open market system. A change in government objectives regarding home ownership for example played a role in the recent crisis that could have been avoided with more early action by the Fed.

This is because panics and crashes are usually caused when people have borrowed money to buy inflated assets. Therefore policy debates about bubbles center on when funding new ventures poses a risk to the financial system due to banks' exposure and leverage that can wipe out their capital such as in 1929 and 2008 but not in the 2000 Internet collapse, the 2008 drop in for-profit universities or social media in 2012. From this perspective strict laws such as margin limits may work better than regulators using their discretion. A middle ground could be setting minimums with regulators only being allowed to be tougher.

The policy objective is keep the financial system especially banks sound while providing the funds needed to support economic growth and new technologies. Given their leverage banks should not provide risk capital. Rather other intermediaries can and should facilitate this process such as brokers, insurance companies, VCs, investment banks, and asset managers. A way to test for this risk is stress tests that look for spillover effects from certain economic or industry scenarios on the banks.

Further part of this analytical and regulatory effort should focus on the assumptions of the market participants and the regulators. That is what may make sense on a micro basis may not when it is done in volume through massive herding effects. Combining growth stocks and risk free assets in a portfolio was a sound financial asset management idea based on history. However, when many asset managers did it in volume during the 1960s and early 1970s, it led to the "nifty fifty" boom and bust. Subprime mortgage lending may have made sense given stable or rising home prices, but when it was done in volume on a national basis it led to the housing boom and bust with foreclosure as a viable exit strategy actually foreclosed because of the number of homes hitting particular markets at the same time with no buyers due to both a reduction in lenders and of potential borrowers.

Increased prices that attract speculators may make lenders and regulators feel good and in turn this will increase asset prices further thus attracting even more participants through an interactive feedback. But once money becomes less available and some speculators leave the market, price volatility increases leading to more exits and some price decline or deceleration [Chapter 8]. Subsequently this decline then at some point creates a panic and with a true price collapse there is a "crash". Therefore price action is the key to understanding a bubble's evolution.

In the real world research indicates that News Stories play

little role in creating a crash though they will certainly try to explain it after the fact. Rather prices in terms of market timing describe the bubble's development where "Financial Innovations" should be suspect, increased leverage should be suspect, complexity should be suspect, concentrated underpriced risk should be suspect, and pro-cyclical regulation should be suspect.

These situations are suspect because they all reflect excessive optimism not only by borrowers but also by lenders and regulators. This three-sided optimism is a bubble cornerstone and becomes reflected in excessive contracting. But once this over-confidence wanes, the prior greed is overcome by fear and panic emerges along with loss of confidence, a crash, financial distress, disillusionment and a financial crisis if there is excessive leverage and bank exposure. Ironically this is when the government usually comes in to deal with the aftermath by bailing out the system or prosecuting the inevitable scams and scandals emerging as the financial tide goes out. Similarly the prior excessive optimism in contracting leads to numerous lawsuits and massive litigation.

Therefore from a prudential policy or regulatory viewpoint there should be a sharp focus on potential banking losses or on other highly leveraged institutions that could impact the national or global financial system such as the SIVs analyzed in Chapter 7. This generally would not include situations where only an investor's capital is at risk such as the Internet or recent Social Media Bubbles where high margin requirements limited

the institutional risk. Conversely one reason the recent subprime mortgage crisis has been so disastrous is because the asset price risk was borne almost entirely by the banks and this was then extended through low margin derivatives to the wider global financial system including foreign exchange markets.

Generally regulators must lean against the wind to counter excessive optimism. But due to possible regulatory co-option using strict rules such as margin requirements or exchanges may be more effective than regulators' discretion or should at least limit it. Such rules should seek to control optimistic contracting through simplicity and transparency requirements that limit leverage through installments or balloon payments. In addition regulators must monitor Aggregation Effects that can lead to concentration of credit risk and counterparty credit issues such as emerged in the case of AIG. Forcing certain transactions through exchanges is meant to address this and to the extent they require margin or collateral this can reduce risk mispricing. But the risk does not go away but only gets shifted. So policy makers must make sure the exchanges are also acting prudentially.

Finally Ponzi Finance where financial costs are covered by increasing financial exposure must be stopped at an early stage especially when it has adverse foreign exchange and balance of payments effects as explained by Professor Aliber

A more systematic policy approach to managing Bubbles resulting from this type of finance as opposed to the current ad hoc one appears needed because bubbles are based in human behavior and market conditions that incorporate actual economic risk taking. Since Ponzi finance substantially reduces borrowers' risk perception and results in over optimism and excessive contracting this must be regulated.

Yet risk taking related to investment and particularly new technologies is an important aspect of the economic growth process when over leverage and risk to the financial system is avoided. At the same time as Colin Clark has explained and verified capital grows faster than other factors of production and economic activity. Thus at various times there will be an excess supply of capital driving down rates of return. This will lead investors to take on more risk seeking a higher return. New technologies, regulatory changes, etc. can attract this capital leading to bubbles that when they collapse return capital availability and pricing to more normal levels.

In sorting out these phenomena including their nature and timing this volume has presented and reviewed both qualitative and quantitative techniques, including some recent statistical and econometric models on bubbles. Both qualitative and quantitative approaches can be important since if an asset bubble can be identified in the early stage of its formation, it can benefit different parties including policy makers, including central bankers, as well as academics and investors. Indeed the two can be interactive and supporting since the qualitative and intuitive recognition may occur first and then quantitative methods can be used as verification and as way to measure its impact. On the other hand quantitative methods even if able to identify a bubble cannot always analyze its type. Further most regulatory initiatives generally work through organizations and a legal framework. So a qualitative understanding of their operations relative to the bubble and its evolution becomes important.

Both approaches however view bubbles as occurring when the price of an asset class rises faster than its economic fundamentals with too fast being the rate that attracts speculators that further drive up prices and destabilize the market.

When this happens just as in *Macbeth* everything for the major participants appears to be going well for awhile, but eventually they will be surprised, exit will become extremely difficult and it will then end in anguish, blood and tears.